Biblical Theology

Biblical Theology

Past, Present, and Future

EDITED BY
Carey Walsh *and* Mark W. Elliott

CASCADE *Books* • Eugene, Oregon

BIBLICAL THEOLOGY
Past, Present, and Future

Copyright © 2016 Wipf and Stock Publishers. All rights reserved. Except for brief quotations in critical publications or reviews, no part of this book may be reproduced in any manner without prior written permission from the publisher. Write: Permissions, Wipf and Stock Publishers, 199 W. 8th Ave., Suite 3, Eugene, OR 97401.

Cascade Books
An Imprint of Wipf and Stock Publishers
199 W. 8th Ave., Suite 3
Eugene, OR 97401

www.wipfandstock.com

Paperback ISBN 978-1-4982-3443-6
Hardcover ISBN: 978-1-4982-3445-0
Ebook ISBN: 978-1-4982-3444-3

Cataloging-in-Publication data:

Names: Walsh, Carey, editor | Elliott, Mark W., editor

Title: Biblical theology : past, present, and future / edited by Carey Walsh and Mark W. Elliott.

Description: Eugene, OR: Cascade Books, 2016 | Includes bibliographical references and index(es).

Identifiers: ISBN 978-1-4982-3443-6 (paperback) | ISBN 978-1-4982-3445-0 (hardcover) | ISBN 978-1-4982-3444-3 (ebook)

Subjects: 1. Bible—Theology. 2. Bible. 3. Theology. I. Title.

Classification: BS543 B5 2016 (print) | BS543 (electronic)

Manufactured in the U.S.A.

Contents

Introduction by Mark W. Elliott vii

I. PAST: HISTORICAL DEVELOPMENTS

1. *Mark W. Elliott.* The Pure and the True Gabler: Questioning a Received Image in the History of Biblical Theology 3
2. *Charles K. Telfer.* Campegius Vitringa Sr. (1659–1722): A Biblical Theologian at the Turn of the Eighteenth Century 18
3. *David Lincicum.* Ferdinand Christian Baur and Biblical Theology 33
4. *Michael C. Legaspi.* Seeing with One Eye: Biblical Interpretation in the Seventeenth and Eighteenth Centuries 51
5. *Philip Sumpter.* Reality, History, and the Old Testament in the Nineteenth Century 63

II. PRESENT: METHODOLOGICAL CONSIDERATIONS FOR BIBLICAL THEOLOGY NOW

6. *Georg Fischer.* Biblical Theology in Transition: An Overview of Recent Works, and a Look Ahead at How to Proceed 79
7. *Darian Lockett.* Some Ways of "Doing" Biblical Theology: Assessments and a Proposal 91
8. *Scott Hafemann.* What's the Point of Biblical Theology?: Reflections Prompted by Brevard Childs 108
9. *Frederik Poulsen.* Church Lectionaries as Biblical Theology 122
10. *Heiko Wenzel.* Sources for Theology Proper 134
11. *N. T. Wright.* Historical Paul and "Systematic Theology": To Start a Discussion 147

III. FUTURE: CONSTRUCTIVE WAYS FORWARD FOR BIBLICAL THEOLOGY

12 *Carey Walsh.* The Wisdom in Rupture: Brueggemann's Notion of Countertestimony for Postmodern Biblical Theology 167
13 *Janghoon Park.* The New Testament as the Covenantal-Liturgical Consummation of the Biblical Story?: A Critical Evaluation of Scott Hahn's Biblical Theology of the New Testament 177
14 *Zvi Shimon.* The Place of God in the Bible: Between Jewish and Christian Theology 190
15 *John Goldingay.* Middle Narratives as an Aspect of Biblical Theology 203
16 *W. Gordon Campbell.* The Book of Revelation and New Testament Theology 214

Introduction

Mark W. Elliott

THE ESSAYS IN THIS volume provide an ample selection of papers presented at the Biblical Theology section of the International Meeting of the Society of Biblical Literature over three years (Amsterdam 2012; St Andrews 2013; Vienna 2014). While "Biblical Theology" is hardly at the cutting edge of fashion in terms of shocking, new movements (it's been around as long as the New Testament, arguably even before), we have been encouraged not only by the attendance at sessions in those three occasions, but also by the pleasing diversity of contributions: Catholic, Evangelical, Reformed varieties of Christian but also Jewish, with a plurality of approaches and ideas operating under those labels. This would be the place to express gratitude to the SBL and their sterling work of organization, especially to Charlie Haws and Trista Krock. Thanks too to Cascade Books' team and to Eric Covington for editorial help at this end.

One overarching idea is that biblical theology cannot allow the study of any part of the Bible to remain forever self-contained and self-referential. There is a post-critical canonical consciousness that accepts that biblical books were composed over a number of years with usually some sort of final redaction (and perhaps one or two penultimate ones), but pushes beyond that. This respects the biblical writings themselves, since these often seem to show awareness of at least *some* other scriptures in their own composition. In the case of the New Testament authors, it means treating phrases, catchwords and ideas as creative catalysts for their own theology and wisdom and although aware of a certain amount of context (if a modified form of C. H. Dodd's famous thesis is to be accepted), these were uprooted and transplanted to serve new arguments

INTRODUCTION

and narratives. Yet to extend correspondences beyond those which can be discerned in quotation, echo, and allusion to the point where one is comparing biblical books at the level of ideas with no such connection (e.g., what Chronicles and 2 Peter say about "x") might seem like treating the Bible as something purely or essentially literary. It might raise a fear that by blending one voice with another we distort or mis-hear the authentic individual voice. Diversity and non-likeness is good, we believe. Even if pre-modern commentators paid lip service to the fourfold witness of the gospel, harmonizing the four was the order of the day, and sometimes that meant John (or sometimes Paul!) had the whip hand and so never really allowed the synoptics to have their say. Yet this is precisely where the modern form of biblical theology can claim to improve upon the pre-modern. No priority is given; instead, there is dialogue and dialectic. But in that "betweenness," akin to the betweenness of Hebrew poetic parallelism, biblical theology can grow.

However in all this attempt to hear a theology, a word for the present, and to approach the text "synchronically," the history in and around the texts is not to be lost in terms of what that history gives to each text in terms of meaning, or constraints of meaning. Now, the charge of denying history *can* justly be leveled at for one the increasingly popular Reception-historical approach where Christianity's favorite Bible texts can be plucked out and observed in the story of their creative interpretation. Brevard Childs has done just this.[1] Just as vulnerable to the accusation is a Ricoeurian moral reading where the canonical reading is decreed not to be final since it is as time-conditioned as any other piece of literature, including those derivative of it, and Scripture is viewed as throwing up imagery waiting to be decoded. Any tendency to be so text-centered, whether one is Wellhausenian or Kermodean, can make one forget the fact that Scripture is properly viewed as testimony, in the sense that that is the self-understanding of those who utterances composed it, and witnessed to things that were in motion back then, even if with continuing force up until now.

According to Childs, a canonical reading (proper to Christian scholars locating themselves within the Church rather than free-floating) is that which turns the reader to Jesus's soteriological identity with the God of Israel. The two testaments are considered together though not to the extent of fusing them: the discrete witness of each must be heard. In

---

1. See Childs, *Church's Guide*, 29, against Luz, "Kanonische Exegese," 40–57.

INTRODUCTION

all this the historical-critical approach needs put in its place as a servant not a master. That method, although necessary, is insufficient if we are to do reach true understanding (*Verstehen*) as that which goes beyond *Erklären* to the substance of the matter and relates to it. Childs was troubled by those who settled for a literary approach to the Bible, and hence could just not understand when Barr, and more so John Barton classified "the Canonical Approach" as a species of this. A reluctance to move through *Historie* to any *Geschichte* in actual events and realities can already be found in traditional historical criticism, separating the genre of *Einleitung* (the history of the literature's development) from the History of Israel, and judging there is no access to the former from the latter, and even less to the history of the ancient world.

For example, the four Gospels do not attempt only to explain the meaning of the gospel, but in different and various ways they bear witness to its contingent yet eternal truth and put the church in touch with it. They move beyond explanation to a higher grasp of the matter, which is revealed at a privileged point in history; thus the faith is supremely historical.

The church, which developed its understanding of canon over many centuries, derived it as a response to the Lordship of Jesus Christ. The apostolic witness to the life, death, and resurrection of Christ in human time and space gained their privileged status to perform their function of bearing testimony to the gospel that had been promised in the Scriptures of Israel (Mark 1:1-3). The canon is a dynamic vehicle by which the Risen Lord continues by the Holy Spirit to guide, instruct and nourish his people.[2]

It does this within an ecumenical context, with Catholic, Protestant and Jewish voices all making a contribution, as we have so far found in our meetings whence the following essays have issued. Karl-Wilhelm Niebuhr has observed: "Wie Kähler, so sieht auch Ratzinger das Entscheidende darin, dass dieser wirkliche, biblische Christus der Jesus der Geschichte ist. Nicht 'historische Jesus' sondern, geschichtliche biblische Christus."[3] Although Niebuhr here possibly over-identifies Ratzinger's position with that of the nineteenth-century Protestant Martin Kähler, the focus on the biblical Christ giving content to the identity of Jesus in his spiritual setting, relationships, effects, and even consciousness

---

2. Childs, *Church's Guide*, 26.
3. Niebuhr, "Der biblische Jesus Christus," 99.

seems worth insisting upon. Nevertheless, the attempts of Catholic and Protestant voices to approach the Bible in a way that not so much settles their doctrinal differences, than sharpens their points and cranks up a dialectic, is to be warmly appreciated.

It might seem that Childs and Ratzinger were once fashionable around the turn of the millennium but their fashion wore out not long into the first decade. Instead, it is not even "the Bible and us" but "we and the Bible," with the Bible providing textual shadows and templates, or mere encouragement to its readers' actions and programs. By contrast any idea of inhabiting the inner "world" of the Bible sounds escapist and pietist. Yet that is just the resource whence the in-between can be supplied for any SBL type of meeting. Roughly speaking, the SBL meeting is made up of sessions on textual minutiae (admittedly, the papers are only twenty-five minutes) and at the other extreme wide-ranging accounts of theory and "issues" affecting the world today. Biblical theology aims to see the big picture but to get there from an account of the details of exegesis of the biblical text. In that sense it can claim to hold the whole thing together. It will not abandon the spiritually important whole in order to stick with textual details or application, but will encourage the activity of shuttling between the two.

Bibliography

Childs, Brevard. *The Church's Guide for Reading Paul: the Canonical Shaping of the Pauline Corpus*. Grand Rapids: Eerdmans, 2008.

Luz, Ulrich. "Kanonische Exegese und Hermeneutik der Wirkungsgeschichte Die Wurzel aller Theologie: Sentire cum Ecclesia": Festschrift zum 60. Geburtstag von Urs von Arx Zürich: Stämpfli, 2003.

Niebuhr, Karl-Wilhelm. "Der biblische Jesus Christus. Zu Joseph Ratzingers Jesus-Buch." In *Das Jesus-Buch des Papstes. Die Antwort der Neutestamentler*, edited by T. Söding, 99–109. Freiburg: Herder, 2007.

I. PAST: HISTORICAL DEVELOPMENTS

The Pure and the True Gabler

Questioning a Received Image in the History of Biblical Theology

Mark W. Elliott

Johann Philipp Gabler

MANY RECENT WORKS (NOT least the *Jahrbuch der biblischen Theologie* of 2010) consider Gabler, particularly in his 1787 inaugural lecture at Altdorf "On the Correct Distinction Between Dogmatic and Biblical Theology and the Right Definition of Their Goals," to represent an exodus of a situated, time-conditioned theological ideology inferred from the biblical date empirically from the old-style dogmatic theology that operated deductively. One can see various versions of this narrative of liberation in accounts by Stuckenbruck (1999), Saebø (1998), and Esler (2005), as well as in the older German scholarship of Smend (1962) and Merk (1972),[1] in which the premise is that the old way of "biblical theology" was broken along with the ties that bound exegesis and theology, so that anything bearing the name "biblical theology" today would have to proceed quite differently (even Childs 1992 shares this view). A dissenting opinion is offered by John Sandys-Wunsch (2005), who argues that Gabler was doing nothing of the sort; unfortunately he devotes less than a paragraph to substantiate his alternative view. Accordingly Gabler

---

1. Stuckenbruck, "Johann Philipp Gabler," 139–57; Saebø, *On the Way to Canon*, 310–27; Esler, *New Testament Theology*; Smend, "Johann Gablers Begründung," 345–57. Merk, *Biblische Theologie*; Childs, *Biblical Theology*; Sandys-Wunsch, *What Have They Done*.

is largely regarded as a marker on the road to the "History of Religions" way of dealing with the content of the Bible, in other words a precursor of Wrede and Gunkel.

In his own day, to the right of Gabler stood G. Zachariä, for whom validity in interpretation must be expressed in terms of traditional loci of systematic theology, while on Gabler's left G. L. Bauer[2] aimed to show the evolution of the theory of religion from the Old Testament to the New Testament, where it would reach its climax with the rational religion of Jesus and the apostles.[3] Bauer's method, once it became standard, meant that the NT and OT became disconnected subject areas.[4] Furthermore the outcome of the fierce discussion at the turn of the 1800s was a confirmation of the historical-critical method, the freeing of biblical theology from the grip of dogmatics, and the marking of a distinction between "historical reconstruction" and "interpretation for every generation."[5] The alternative sketched by Zachariä was ignored.

Yet it is often assumed that Gabler was the one who sounded the death knell for biblical theology in a sense of any theology for the present being derivable from the Bible.[6] His "rein biblische Theologie" (that which has validity long after the period of its origin) is often viewed as something quite sealed off from the "wahr biblische Theologie" (the larger amount of theological content represented in the Bible), and the latter is then seen in terms of religious self-expression or theological ideology, according to the *Religionsgeschichtliche Schule*. Wrede in particular reckoned that the theology from the Bible would be better parsed as "religion." It is no coincidence that in that spirit D. F. Strauss also wrote in his *Glaubenslehre* (1841) a section called "Vergängliches und Bleibendes im Christenthum." However, Strauss was not Gabler. Yet, perhaps regrettably, it is the majority opinion that Gabler began a process

---

2. Professor of Philosophy and Oriental languages at the University of Altdorf from 1789, and in 1805 professor at the University of Heidelberg,

3. In his *Theologie des Alten Testaments*.

4. Segalla, "Teologia biblica," 1534f: "Zachariä rifuta il metodo precedente dei 'dicta probantia.' Non basta riportare i testi biblici. *Bisogna interpretarli* in modo da vedere ciò che è valido o meno nella teologia sistematica' and Bauer 'vuol dimostrare l'evoluzione della teoria della religione dall' A al NT, dove raggiunge il suo culmine con la religione razionale . . .'"

5. Merk, *Biblische Theologie*, 272. Otto Merk here makes reference to G. Ebeling's essay on Historical-Critical Theology, "Die Bedeutung der historisch-kritischen Methode," 1–46, and to H. Schlier, "Biblische und dogmatische Theologie," 425–37.

6. Frey, "Zum Problem."

of emancipation from dogmatic categories, leading to the independence of exegesis and the rise of the historical-critical method.[7]

It needs to be admitted that Gabler was thoroughly religiously motivated, and was not interested in establishing the original meaning of the texts as end in itself. It mattered to him that there was also a second step (to use a term of John Barton's) to be taken towards establishing biblical concepts of ongoing validity, but at neither of those steps was he seeking a religious or theological neutrality. Hence whatever the nature of his close association with Eichhorn, it is to be doubted that Gabler can be held responsible for the *Religionsgeschichtliche Schule*. Lauster himself describes the constructive side of Enlightenment exegesis: what academics did was to make preaching informative and informed, while also lending weight to the truth-content of what is preached.[8] Gabler then associated the Bible with the unchanging religion of Christianity as its source. Also, the intention to rid biblical study and theology from dogmatic categories was accompanied by a conviction that dogmatic theology was not well-served by the use of *dicta probantia*. Gabler aimed to free practical dogmatics (in preaching and catechizing) from a proof-texting way of using the Bible, but he also wanted to go further, by allowing biblical concepts, hermeneutically re-cast to inform dogmatics.

The Other Path from Gabler

Johann Christian Konrad von Hofmann

Half a century later we meet the phenomenon of *Vermittlungstheologie* (or "middle way theology") and a particular version of that, one which privileged the Bible, and is neatly called "the Erlangen school." It is no coincidence that the University of Erlangen became the replacement for the redundant Altdorf, less than twenty kilometres away. In F. W. Kantzenbach's summary of the key descriptors of Erlangen theology, echoes

---

7. Lauster, *Prinzip und methode*, 32: "Man wähnt hier mit gutem Grund den Anfangspunkt eines Emanzipationsprozesses, in dem sich die Erforschung der Bibel von der schematischen Auslegung durch die Vorgaben der dogmatischen Lehrbegriffe zu befreien versucht, was dann letztlich zur Ausbildung der Exegese als eigenständiger Disziplin und damit zum Aufstieg der historischen-kritischen Methode führt..."

8. Ibid., 166: "Gelehrte Theologie, so darf man folgern, nützt der christlichen Religion, weil letztere ihren Erkenntnisgrund in der Heiligen Schrift findet. Es ist die gelehrte Theologie, welche durch Exegese und Hermeneutik zum rechten Schriftverständnis anleiten kann."

of Gabler's own manifesto can be heard. First, there was a disdain for the *loci communes* method and proof texts. Only timeless truths *coming directly from the Bible itself* could be used in theology. Like Gabler and possibly Luther, there is a sense that the Bible has concepts, which once shorn of their particular historical accoutrements still have substance as guiding notions for contemporary Christian thought. Second, and, concomitant with the first, against the claims of "supranaturalists," miracles were to be explained "naturally," in such a way as to maintain and defend their historicity as events.

There was a spirit of moderate enlightenment: a *Christian* rationalism modified by an interest in the particular, and special history was asserted over against rationalist accounts.[9] What is more than coincidental is that the father of the founder of Erlangen theology, Gottfried Thomasius, taught in Gabler's Altdorf School before moving to Erlangen. Likewise, P. J. S. Vogel was a junior colleague of Gabler, and an antirationalist who relocated to Erlangen in 1808, to attempt his own version of a middle way.[10] Kantzenbach concludes that the Erlangen Bible Professors Ammon and Seiler held Erlangen theology in a Kantian grip during the two decades on either side of 1800, and more so after the premature death of Vogel.[11] Further, with their rationalist successor D. L. Bertholdt using proof texts to make philosophical points, it would take J. C. K. von Hofmann really to grasp what Gabler was after, and reverse this trend of misinterpretation.[12] In this he was helped by Prof Gottlieb P. Chr. Kaiser who in the spirit of revivalism and Romanticism prepared the way for the new Erlangen theology in the 1820s and 1830s by determining that theology and ethics must be rooted in Scripture and Confession.[13]

Writing about the mid-nineteenth century *Vermittlungstheologie* as a whole, Ragnar Holte contends that the material principle of this brand of Protestantism was "free divine grace in Christ and justification through

---

9. Kantzenbach, *Die Erlanger Theologie*, 66. Cf. also Beyschlag, *Die Erlanger Theologie*); Simon, "Die innere Erneuerung."

10. Kantzenbach, *Die Erlanger Theologie*, 67.

11. Ibid., 66: "Zusammenfassend kann man urteilen, daß Seiler und Ammon für die Periode der Erlanger Theologie von ca.1770–1817 die charakteristischen Gestalten sind."

12. Ibid., 76: "Die von Gabler angepragerte Loci-methode hat Bertholdt noch nicht überwunden. Das Alte Testament steht für ihn oft unterschiedlos eben dem Neuen Testament. Eine Welt trennt ihn von Johannes von Hofmann."

13. Ibid., 97.

faith," while the formal principle was one of autonomy, a passion for the truth, and honesty of conscience.[14] In other words, there was a compromise of traditional Protestant theology and Enlightenment principles. However, the Erlangen Lutherans wanted to add something to this, so as to arrive at their own version of a "middle way," and that was an insistence on the discrete witness of both biblical testaments. In one of his last works,[15] Brevard Childs came to appreciate the mediating approach of that most famous of Erlangen exegetes, von Hofmann, especially in his approach to the OT "prophecies" as more like typological statements in their original intention, which then exerted a pressure on the later NT writers. Indeed much was made of this in Hofmann's *Weissagung und Erfüllung im Alten und im Neuen Testamente: ein theologischer Versuch*. Hofmann also laid emphasis on the term *Thatbestand*, i.e., the believer's present factual situation as the experience of the Risen Christ, "which has realized itself objectively in me," in other words the present Christ received through ecclesial community.[16]

It is not "my self-consciousness" that matters, but rather an ecclesially shared relationship to the history of salvation and to the Trinitarian God behind it, with the Son as the one who is always in a form of becoming. The priority of the ecclesial becomes especially clear in Hofmann's *Schriftbeweis*.[17] All parts of the NT are equally close to Christ. As with Gabler there is no attempt to get behind the gospels to some purer history, whereas while the OT is a mystery (*Verhüllung*) to "them" (Steck thinks Hofmann means both Hengstenberg and Schleiermacher here), "to us it is the revelation of the essential relationship between God and humanity."[18] He thinks readers must accompany Scripture through its

---

14. Holte, Die *Vermittlungstheologie*, 160: "Das Princip des Protestantismus als Erscheinung (*materiales Princip*) ist die Lehre von der *freyen Gnade Gottes in Christo und der Rechtfertigung durch den Glauben*. . . . Das *formale* (subjective, erzeugende) Princip ist *Selbständigkeit, Wahrheitsliebe, Regsamkeit des Gewissens, sittlicher Ernst*."

15. Childs, *Struggle to Understand Isaiah*, 320.

16. Steck, *Die Idee der Heilsgeschichte*, 38: cf. Steck, "Johann Christian Konrad von Hofmann"; Swarat, "Die heilsgeschichtliche Konzeption"; Slenczka, "Johann Christian Konrad von Hofmann"; Becker, *Self-Giving God*.

17. The church is to be thought of as neither individuals collected nor an institution, "sondern das Gemeinwesen Christi, welches durch den in den Gnadenmitteln gegenwärtigen Christus hergestellt wird, und deshalb immer früher ist, als die einzelnen durch den Dienst dieses Gemeinwesens gewonnenen Christen." Hofmann, *Der Schriftbeweis*, 17.

18. ". . . uns es ist seine Offenbarung des wesentlichen Verhältnisses zwischen Gott

stages to see how the latter and former parts interconnect. Moreover, that Israel was the chosen people means its book is the Word of God for us: we should not see it as needing its Israelite nature removed in order to see its usefulness theologically. And we need the whole of it, and not just the New Testament as that part of the Bible corresponding more obviously to Christian experience. As he put it programmatically, "the systematic project as I intend it is not a description of the Christian-religious condition of feeling, nor a version of the content of scriptural and ecclesial teaching, but as an unfolding of the simple actual condition which makes a Christian a Christian."[19]

Hofmann was one whose theology shuttled and mediated between objective and subjective forms of truth. Theology had to show how truth was located in faith, yet it must also demonstrate how historical truth and scriptural truth corresponded.[20] Scripture came out of real human situations and needs,[21] yet the content of saving truth made Scripture different from, say, Herodotus's *History* for Scripture promoted *Heilsgewissheit* in actual lives. It was not through historical criticism that one could receive the saving *Tatsachen*. Hofmann suspected that the approach of his contemporary, the liberal pietistic (Schleiermacherian) Richard Rothe made the Spirit and experience dependent on the objective revealing of the biblical texts in the light of the historical Jesus. No, Hofmann objected, that would make experience dependent on the results of historical enquiry when it should be a methodically unapproachable moment of *religiose Gewißheitserfahrung*. The Spirit-induced experience should come first, biblical theology second and subordinately.[22]

There is an immediate awareness of being in relation to Christ and God, but in terms of the order of being the experience presupposes what God has done in creating relationship from Abraham onwards. Scriptural

---

und der Menschheit" (ibid., 26), quoted in Steck, *Idee*, 104.

19. *Der Schriftbeweis*, 11: "Die systematische Thätigkeit, welche ich meine, ist nun weder Beschreibung der christlich-religiösen Gemüthszustände, noch Wiedergabe des Inhalts der Schriftlehre und Kirchenlehre . . . sondern Entfaltung des einfachen Thatbestand, welcher den Christen zum Christen macht."

20. On this relationship between history and faith in Hofmann, see Lauster, *Prinzip*, 173: "Diese Mittelstellung resultiert aus dem Bemühen, die beiden eingangs erwähnten Dimensionen einer subjektiven, d.h. an der individuellen Erfahrung festzumachenden und einer objektiven, d.h. an den historischen Ereignissen auszuweisenden Schriftlehre miteinander in Einklang zu bringen."

21. von Hofmann, *Weissagung* I, 48.

22. Lauster, *Prinzip*, 182–83, with reference to Lauster, *Die heilige Schrift*, 40.

exegesis is thus a means to assurance of faith (*Vergewisserung*).[23] In so doing the aim is not to know there is a God, but that he is the one who raised Christ from the dead. Scriptural understanding adds fullness to faith. Hofmann also composed a biblical hermeneutics which maintained that the two testaments were of equal value and warned the reader not to discard the Old as Schleiermacher would have one do. Yet there is, he asserts, a threefold distinction of content in the Bible which operates regardless of which Testament we are in, since Scripture is not a sort of textbook of conceptual truths, but the source of our knowledge of a history in which it itself originates. These can be of three genres: reports of events in the past, statements about the present, and oracles about the future.[24]

Christoph Senft observes how Hofmann was aware of having to avoid the extremes represented by Semler, that of reading the Bible just as any other book, and of Orthodoxy (or Pietism for that matter) which would ignore the historical nature of the Word of Revelation.[25] For to be able to grasp the point we have to enter into the whole of the historical network. God's revelation conditioned itself to human conditions.[26] Hence biblical theology centers on the relationship of faith to the revealed history, not a feeling of absolute dependence, from which it moves forward. Senft goes on, unfairly in my view, to argue that Hofmann was caught between a dedication to history and a conservative churchmanship. For in fact the two go together well: conservatives have never been able to do without history.

It is not too bold a claim to conclude that Hofmann stood firmly in the Gablerian tradition. One might be put off the scent of a Lutheran

---

23. Slenczka, "Johann Christian Konrad von Hofmann," 149: "Dogmatische Theologie ist nichts anderes als die Explikation dessen, was im Bewusstsein des wieder geborenen Christen gesetzt ist, und zweitens die Überprüfing der Übereinstimmung desselben mit der Schrift."

24. Hofmann, *Biblische Hermeneutik*, 225: "Es geht nun aber auch durch beide Hälften eine Unterschiedlichkeit des Inhalts hindurch, welche darin ihren Grund hat, daß die Schrift kein Lehrbuch begrifflicher Wahrheiten, sondern Urkunde einer Geschichte und inmitten derselben entstanden ist, indem dies mit sich bringt, daß ihr Heilszeugnis theils Bericht von Geschehenem, theils Aussage von Gegenwärtigem und theils Vorhersagung von Zukünftigem ist."

25. Summed up by Senft, *Wahrhaftigkeit und Wahrheit*, 90, as: "erstens die ruhige *Anerkennung der Geschichtlichkeit der Schrift*, zweitens ein *lebensmäßiges Verhältnis zur bezeugten Wahrheit*."

26. As Senft put it (ibid., 95), Hofmann saw his job as holding together the freedom of those who were inspired, the historical "conditionedness" of divine revelation and the correspondence between the historical manifestation and the divine intention.

and Gablerian trail running through to Hofmann by the claim that he was open to non-Lutheran forces; long ago, G. Schrenk[27] made the case that "Hofmann's views are profoundly rooted in the covenant theology of Cocceius mediated to Hofmann through the Reformed Erlangen professor and pastor Christian Krafft." Or as Albrecht Ritschl claimed: "Cocceius [was] the rich uncle whose inheritance went to Bengel and Hofmann."[28] Unlike Bengel, the Bible for Hofmann was not to be read synchronically as a whole, but with attention to its diachronic sequence.[29] In that he was not so much "Reformed" as post-Gablerian. Hofmann, in contrast to Cullmann, considered *Heilsgeschichte* to be a more comprehensive category than "world history."

Scripture as a whole is God's word—it is not the case that some bits are closer to Christ than others. If we want to have a *Denkmal* of the whole history in its religious aspect, then we must read each part in relation to the whole.[30] And human history will change for the better if it learns from the Old Testament. One obvious way to answer the question of Hofmann's debt to Gabler is to look at where the former actually mentioned the latter. Hofmann's own view of Gabler is revealed in his own account of biblical theology. The distinction between rational truth and time-conditioned ideas he found already discussed in Zächaria (1771). But, says Hofmann, Gabler called for two sciences: one historical, the other didactic, and he demanded for the former a consideration of the historical fixedness with which the individual teachers and writers offered that which one takes from Scripture. Only then, once all has been grasped and received in its historical context, did he allow for a comparison between these where they were similar.

However the next generation, was more influenced by Semler than Gabler, such that, the more biblical theology was treated as a historical religion, the more it was treated as a branch of the history of religion, as with Bauer and Kayser.[31] De Wette's project in reducing biblical dogmatics

---

27. Schrenk, *Gottesreich*, 330.
28. Quoted by Schrenk, ibid., 331.
29. Cf. Kantzenbach, *Der Weg der evangelischen Kirche*, 80.
30. Hofmann, *Die biblische Theologie des Neuen Testaments*, 3: "Ist die Schrift als Ganze Gottes Wort, so hat sie überall gleicher Maßen Beweiskraft."
31. Ibid., 4: "Das größte Verdienst um eine richtigere Fassung der Aufgabe unserer Disciplin hat sich Gabler erworben durch seine Nebe *de justo discrimine theol. bibl. et dogm. regundisque recte utriusque finibus* (Altdorf 1789). Er nennt jene eine historische, diese eine didaktische Wissenschaft und fordert für jene Beachtung der

to ideas of pure religion without much regard for historical realities was far from Gabler's vision, one which went largely unfulfilled.[32] Hofmann regarded Gabler as a glorious failure, but that was not due to his own fault. With Hofmann one can at least see a basic sympathy for Gabler's manifesto. Recent Lutheran exegetes have not always extended the same degree of kindness to Hofmann in turn. Peter Stuhlmacher regards him as one of the essential fathers of a 'Hermeneutik des Einverständnisses'; yet he receives a not wholly positive verdict from the Tübingen biblical theologian: indeed, according to Stuhlmacher, Beck and Hofmann's activity led to "eine innergläubige Isolierung."[33]

Just as critical is the study of Eberhard Hübner,[34] for whom Hofmann's theology was really too much like an anthropology, and his notion of "salvation history" allowed too much to "development," with Christ's work as mere fulfilment of human need. Hübner finds problematic Hofmann's idea that Christ is not so much the model of the relationship between God and humans, but is the relationship of God and humans itself.[35] In Hofmann's own day he was attacked more from the right: his insistence that E. Hengstenberg's *a priori* dismissal of historical-critical

---

geschichtlichen Bestimmtheit, mit der die einzelnen Lehrer und Schriftsteller das bieten, was man aus der Schrift entnimmt, und erst, nachdem man auf diese Weise Alles in seiner geschichtlichen Umgebung erfaßt und erhoben hat, laßt er eine Vergleichung zu zwischen ihnen hinsichtlich des Gemeinsamen. Da nun aber seit Semler kein spezifischer Unterschied mehr behauptet wurde zwischen der in der Schrift beurkundeten Religion und den Religionen anderer Völker, so wurde die bibl. Theologie, je mehr man sie als historische Disciplin faßte, als Zweig der allgemeinen Religionsgeschichte behandelt, wie von L. Bauer (Bibl. Theol. der. N.T. 1800–2) und Kayser (Bibl. Theol. od. Judaismus u. Christianismus 1813)."

32. "De Wette bemißt in seiner bibl. Dogmatik 1813, was reine Religon ist, nach der Fries'schen Philosophie und nach dem, was so reine Religion ist, bemißt er die Wirklichkeit der Thatsachen der h. Geschichte und nach diesem Ergebnis das Alter und die Entstehungsgeschichte der biblischen Schriften. Bei solchem Verfahren erfüllte man doch nicht Gablers Forderung." (ibid., 50)

33. Stuhlmacher, *Vom Verstehen des Neuen Testaments*, 156–59.

34. übner, *Schrift und Theologie*, 123: "also auch die Heiligung als der nun dominierende Inhalt der Heilsgeschichte, nicht mehr theologisch, sondern anthropologisch fundamentiert ist."

35. "... nicht mehr Vorbild des Verhältnisses Gottes und des Menschen, sondern *Verhältnis Gottes und des Menschen selbst* ist" (Hofmann, *Schriftbeweis*, 45; quoted in Hübner, *Schrift und Theologie*, 127). Of course this Christocentricity, whereby Christ occupies the God-Humanity "betweenness," contrasts with Harrisville's assessment, who in his entry on Hofmann in the *Handbook of Major Biblical Interpreters* identifies Hofmann with Jacob Boehme.

method was misconceived lost him friends, and it seemed that his opposition to traditional satisfaction accounts of the Cross of Christ paved the way for Ritschl's theory.[36] If Hofmann's biblical theology stood halfway between a pure dogmatic and pure historic approach, this was in the spirit of Gabler's manifesto, but again, caught in the middle ground, it too was a failure, even an inglorious one.

Martin Kähler

According to J. Wirsching, the Halle theologian Martin Kähler adopted the central piece of Christian theism, viz., the revealing of God's personhood through analogy with our own.[37] With help from Hofmann, Kähler was able to resist the tendency of others such as Tholuck at Halle to split the OT off from the NT. The whole Bible displays God's own personal economy, yet one which also worked in the hearts of humans. However, in his dictionary article "Biblische Theologie," Kähler came to view Gabler as a neologist preparing the way for those who would reduce biblical revelation to a rationalistic religious teaching. Kähler's view of Gabler is clearly far less positive than that of Hofmann. Ever since, he writes, the historical critics suppose that edifying truth can emerge from the ashes of historical doubt; but all historical knowledge is itself to be doubted, and what one has to find is a constructive way of relating the biblical material to the course of the events of saving history.

---

36. Pfleiderer, *Die Entwicklung der protestantischen Theologie*, 178: "Noch weiter entfernt sich die Lehre des Erlanger Theologen Chr. Von Hofmann von der kirchlichen Dogmatik.... Im Gründe ist dieser 'Schriftbeweis' das supranaturalistische Seitenstück zur Hegel'schen Philosophie der Geschichte; beiderseits dasselbe Verfahren einer Deduktion der Geschichte aus apriorischen Ideen." (English Translation: *The Development of Theology in Germany*, 174.) Or Kliefoth, *Der Schriftbeweis von Dr J. Chr. K. von Hofmann*, 559: "Es ist die Theologie v.H.'s ein theosophisches System, daß unter Vergewaltigung der Schrift die Heilsgeschichte durch phantasiereiche, aber unwahre Kombinationen entstellt, und das kirchliche Lehrgebäude in der gedoppelten Richtung zersetzt, daß es die mehr theoretischen Dogmen von Gott, der Trinität, der Schöpfung, dem Menschen, der Person und den Naturen und den Ständen Christi durch eingewobene theosophische Elemente entstellt, und in der mehr praktischen Dogmen von der Sünde, der Erlösung und Versöhnung, dem Werk der Gnade, der Aneigung des Heils Alles abschwächt."

37. Wirsching, *Gott in Der Geschichte*, 53: "Kähler habe auch unbedenklich das Kernstuck des christlichen Theismus, die Erschließung der Persönlichkeit Gottes nach Analogie des unsrigen, übernommen." See also Link, *Geschichte Jesu und Bild Christi*; Wimmer, *Geistestheologie*.

For Kähler, the Bible expresses an original life of faith in pristine authenticity and uninterrupted autonomy.[38] "Historical" should be the byword not the main word, the qualifier, not the substantive: theology has own rules in order to be scientific and should not be in thrall to history. *Bibelreligion* was not just about establishing some facts from past but a "wirksame Thatsache der Gegenwart," something having power in enduring church life. History had no right to stand between exegesis and theology. Biblical theology's task was to raise the Bible into academic definition and fullness and to serve the Word in caring for the church.[39] That this is more about application than universal interpretation is implied in his concession that of course any biblical theology will be a child of its age. Rather than "Systematics" to keep biblical theology from historicism, we need to preach the biblical material in all its width and range, he contends. Kähler concludes that it is arguably unhistorical to treat the Bible as document with which to reconstruct history of religion: the Bible was meant to be heard, not discussed, and for the NT this means to appreciate the traditions coming from Jesus, and not just "the gospel." A belief in the inspiration of the Bible as whole was one reason for not attacking it on points of detail. Yet a division of the two Testaments is necessary, since each belongs to a different stage of revelation, and one should be taught by what the NT does with the OT, e.g., filtering out its wilder bits.

It is unclear whether Kähler surrendered Gabler to the *Religionsgeschichtliche Schule*, or whether (more likely) Gabler had already been appropriated. When one looks back from the work that Kähler continues to be known for, the *Der sogenannte historische Jesus und der geschichtliche, biblische Christus* (1892) to his statement of theology *Die Wissenschaft der christlichen Lehre von dem evangelischen Grundartikel aus* (1883), with a series of additions,[40] one can only see a fairly dry systematic work, hardly redolent of the theology informed by the Bible understood historically, in the spirit of Gabler and Hofmann. In this earlier, foundational work Scripture is usually mentioned in the last paragraph of a section as a

---

38. Kähler, "Biblische Theologie," 197: "Sie geht von dem Eindruck aus, daß sich in der Bibel ein ursprüngliches Glaubensleben in unverfälschter Eigenheit und ungebrochener Selbständigkeit ausgesprochen hat und in seiner Bezeugung eine im Grunde einheitliche Anschauungsweise darlegt."

39. "Die biblische Theologie soll das Wort Gottes so, wie die Bibel es überliefert, in wissenschaftlicher Bestimmtheit und Vollständigkeit erheben und dem Dienst am Wort übermitteln, sowohl seiner verschiedenartigen Ausrichtung in der Gemeindepflege" (ibid., 199).

40. Kähler, *Dogmatische Zeitfragen*.

way of checking the content of confessional theology.⁴¹ In his famous *Der sogenannte historische Jesus* (1896), although some biblical texts do come to the fore, the scriptural content is reduced to a point where there is little "rein" biblical theology, since there is little "wahr" biblical theology for it to draw on.

Conclusion

This essay not only calls into question the wholesale misappropriation of Gabler, or the substitution of half-Gabler for whole Gabler, it also should make one pause before accepting Robert Yarborough's hypothesis⁴² of an "alternative" line running from Von Hofmann through Kähler to Schlatter to Goppelt (who of course inherited the notion of "typology") and on to Cullmann. Kähler's "whole Jesus clothed in his tradition" (not a "Jesus of faith") and *"Grundthatsachen,"* which gives assurance but not living faith, owes *something* to Hofmann, but is far less attractive.⁴³ While Kähler believed the objective faith saved, and the experience assured us, not vice versa,⁴⁴ for Hofmann personal assurance was Christian faith, even while dependent of the fellowship with God objectively gained in Christ, whose content is revealed in Scripture's witness.⁴⁵ In that sense Hofmann's hermeneutical method moved, as Gabler's would, from the spiritual, living, and historical particular faith of the ancient people of God towards the principles that would in turn inform living faith in this day. Hence Hofmann, but not Kähler and his successors, was truer to the spirit of Gabler, as one whose approach started with faith and ended with theology for faith.

41. Ibid., 51: ". . . ihre Geltung als höchsten Maßstabes für den kirchlichen Unterricht." Hence, the Bible gives assurance not faith: the idea is of an uninterrupted church history of salvation; he contends against any Biblicism, and ("sogenannte") biblical theology exists to serve exegesis.

42. Yarbrough, *Salvation Historical Fallacy?*

43. Merk, "Theologie des Neuen Testaments."

44. Mildenburger, "Martin Kähler."

45. Schwöbel, "Heilsgeschichte," 747: "Die christliche Glaube ist für v. Hofmann allerdings—wie für F. H. R Frank, . . . persönliche Gewissheit. Diese Gewissheit aber ist die subjective Gewiss-Sein einer objektiven Wahrheit, der Wahrheit der in Christus realisierten Gemeinschaft mit Gott, deren Inhalte durch das Zeugnis der Schrift dem christlichen Glauben zu verstehen gegeben wird.' See also in the same volume the essay by Johannes Wischmeyer: 'Heilsgeschichte im Zeitalter des Historismus: das geschichtstheologische Programm Johann Christian Konrad Hofmanns."

Bibliography

Bauer, Georg Lorenz. *Theologie des Alten Testaments oder Abriß der religiösen Begriffe der alten Hebräer*. Leipzig: Weigand, 1796.

Becker, Matthew. *The Self-Giving God and Salvation History: The Trinitarian Theology of Johannes Von Hofmann*. London: T. & T. Clark, 2004.

Beyschlag, Karlmann. *Die Erlanger Theologie*. Erlangen: Verlag für Kirchengeschichte Bayerns, 1993.

Childs, Brevard S. *Biblical Theology of Old and New Testaments*. Minneapolis: Fortress, 1992.

———. *The Struggle to Understand Isaiah as Christian Scripture*. Grand Rapids: Eerdmans, 2004.

Ebeling, Gerhard. "Die Bedeutung der historisch-kritischen Methode für die protestantische Theologie und Kirche." *Zeitschrift für Theologie und Kirche* 47 (1950) 1–46.

Esler, Philip. *New Testament Theology: Communion and Community*. Minneapolis: Fortress, 2004.

Gabler, Johann Philipp. *De justo discrimine theol. bibl. et dogm. regundisque recte utriusque finibus*. Altdorf, 1789.

Frey, Jörg. "Zum Problem der Aufgabe und Durchführung einer Theologie des Neuen Testaments." In *Aufgabe und Durchführung einer Theologie des Neuen Testaments*, edited by Cilliers Breytenbach and Jörg Frey, 3–45. Tübingen: Mohr Siebeck, 2007.

Harrisville, Roy. "Hofmann, Johann Christian Konrad von." In Dictionary of Major Biblical Interpreters, edited by Donald McKim, 533–37. Downers Grove, IL: InterVarsity, 2007.

Hofmann, Johann Christian Konrad von. *Der Schriftbeweis: Ein theologische. Versuch*, Nördlingen: C. H. Beck, 1852.

———. *Biblische Hermeneutik Nach Manuscripten und Vorlesungen* (=Die heilige Schrift neuen Testaments, zusammenhängend untersucht, Bd. 11; hrsg. von W. Volck: Nördlingen Beck, 1886.

———. *Die heilige Schrift neuen Testaments zusammenhängend untersucht*. Vol. 1. Nördlingen: C. H. Beck, 1862.

Holte, Ragner. *Die Vermittlungstheologie*. Uppsala: Almquist, 1965.

Hübner, Eberhard, *Schrift und Theologie. Eine Untersuchung zur Theologie JCK von Hofmanns*. München: Kaiser, 1956.

Kähler, Martin. "Biblische Theologie." In *Realencyklopädie für protestantische Theologie und Kirche*, vol. 3, edited by J. J. Herzog, Albert Hauck, and Hermann Caselmann, 192–200. Leipzig: J. C. Hinrich, 1896–1913.

———. *Dogmatische Zeitfragen. Alte und neue Ausführungen zur Wissenschaft der christlichen Lehre* 1. Heft. Leipzig 1898 2. Heft: Zur Lehre von der Versöhnung. Leipzig 1898; 2. Band: Angewandte Dogmen, Leipzig 1908; 3. Band: Zeit und Ewigkeit, Leipzig 1913.

Kantzenbach, Friedrich Wilhelm. *Die Erlanger Theologie. Grundlinien ihrer Entwicklung im Rahmen der Geschichte der Theologischen Fakultät 1743–1877*. München: Evangelische Presseverband für Bayern, 1960.

———. *Der Weg der evangelischen Kirche vom 19. Zum 20. Jahrhundert* Gutersloh: Mohn, 1968.

Kliefoth, Friedrich D. *Der Schriftbeweis von Dr J. Chr. K. von Hofmann.* Schwerin: Otto, 1859.
Lauster, Jörg. *Prinzip und methode, Die Transformation des protestantischen Schriftprinzips durch die historische Kritik von Schleiermacher bis zur Gegenwart.* Tübingen: Mohr Siebeck, 2004.
Link, Hans-Georg. *Geschichte Jesu und Bild Christi. Die Entwicklung der Christologie Martin Kählers in Auseinandersetzung mit der Leben-Jesu-Theologie und der Ritschl-Schule* Neukirchen-Vluyn: Neukirchner, 1975.
Merk, Otto. *Biblische Theologie des Neuen Testaments in ihrer Anfangszeit: ihre methodischen Probleme bei Johann Philipp Gabler und Georg Lorenz Bauer und deren Nachwirkungen.* Marburg: Elwert, 1972.
———. "Theologie des Neuen Testaments und biblische Theologie." In *Wissenschaftsgeschichte und Exegese,* 98–129. Beihefte Zur Zeitschrift für die Neutestamentliche Wissenschaft 95. Berlin: De Gruyter, 1998.
Mildenburger, Friedrich. "Martin Kähler." In *Gestalten der Kirchengeschichte. Bd. 9.2. Die neueste Zeit II.,* edited by Martin Greschat, 278–88. Stuttgart: Kohlhammer, 1985.
Pfleiderer, Otto. *Die Entwicklung der protestantischen Theologie in Deutschland seit Kant und in Grossbritannien seit 1825.* Tübingen: Mohr, 1891.
———. *The Development of Theology in Germany Since Kant: And Its Progress in Great Britain Since 1825.* London: S. Sonnenschein, 1890.
Sandys-Wunsch, John. *What Have They Done to the Bible? A History of Modern Biblical Interpretation.* Collegeville, MN: Liturgical, 2005.
Saebø, Magne. *On the Way to Canon, Creative Tradition History in the Old Testament.* London: T. & T. Clark, 1998.
Schlier, Heinrich. "Biblische und dogmatische Theologie." In *Besinnung auf das Neuen Testament: Gesammelte Aufsätze II,* 25–34. Freiburg: Herder, 1964.
Schrenck, Gottlob. *Gottesreich und Bund im älteren Protestantismus vornehmlich bei Johannes Coccejus. Zugleich ein Beitrag zur Geschichte des Pietismus.* Gütersloh: Bertelsmann, 1923.
Schwöbel, Christoph. "'Heilsgeschichte' Zur Anatomie eines umstrittenen theologischen Konzepts." In *Heil und Geschichte: Die Geschichtsbezogenheit des Heils und das Problem der Heilsgeschichte in der biblischen Tradition und in der theologischen Deutung,* edited by Jörg Frey, Stefan Krauter and Hermann Lichtenberger, 745–57. Tübingen: Mohr Siebeck, 2009.
Segalla, Giuseppe. "Teologia biblica." In *Nuovo Dizionario di biblica teologia,* 1533–39. Milano: San Paolo, 1988.
Senft, Christoph. *Wahrhaftigkeit und Wahrheit. Die Theologie des 19. Jh zwischen Orthodoxie und Aufklärung.* Beiträge zur hisorischen Theologie 22. Tübingen: Mohr Siebeck, 1956.
Simon, Matthias. "Die innere Erneuerung der Theologischen Fakultät Erlangen im Jahr 1833." *Zeitschrift für bayerische Kirchengeschichte* 30 (1961) 51–69.
Slenczka, Notger. "Eine neue Weise, alte Wahrheit zu lehren." In *Theologen des 19. Jahrhunderts,* edited by Peter Neuner and Gunther Wenz, 144–64 Darmstadt: WBG, 2002.
Smend, Rudolf. "Johann Gablers Begründung der biblischen Theologie." *Evangelische Theologie* 22 (1962).

Steck, Karl. *Die Idee der Heilsgeschichte: Hofmann-Schlatter-Cullmann.* Zollikon: Evangelischer Verlag, 1959.

———. "Johann Christian Konrad von Hofmann (1819–1877)." In *Theologen des Protestantismus im 19. und 20, Jahrhundert*, edited by Martin Greschat, 99–112. Stuttgart: Kohlhammer, 1978.

Stuckenbruck, Loren, T. "Johann Philipp Gabler and the Delineation of Biblical Theology." *Scottish Journal of Theology* 52 (1999).

Stuhlmacher, Peter. *Vom Verstehen des Neuen Testaments. Eine Hermeneutik, Grundrisse zum Neuen Testament*; NTD Ergänzungsreihe (Band 6). Auflage: Göttingen 1986.

Swarat, Uwe. "Die heilsgeschichtliche Konzeption Johannes Chr. K. von Hofmanns." In *Glaube und Geschichte. Heilsgeschichte als Thema der Theologie*, edited by Helge Stadelmann, 211–39. Gießen (u. a.), 1986.

Wimmer, Ulrich. *Geistestheologie. Eine Untersuchung zur Grundlegung der Theologie und zur Pneumatologie bei Martin Kähler* Neuss: Päffgen, 1978.

Wirsching, J. *Gott in Der Geschichte.* München: Kaiser, 1963.

Wischmeyer, Johannes. "Heilsgeschichte im Zeitalter des Historismus: das geschichtstheologische Programm Johann Christian Konrad Hofmanns." In *Heil und Geschichte: Die Geschichtsbezogenheit des Heils und das Problem der Heilsgeschichte in der biblischen Tradition und in der theologischen Deutung*, edited by Jörg Frey, Stefan Krauter and Hermann Lichtenberger, 633–46. Tübingen: Mohr Siebeck, 2009.

Yarbrough, Robert W. *The Salvation Historical Fallacy? Reassessing the History of New Testament Theology.* Leiden: Deo, 2004.

Campegius Vitringa Sr. (1659–1722)

A Biblical Theologian at the Turn of the Eighteenth Century[1]

Charles K. Telfer

THIRTY YEARS AFTER VITRINGA's death, far off in the Americas, Jonathan Edwards cited a letter from his Scottish correspondent, John Erskine, stating, "Perhaps there was never a commentary published on any part of Sacred Scripture equal in learning and judgment to Vitringa on Isaiah and in which so much valuable light is thrown on many difficult texts."[2] Vitringa's massive commentary on Isaiah (1772 folio pages) was the product of thirty years of effort. The philological and historical research it represents was widely respected, even by reviewers such as Jean LeClerc.[3] All the careful details of this work, down to the extensive indices, show that this was a labor of love, published in Latin in 1714 with the second volume in 1720. The work was translated into Dutch and German and

---

1. I would like to devote this essay to the memory of Dr. Willem van Asselt. The expected participation of Dr. van Asselt was sorely missed at our SBL sessions in Amsterdam. His death has robbed the scholarly community of one of its foremost workmen in the field of post-Reformation studies. I personally am indebted to Dr. van Asselt for his work on Cocceius, which became a point of entry for me into Vitringa studies, and for his warm hospitality during a visit to the University of Utrecht around the time of our conference.

2. Edwards, "'Catalogue' of Reading," 277. Here Edwards cites the Rev. John Erskine (a Scottish correspondent of JE's) "in a letter to me dated May 13, 1752."

3. Jean LeClerc, a notable biblical scholar and one of the gatekeepers of the "Republic of Letters," highly valued Vitringa's learning and judgment as well. In a review of a certain book LeClerc notes the support of, "Monsieur Vitringa, the Elder, who [is] a very excellent judge . . . and whose impartiality [is] universally confessed." Golden, *Jean LeClerc*, 51.

had a wide influence throughout the eighteenth century, especially in Germany.[4] Even Gesenius commended this "masterpiece of historical exegesis," speaking highly of the methodology it exemplified.[5] According to Brevard Childs, the Isaiah commentary "dominated the field for a century."[6]

Work

In his day, Vitringa was internationally-known for many of his publications. His *De synagoga vetere* emerged out of a controversy with Lightfoot over the relationship of the synagogue to the church.[7] His *Dissertatio theologica de generatione filii* came from the controversy with his colleague Herman Alexander Roëll who showed tendencies toward rationalism.[8] Vitringa published a short systematic theology in 1693 which was widely used by students.[9] He produced a substantial commentary on the Book of Revelation, which laid a foundation for his further interpretative work in the OT prophets.[10] He wrote a work on the need and authority of church synods and a guidebook for preaching.[11] As Richard Muller notes, Vitringa was well-appreciated as a biblical chronographer and chorographer, producing a summary of world and biblical history through the first century AD, and, among his posthumous works, a *Geographia sacra*.[12] From exegetical studies throughout his career he published a six-volume *Observationum sacrarum*, which J. F. Buddeus, in a 1737 review called "books bursting with remarkable learning."[13]

4. Witteveen, "Campegius Vitringa," 359.

5. Ibid., 357.

6. Childs, "Hermeneutical Reflections," 89.

7. Vitringa, *De synagoga vetere*. Cf. the severe English abridgment: *The Synagogue and the Church*.

8. Roell and Vitringa, *De generatione Filii*.

9. Vitringa, *Doctrina christianae religionis*.

10. Vitringa, *Anacrisis Apocalypseos*.

11. Vitringa, *Oratio de synodes*, and *Animadversiones ad methodum homiliarum ecclesiasticarum*.

12. "His importance as an exegete lay in his philological skills and his examination of historical and geographical background in the interpretation of texts. He stands in the tradition of seventeenth-century chronologists and chorographers, among whom Ussher and Lightfoot are also to be numbered" (Muller, "Biblical Interpretation," 40).

13. Büsching, "Lebenslauf," 36.

Among his many other works is *Typus doctrinae propheticae* in which he outlines a methodology for interpreting prophetic texts, a work of special interest for describing his hermeneutics.[14]

Vita

According to Anton Friederich Büsching, who authored his *Lebenslauf* and translated his Isaiah commentary, Vitringa was a *Wunderkind* with languages, mastering much of the Greek New Testament and Hebrew Old Testament as a teenager. When he was sixteen he gave an oration in Latin entitled "On Christian Patience" which was delivered "with such skill and . . . brilliance that the hearers were left astonished. The famous Herman Witsius (who was still a preacher in Leeuwarden at that time) . . . was so moved . . . that he could not restrain himself from weeping."[15] Witsius became a close teacher and patron of Vitringa. Vitringa studied at Franeker not only with Witsius, but also with Arnold, and Mardius. He continued his studies at Leiden under Spanheim, Wittichius, and Le Monne. In 1680, he became professor of Hebrew Language and Holy Antiquities at the University of Franeker at the age of twenty-one, and his inaugural address was "On the Duty of a Proper Interpreter of the Holy Scriptures." Thirteen years later he also became professor of Sacred History.

Though he was twice invited to take up a post at the University of Leiden, and offered an overwhelmingly generous salary as an enticement (the story of which involves Statholder William III, of William and Mary fame), Vitringa began and ended his teaching career at the University of Franeker in Friesland. His son Campegius Jr. succeeded him in his professorate, but succumbed to death himself a year later in 1723.

Secondary Literature

Historically, however—and particularly in the twentieth century and in English-speaking countries—Vitringa has often been overlooked. Perhaps this is because many so-called, "pre-critical" exegetes have long been considered as having little to contribute to scholarly biblical studies. Perhaps this is because of a lamentable ignorance of Latin, especially in

---

14. Vitringa, *Typus doctrinae propheticae*.
15. Büsching, "Lebenslauf," 27.

the United States. Brevard Childs of Yale is a notable exception to these tendencies, having written the article, "Hermeneutical Reflections on Campegius Vitringa, Eighteenth-Century Interpreter of Isaiah" in 1999, which was modified and included in his 2004 monograph: *The Struggle to Understand Isaiah as Christian Scripture*.[16] John Sandys-Wunsch of Victoria BC treats Vitringa briefly as one of the "Early Old Testament Critics on the Continent" as a part of the vast Vandenhoeck and Ruprecht series on the *Hebrew Bible/Old Testament: The History of Its Interpretation*.[17] More substantially, two Dutch scholars in the 90s directed their attentions to Vitringa: Klaas Marten Witteween in a 1993 article, "Campegius Vitringa und die prophetische Theologie," and Ernestine van der Wall in a 1994 contribution entitled, "Between Grotius and Cocceius: The 'Theologia Prophetica' of Campegius Vitringa (1659-1722)."[18]

Previous to these excellent contributions, other continental studies, particularly by German scholars, have dealt with Vitringa, but they often dwell on narrower concerns, in particular, his contributions to Pietism. Bauch and Schrenk make valuable contributions in this area.[19] Still earlier, Diestel dedicates a number of pages to Vitringa as one of the major interpreters of the Reformed church in his 1869 encyclopedic survey *Geschichte des Alten Testamentes in der christlichen Kirche*.[20] The only monograph-length study on Vitringa until my own work has been Willem F. C. J. van Heel's 1865 Utrecht dissertation: *Campegius Vitringa Sr. als Godgeleerde Beschouwd*—Vitringa considered as a theologian.[21]

There is a consensus of scholarship that Vitringa's approach to the interpretation of the Bible lies between that of two major conversation partners: Hugo Grotius and Johannnes Cocceius. The major disagreements among Vitringa scholars can perhaps be summarized in two questions. First, to which of these predecessors is Vitringa more indebted? To put it crudely, is he obligated more to the historical emphasis of Grotius or the Christological emphasis of Cocceius? A closely connected second

---

16. Childs, *Struggle to Understand Isaiah*.

17. Sandys-Wunsch, "Early Old Testament Critics," 971-76.

18. Witteveen, "Campegius Vitringa," and Wall, "Between Grotius and Cocceius," 195-215.

19. Bauch, *Die Lehre vom Wirken des Heiligen Geistes im Frühpietismus*, and Schrenk, *Gottesreich und Bund*.

20. Diestel, *Geschichte des Alten Testamentes in der Christlichen Kirche*.

21. Heel, "Campegius Vitringa Sr. als Godgeleerd." For a detailed examination of Vitringa's exegetical method in theory and in practice see my *Wrestling with Isaiah*.

question is this: Does Vitringa's interpretative method shift significantly over the course of his lifetime? Some scholars want to see Vitringa as essentially Grotian, committed to an emerging Enlightenment approach, seeing the light more and more clearly and leaving churchly interpretative schemes behind. Along these lines Heel remarks, "In his early years as a young Cocceian, typological exegesis [*die Typik*] captivated him, but as he grew older, however, he saw ever more clearly what was the proper duty (task) of an exegete, and his Isaiah commentary is the fruit thereof."[22] And even Diestel remarks, "Not infrequently it seems as if in giving these kinds of [spiritual] interpretations he is bending unwillingly to the spirit of his age."[23] In other words, Vitringa was committed to emerging modernist canons of biblical interpretation, but concern for his readers kept him in traditional ruts. Unfortunately, such a view seems to reflect a certain triumphalistic historiography, charting the inevitable emergence of the historical-critical method over unscientific, more traditional approaches to the Bible. Witteveen dispels the rosy misconception that there was a notable change in the mature Vitringa by comparing the earlier work on the Apocalypse and his later work on Isaiah. There is no decisive shift in approach—rather, there is a large continuity between the two works.[24]

His Views of Grotius

Vitringa calls Grotius "a man of immortal merit in the world of letters."[25] He sympathizes with Grotius's concern to find the fulfillment of prophecy near to the time in which it was uttered. Vitringa agrees with Grotius's complaint against interpreters who, when they find something difficult to understand in the text, immediately refer its fulfillment to NT times or the end times. Vitringa takes historical fulfillment just as seriously as Grotius does. He is sympathetic that the prophecies of Isaiah were intended for the Jewish people of his day and addressed immanent questions.[26]

Nevertheless, there is an unbridgeable chasm between the hermeneutics of Grotius and of Vitringa, who writes, "If the hypothesis of

---

22. Witteveen, "Campegius Vitringa und die prophetische Theologie," 356–57.
23. Ibid., 357.
24. Ibid., 347.
25. Vitringa, "Praefatio Ad Lectorem," 13.
26. Ibid., 13–15.

Grotius prevails, Isaiah in his entire book of prophecies contains no direct, proper and clear prophecy about Christ Jesus and his kingdom anywhere."[27] Grotius's caveat that there exists a "sublime" sense is unproductive.[28] Even when Grotius is dealing with something which clearly and solidly points to Christ, it vanishes under his treatment. Grotius falls under the condemnation of the Lord Jesus himself who rebuked those "who were slow in reading the prophetic word with a prudent and spiritual eye," since all the Scriptures were written concerning him (cf. Luke 24:27).[29]

For Vitringa, Christian interpreters find a definitive hermeneutic in the approach of Jesus recorded in the gospels and of the apostles. For example, Vitringa quotes John 1:45 (that Christ is the one of whom Moses in the law and also the prophets wrote), Acts 10:43 (where Peter affirms that "to him all the prophets witness"), and 1 Peter 1:10–11 (that the Spirit of Christ in the prophets "testified beforehand to the sufferings of Christ and the glories that would follow"). The tension between Vitringa and Grotius is of course one of the great hermeneutical questions posed through the ages: how normative is the approach of Jesus and the apostles for the interpretation of OT texts? In perhaps Grotius's most egregious example of a sub-Christian approach to Isaiah, he attributes the descriptions of a suffering servant in Isa 52:12 through 53 as referring to Jeremiah, and not to Jesus Christ. Vitringa notes, "Shame, not reason, drives learned men to this opinion." Grotius's approach is a "new way, thus far walked by no Christian."[30] There can be no proper interpretive horizons for the prophets apart from a connection to the New Testament. According to Vitringa, Grotius falls short because his work produces no special reverence for Jesus Christ and is outside the tradition of Christian interpretation; in fact, he "did so much to detract from the lustre of the prophecies."[31] He has in effect bolstered the Roman Catholic position on Scripture.[32] Grotius's hermeneutical method concerning biblical prophecies became part of the debates over the rational validity of the

---

27. Vitringa, "Praefatio ad lectorem," 15–16.

28. "Admittedly Grotius knows of a 'sensus sublimior,' but he pays so little attention to it and, if he does, talks about it in such a cold manner that it does not seem to play any particular role in his exegesis." Wall, "Between Grotius and Cocceius," 199.

29. Vitringa, "Praefatio Ad Lectorem," 15.

30. Ibid., 15–16.

31. Wall, "Between Grotius and Cocceius," 211.

32. By undermining the perspicuity of Scripture. Ibid., 209.

Christian faith in the late seventeenth-century Dutch Republic. And he was widely used by the opponents of orthodox Protestant Christianity, which of course caused Vitringa deep concern, in part because Grotius undermined an important basis for Christian apologetics with the Jews.[33]

His Views of Cocceius

By contrast, Vitringa speaks of "the eminent Cocceius, by whose labors and merit (which have been so valued by the church), let it be said, I have been influenced."[34] He "brought [to his work] literary learning and a cultivation in history that is required of a meritorious interpreter of prophecies."[35] Cocceius had great "wisdom in the word of God and skill in spiritual things."[36] And "certainly he was second to none of the learned teachers of his time. He had a marvelous perception of the comprehensive wisdom of the Word of God."[37] Perhaps what Vitringa most appreciated about Cocceius was his view that the prophetic word ultimately "was concerned with the person and kingdom of Jesus Christ, and the beginnings, progress and destinies of his kingdom."[38] Vitringa defends Cocceius from the charge of finding the source of his interpretations in Origen. In Cocceius's view, for example, references in Isaiah to Ephraim, Judah, Moab, Egypt, Tyre, etc. admit to only a single sense (rather than multiple senses as in Origen) which is a "proper, historical sense." But that sense for Cocceius often refers to events from times significantly later than those of the prophets themselves, and, somewhat idiosyncratically, at times to developments in post-biblical church history.[39] Vitringa appreciates the diligent search for a historical reference, but is not willing

---

33. "Grotius' ideas about the biblical prophecies could be most appropriately used in the enlightened assault upon scriptural authority and so challenge the traditional beliefs of Christianity. It was precisely this use which could be made of Grotius that long rendered him so unpopular in the eyes of the orthodox divines." Ibid., 195.

34. Ibid., 21.

35. Vitringa, "Praefatio Ad Lectorem," 13.

36. Vitringa, "On the Interpretation of Prophecy," 169.

37. Vitringa, "Praefatio Ad Lectorem," 13.

38. Ibid.

39. Vitringa is hesitant to follow his predecessor in many applications of OT texts to the historical experiences of the Christian church (for example when Cocceius sees in Hosea a prophecy of the division of the Christian church into Western and Eastern halves). Vitringa, "Praefatio Ad Lectorem," 13.

to exclude a nearer historical fulfillment, as well as a fulfillment in the destinies of Christ and his NT church.[40]

Ernestine van der Wall summarizes accurately,

> For most divines in the (early) Enlightenment the choice between the preterist approach of Grotius and the historicist method of Cocceius was not a difficult one: there was a strong predilection for the latter. Campegius Vitringa was no exception to the rule. Though he often praised Grotius' philological achievements ... and seriously tried to connect Grotius' hermeneutics with those of Cocceius, he undoubtedly preferred the Cocceian view of history. Nevertheless he wanted to curb the typological extravagances of Cocceian exegesis. In this he surely followed in the footsteps of his teacher Herman Witsius.[41]

Vitringa explicitly sets himself to walk a *via media*. Following Grotius, Vitringa intends to listen fully and carefully to the prophets as they speak of events in their days, but following Cocceius he sees Christ as the *primarium objectum prophetiarum*, the principal focus of prophetic passages. Biblical writers were inspired by the same Holy Spirit and had the same ultimate subject—Christ and his kingdom. Vitringa expresses his delight, quoting the Song of Songs, in interpreting the prophetic text as showing forth Christ, "the one for whom our souls long."[42]

Canones Hermeneuticos

Vitringa is very transparent in setting forth his own ideal approach to the Bible. In his *Typus doctrinae propheticae* he sets forth various *canones hermeneuticos* that, fortunately, have been translated into English as "Canons for Rightly Expounding Prophecy."[43] Vitringa emphasizes the importance of determining the topic under discussion with the ut-

---

40. "[Cocceius'] *Ultima Mosis* [was a work] in which he labored very diligently. As regards the prophecies of the Old Testament, his work is inestimable; and as regards the New Testament, many things are doubtless ably and piously taught by this learned and accomplished divine; though he might nevertheless have chosen from the prophecies of the Old Testament subjects better adapted to illustrate the fortunes of the New Testament church, than the song and blessing of Moses." Vitringa, "On the Interpretation of Prophecy," 174–75.

41. Wall, "Between Grotius and Cocceius," 202.

42. Vitringa, "Praefatio Ad Lectorem," 15.

43. Vitringa, "On the Interpretation of Prophecy," 157–69.

most clarity. He introduces his basic, bipartite division between "literal/ historical/grammatical/proper" and "mystical/spiritual/prophetic" approaches to interpretation.[44] He calls for attention to all the attributes of the subject in the prophecy and for holding to a literal approach. If this is impossible, one may look for "parallels" and correspondence between type and antitype. Prophecy is history foretold, and history is prophecy fulfilled; they are correlates of one another. Particularly when the language is unbounded, there must be a larger reference. Because of the unity of the canon (due to its plenary inspiration by the Spirit) the interpretation that gives the richer meaning of the text is to be preferred. Not only must we "acquiesce in the judgment" of NT authors when they handle specific OT texts, but we must "take their interpretation as a rule for our own."[45] Therefore Christ and his kingdom is ultimately the center of all prophecy.[46] In this respect Calvin has "not been sufficiently liberal in [his] interpretation of prophecy, although more so than Grotius."[47] When the text asserts something superlative about an individual not mentioned by name, it may be a reference to Christ. Also, Vitringa counsels caution in "overly feeding" speculations regarding future events.[48]

Reoccurring principles underlined in these canons as well as in the *Praefatio* to the Isaiah commentary include an emphasis on the literal/grammatical sense of the text, the search for historical fulfillment in a near period, the need to establish all assertions through rational demonstration, and the importance of comparing each element of the text with its natural parallels (including those in the New Testament).[49]

Vitringa goes on to commend a series of resources and virtues for those who would be good interpreters. They should know Hebrew in particular, and have a "tolerable acquaintance with history."[50] Most importantly, interpreters must compare Scripture with Scripture and consider

44. Ibid., 157.

45. Ibid., 166-67.

46. "It is the business of a good interpreter, first diligently to seek Christ in the word of prophecy . . . and never purposely to avoid, instead of willingly seizing, an opportunity when it offers itself [to point him out]." Ibid., 165.

47. Ibid., 164.

48. Ibid., 157-69.

49. Vitringa sets forth similar concerns in the *Praefatio* to his Revelation commentary as well. Cf. Wall, "Between Grotius and Cocceius," 210.

50. "Such men as Scalinger, Usher, Conring, Marsham, and Vorstius deserve to be mentioned with special commendation in this particular." Vitringa, "On the Interpretation of Prophecy," 172.

the whole in the interpretation of the parts. The basis for Vitringa's efforts in "biblical theology" stem from his assumption of a Spirit-breathed canon.

> Of this we cannot doubt, that the matter, scope and argument of all the prophecies—yea of all Scripture—is the same; that they proceeded from one author, viz. the Holy Spirit; and that therefore they cannot but mutually illustrate each other. Moses, Elijah—yea David, Isaiah, and the whole company of the prophets—here "converse with each other and with Christ;" so that . . . "among them there is nothing but harmony, concord and unanimity: all breathing the same sentiments; and speaking nothing individually which they speak not universally."[51]

More controversially, Cocceius commends the "system of prophetic theology developed in recent times in which prophecies are arranged in accordance with the periods of church history."[52]

There is a pastoral and devotional quality to all of Vitringa's work. His final commendation to biblical scholars is to

> bring to the study a mind chaste, pure, modest, free from willful prejudice, affected with due reverence toward God and his word, entertaining no mean ideas of his revelation, and ready to

---

51. Ibid., 174. As the Schaff-Herzog Encyclopedia puts it, "His views of the Scriptures and their inspiration were in accord with post-Reformation orthodoxy." Kautzsch, "Vitringa," 219.

52. Vitringa, "On The Interpretation of Prophecy," 175:
> In our own age and that immediately preceding, the knowledge of the prophetic word began to be digested into a certain body or systematic form of doctrine, by which the periods of church history are divided, and every prophecy arranged under its own proper time; doubtless the learner will act wisely, in seeking the necessary aids and directions from those books which treat of them, and avail himself of them as useful guides in the reading of the prophecies. . . . Gulichus, Momma, Heidegger, and others whose praise is in the church, have followed closely in the footsteps of Cocceius; and after the essays of these, in the age immediately preceding, the eminent Nich. Gurtler, in our own age, and our own colleague in the Lord, has put forth an excellent *system of prophetic theology*, as well from its being skillfully and diligently composed, as ably digested, and adorned with the needful erudition. In regard to the seven periods of the Church also, our brother and most honoured fellow labourer in Christ, Tillius, following the hypothesis of Cocceius of blessed memory, has pointed out and discussed many things with remarkable discretion and judgment in a tract upon this subject.

Witteveen summarizes Vitringa on this point as promoting "eine typologische, emblematische, änigmatische und prophetische Theologie." Witteveen, "Campegius Vitringa und die prophetische Theologie," 345.

receive with humble and obedient faith every intimation of the divine will.... As this can only be the result of divine grace, the aid of the Holy Spirit must be most earnestly implored, as well to produce those holy affections of the mind, and to preserve them when produced; as to illuminate the mind, and remove the veil of prejudice, directing it to what is right, and withdrawing it from what is contrary; which operation of the Spirit of God good and holy men have at all times acknowledged.... In the light of God we can alone see light; and whosoever is deficient of that divine teaching is in darkness, however wise he may be in his own conceit.... The guidance therefore of the Holy Spirit is especially required in those prophecies the subject of which being *spiritual*, is opposed to the natural prejudices and affections of the carnal man. Thus the true and hidden sense of those predictions which speak of Christ's kingdom, and of the benefits and privileges thereof, cannot be perceived, except by a spiritual man who walks in the faith, and has an *experience*, as well as knowledge of these things.[53]

Vitringa's Influence

Vitringa's students appear again and again in the "Who's Who" biographies of the Netherlands in the eighteenth century.[54] His successor at Franeker (and son-in-law) Herman Venema continued the main trajectory of his approach through much of the eighteenth century.

---

53. Ibid., 175–76.

54. Van der Wall makes a bold but credible summary: "[Vitringa] was known for his vast scholarship that went hand in hand with a deep piety and an irenic mind. As a disciple of Johannes Cocceius Vitringa was an exponent of the federal theology, which possessed elements similar to Grotius' ideas on natural law. Belonging to the so-called 'serious' or pietistic Cocceians, he showed great interest in practical theology, mysticism, quietism, and asceticism. Through his works, which were translated into various languages, and his many students from the Dutch Republic as well as from abroad (Hungary, Poland, France, Germany, Scotland), Vitringa's influence made itself felt for a long time, lasting well into the nineteenth century. Above all his eschatological ideas were influential among such famous pietists as Philipp Jakob Spener, August Hermann Francke, and Johann Albrecht Bengel. His dogmatic work, entitled *Aphorismi quibus fundamenta S. theologiae comprehenduntur*, was reprinted several times. His *Commentarius in librum prophetiarum Jesaiae* was highly praised by contemporary and later exegetes." Wall, "Between Grotius and Cocceius," 197–98.

Witteween sees Vitringa as an important representative of the "Dutch-Reformed Enlightenment" and draws breathtaking conclusions about his influence,

> One can thus draw several lines [of influence] from Vitringa. One of them runs across A. H. Franke and Joachim Lange to J. A. Bengel; and it continues further . . . to von Oetinger, J. L. Fricker, Jung-Stilling onward to Lessing, Herder, and German Idealism. A second line runs across Albert Schultens, Herman Venema, J. J. Schultens, Joan Alberti, P. Conradi, S. H. Manger, and Ew. Hollebeek to the point of nineteenth-century exegesis. Vitringa showed the way towards a historical-critical exegesis by having become so very careful (deliberate) in his scientific methodology.[55]

Surely Vitringa's careful linguistic scholarship won him many followers. Childs notes that, even,

> Such an acerbic and demanding grammarian as Gesenius spoke of Vitringa with great respect and even awe regarding his philological and historical prowess. Moreover, throughout much of the nineteenth century he continued to be cited with approval by Rosenmüller, Deilitzsch and Dillman.[56]

He further comments:

> Vitringa's massive apologetic defense of the literal coherence between biblical text and historical reference became widespread by the early eighteenth century, especially in England, Scotland, and North America. A multitude of books in this genre flooded the British marked in the works of Thomas Sherlock, Thomas Newton, and Alexander Keith, to name but a few. . . . In North America Vitringa's approach was most systematically developed by the old Princeton School, emerging in full form already in one of its founders, A. A. Alexander.[57]

In his own day perhaps it was the experiential emphasis in Vitringa's writings which was most appreciated, particularly by those in the Pietistic movement. His guide to the spiritual life (*Typus theologiae praticae, sive de vita spirituali*)—so well-loved that it was translated not only into Dutch, but also into German, Hungarian, and French—breathes the air

---

55. Witteveen, "Campegius Vitringa," 359.
56. Childs, "Hermeneutical Reflections," 90.
57. Ibid., 97.

of *Nadere Reformatie* spirituality with its concern for vital religion. Albert Schultens calls it, "A very worthy book that should live and be carried around in our eyes, hands, bosoms and even our very bones and hearts."[58]

In the twentieth century, as the ability of scholars to read Latin plummeted (particularly in the United States) and as historical-critical approaches less sympathetic to his orthodoxy carried the day, Vitringa eventually became passé and was often overlooked, even as a commentator on Isaiah, his magnum opus. But with shifting tides in late twentieth and early twenty-first century biblical studies, Vitringa seems to be be returning to some prominence once again.[59]

Bibliography

Asselt, W. J. van. *Introduction to Reformed Scholasticism*. Translated by A. Gootjes. Grand Rapids: Reformation Heritage, 2011.

Bauch, Hermann. *Die Lehre vom Wirken des Heiligen Geistes im Frühpietismus: Studien zur Pneumatologie und Eschatologie von Campegius Vitringa, Philipp Jakob Spener und Johann Albrecht Bengel*. Theologische Forschung: wissenschaftliche Beiträge zur kirchlich-evangelischen Lehre 55. Hamburg-Bergstedt: H. Reich, 1974.

Beuken, Willem A. M. *Isaiah: Part II*. Leuven: Peeters, 2000.

———. *Jesaja*. Vol. IIA-B, IIIA-B. De prediking van het Oude Testament. Nijkerk: Callenbach, 1979.

Büsching, Anton Friederich. "Fortsetzung des Lebenslaufs des selige Herrn Vitringa: von seinem natürlichen und sitlichen Character." In Campegius Vitringa, *Auslegung der Weissagung Jesaiae*, edited by Anton Friederich Büsching, 7–16. Vol. II. Halle: Bierwirth, 1749.

———. "Lebenslauf des Verfassers dieser Auslegung." In *Auslegung der Weissagung Jesaiae*, edited by Anton Friederich Büsching and Campegius Vitringa, 25–52. Vol. I. Halle: Johann Gottlob Bierwirth, 1749.

Childs, Brevard S. "Hermeneutical Reflections on Campegius Vitringa, Eighteenth-Century Interpreter of Isaiah." In *In Search of True Wisdom: Essays in Old Testament Interpretation in Honour of Ronald E. Clements*, edited by Edward Ball, 89–98. Sheffield: Sheffield Academic, 1999.

———. *Isaiah*. Louisville, KY: WJK, 2001.

Diestel, Ludwig. *Geschichte des alten Testamentes in der christlichen Kirche*. Jena: Mauke, 1869.

---

58. Büsching, "Lebenslauf Des Verfassers Dieser Auslegung," 49. Cf. Schultens, *Laudatio funebris*.

59. Cf. e.g., the commentaries of Beuken, *Jesaja*, and Childs, *Isaiah*, both of whom cite Vitringa appreciatively. Cf. Telfer, "Campegius Vitringa" and *Wrestling with Isaiah*.

Edwards, Jonathan. "'Catalogue' of Reading." In *Catalogues of Books*, edited by Peter J. Theusen, 117–318. *The Works of Jonathan Edwards*. Vol. 26. New Haven, CT: Yale, 2008.
Golden, Samuel A. *Jean LeClerc*. New York: Twayne, 1972.
Heel, Willem Frederik Caspar Johannes van. "Campegius Vitringa Sr. Als Godgeleerde Beschouwd." PhD dissertation. Gravenhage: Utrecht, 1865.
Kautzsch, Emil Friedrich. "Vitringa, Campegius." *The New Schaff-Herzog Encyclopedia of Religious Knowledge*, 218–219. Vol. XII. New York: Funk and Wagnalls, 1912.
Muller, Richard A. *After Calvin: Studies in the Development of a Theological Tradition*. New York: Oxford University Press, 2003.
———. "Biblical Interpretation in the Sixteenth and Seventeenth Centuries." In *Dictionary of Major Biblical Interpreters*, edited by Donald K. McKim, 22–44. Downers Grove, IL: InterVarsity, 2007.
Roell, Herman Alexander, and Campegius Vitringa. *Dissertatio theologica de generatione Filii, et morte fidelium temporali: qua suas de iis theses plenius explicat, & contra clarissimi viri Campegii Vitringa objectiones defendit: opposita epilogo Campegii Vitringa*. Franeker: Gyselaar, 1689.
Sandys-Wunsch, John. "Early Old Testament Critics on the Continent." In *Hebrew Bible/Old Testament: The History of Its Interpretation: From the Renaissance to the Enlightenment*, edited by Magnae Sæbø et al., 971–76. Vol. II. Göttingen: Vandenhoeck and Ruprecht, 2008.
Schrenk, Gottlob. *Gottesreich und Bund im älteren Protestantismus: vornehmlich bei Johannes Coccejus; zugleich ein Beitrag zur Geschichte des Pietismus und der heilsgeschichtlichen Theologie*. Gütersloh: Beretelsmann, 1923.
Schultens, Albert. *Laudatio funebris in memoriam Campegii Vitringa, theol. prof.* Franeker: Halma, 1722.
Telfer, Charles K. "Campegius Vitringa." In *Handbuch der Bibelhermeneutiken*, edited by Oda Wischmeyer, 435–49. Berlin: De Gruyter, forthcoming.
———. "The Exegetical Methodology of Campegius Vitringa (1659–1722), Especially as Expressed in His Commentarius in Librum Prophetiarum Jesaiae." PhD diss., Trinity Evangelical Divinity School, 2015.
———. *Wrestling with Isaiah: the Exegetical Methodology of Campegius Vitringa (1659-1722)*. Göttingen: Vandenhoeck and Ruprecht, forthcoming 2016.
Vitringa, Campegius. *Anacrisis apocalypseos Joannis Apostoli: qua in veras interpretandae ejus hypotheses diligenter inquiritur & ex iisdem interpretation facta, certis historiarum monumentis confirmamur atque illustratur*. Franeker: Halma, 1705.
———. *Commentarius in librum prophetiarum Jesaiae*. 2 vols. Leeuwarden: Halma, 1722.
———. *De synagoga vetere, libri tres : quibus tum de nominibus, structura, origine, præfectis, ministris, et sacris synagogarum, Agitur; tum præcipue, formam regiminis et ministerii earum in ecclesiam christianam translatam esse, demonstratur*. 2 vols. Franeker: Gyselaar, 1694.
———. *Doctrina christianae religionis, per aphorismos summatim descripta*. Franeker: Halma, 1690.
———. *Hypotyposis historiae et chronologiae sacrae, a M[undo] C[ondito] usque ad finem sæc[uli] I. Æ[tatis] V*. Franeker : Halma, 1698–1716.

———. *Observationum sacrarum libri septem in quo de rebus varii argumenti, et utilissimæ investigationis, critice ac theologice, disseritur.* Amsterdam: Horreum, 1683–1727.

———. "On the Interpretation of Prophecy." *The Interpreter* 4 (1835) 153–76.

———. *Oratio de synodes, earumque utilitate, necessitatem auctoritate.* Franeker: Halma, 1706.

———. *The Synagogue and the Church: Being an Attempt to Show That the Government, Ministries and Services of the Church Were Derived from Those of the Synagogue.* Translated by Joshua L. Bernard. London: Fellowes, 1842.

———. *Typus doctrinae propheticae, in quo de prophetis et prophetiis agitur, hujusque scientiae praecepta traduntur.* Franeker: Halma, 1708.

———. *Typus theologiae praticae, sive de vita spirituali, ejusque affectionibus commentatio; et Oratio de synodis etc.* Franeker: Bleck, 1716. Translated as *Essai de Theologie Pratique, on Traité de la Vie Spirituelle et de ses Characteres, Traduit du Latin Par M. (H. P.) De Limiers.* Amsterdam: Strik, 1721.

Wall, Ernestine G E van der. "Between Grotius and Cocceius: The 'Theologia Prophetica' of Campegius Vitringa (1659–1722)." In *Hugo Grotius, Theologian*, edited by Henk J. M. Nellen, 195–215. Leiden: Brill, 1994.

Witteveen, Klaas Marten. "Campegius Vitringa Und Die Prophetische Theologie." *Zwingliana* 19.2 (1993) 343–59.

Ferdinand Christian Baur and Biblical Theology*

David Lincicum

1. Introduction

WHEN RUDOLF BULTMANN REFLECTED on the task of New Testament Theology, he suggested:

> The question may be raised whether it is more appropriate to treat the theological thoughts of the New Testament writings as a systematically ordered *unity*—a New Testament system of dogmatics, so to speak—or to treat them in their *variety* (*Verschiedenheit*), each writing or group of writings by itself, in which case the individual writings can then be understood as members of a historical context (*eines geschichtlichen Zusammenhangs*).[1]

In opting for the latter of these alternatives, Bultmann was placing himself and his own influential work squarely in the line of Ferdinand Christian Baur.[2] The idea of treating the New Testament writings in their

---

* This paper was first presented at the Society of Biblical Literature Annual Meeting in Amsterdam, 2012. I am grateful to Mark Elliott for the invitation to present, and to David Moffitt for reading the paper in my absence and conveying useful feedback. The research for this paper was undertaken with the support of an Early Career Fellowship from the Leverhulme Trust, and it is a pleasure to record my gratitude here. An earlier version was published in *Annali di Storia dell'Esegesi* 30 (2013) 79–92.

1. Bultmann, *Theology of the New Testament*, 2.237 (translation modified); *Theologie des Neuen Testaments*, 585.

2. There are other interesting similarities between Baur and Bultmann, not least concerning the question of the relationship of Jesus and his teachings to New Testament theology. As in a certain sense also for Bultmann, for Baur Jesus belongs to the presupposition of New Testament theology, since he founds a religion rather than a

variety but united by the genealogical connection of a historical relationship is in fact a precise reflection of Baur's challenge to the enterprise of biblical theology and his reconfiguration of the discipline in a new key.

It is fair to say that F. C. Baur holds an ambiguous place in the history of the discipline of biblical theology. On the one hand, his *Tendenzkritik* ("tendency criticism") proceeds on the assumption of an irreconcilable plurality in the historical sources of early Christianity, and so constitutes a challenge to the attempt to find a unified New Testament theology, to say nothing of a pan-biblical theology. On the other hand, his own historical reconstruction of the development of early Christianity does have a certain unity in the historical process of overcoming conflict. This contribution seeks to explore this ambiguity as a way of locating Baur in the history of biblical theology. After setting forth Baur's conception of biblical theology briefly, I will outline some of Baur's major challenges to unified conceptions of biblical theology, and then go on as a second stage to pose the question of whether and in what sense might Baur nevertheless be seen as concerned with a certain form of unity, though in a differentiated historical rather than theological sense.

2. Baur on Biblical Theology

Baur's most important exegetical works were undertaken in the 1830s and 1840s, with his lectures on New Testament theology given in the last decade of his life and published in 1864, four years after his death, by his son.[3] It is in these posthumously published lectures that we find Baur's most systematic reflections on biblical and New Testament theology, though they sum up emphases that he developed throughout his life. We will turn to these lectures shortly, but it is worth noting beforehand that Baur's first publication (out of an eventual 16,000 printed pages, in Emanuel Hirsch's reckoning) was a long review of the first two volumes of Gottlob Philipp Christian Kaiser's rationalistic *Die biblische Theologie* for Bengel's *Archiv* in 1818.[4] In this early piece, Baur has not yet developed

---

doctrinal system; see Baur, *Vorlesungen*, 45–46; on which see Hodgson, *Formation of Historical*, 221–34; Balla, *Challenges to New Testament Theology*, 172. But the rest of the New Testament does reflect the messianic self-consciousness and teachings of its founder.

3. Baur, *Vorlesungen*. An English translation is being prepared by Peter Hodgson and Robert Brown, though translations here are my own unless otherwise noted.

4. Kaiser, *Die biblische Theologie*. Baur reviewed the first two volumes (1813, 1814)

the way to move beyond the impasse he sees between rationalism and supernaturalism, but we do see him attempting methodically to work out a consistent, historical approach to biblical theology.[5]

By the end of his career, and after his foundational exegetical insights in the 1830s especially, Baur had developed such a historical approach. In his lectures on New Testament theology, he conceives of biblical theology as a "purely historical science (*eine rein geschichtliche Wissenschaft*), emancipated from the constraints of the dogmatic system of the church".[6] Biblical theology should focus on the process of development of biblical concepts of religion in chronological succession, and on the precise differences among individual authors.[7] New Testament theology is "that part of historical theology which has to portray both the teachings of Jesus as well as the doctrinal concepts based upon them in the context of their historical development and according to the individual character by which they are to be distinguished from one another, as far as this can be done on the basis of the New Testament writings."[8] There are several salient points to note in this concept of biblical theology. First, it should be historical rather than normative in character. He criticizes both G. L. Bauer and W. M. L. de Wette for failing to overcome the determination of questions for New Testament theology by their contemporary situation, even if the questions are now rationalistic rather than the traditional dogmatic ones. Rather, Baur draws an analogy to the study of the history of dogma:

> As in the history of dogma one does not ask whether what it has to portray is also true in itself and must be made an object of faith for us, but generally only what is taught—not what we ourselves should believe but what others held to be true and believed—so it is with New Testament theology. One wants to know only what the writings of the New Testament contain by way of doctrine, and what forms in their doctrinal content can be distinguished from one another through their characteristic individuality. . . . How is a historical treatment possible if one simply wants to find in history what one has to believe . . . ?[9]

---

in 1818, on which see Harris, *Tübingen School*, 140–43; Hopper, "Historical Theology," 20–23.

5. Merk, *Biblische Theologie*, 215.
6. Baur, *Vorlesungen*, 1.
7. Ibid., 8.
8. Ibid., 28.
9. Ibid., 33.

Since he also rejects approaches to New Testament theology that proceed on the basis of the revelatory character (*Offenbarungscharakter*) of the New Testament,[10] this in some sense reduces the importance of New Testament theology to the theological importance of history as such, albeit a unique period in the development of religious consciousness, to which we will return.

Second, Baur is concerned with doctrinal concepts (*Lehrbegriffe*) rather than with religion or history in itself.[11] What is more, the concept of development is key to Baur's definition. One should not simply distinguish individual doctrinal concepts from one another and set them side by side; rather, the task of New Testament theology is to sketch a process of theological development.[12] This concept of development, in fact, is one of Baur's new emphases and informs one of his major challenges to the discipline of biblical theology. It is to these challenges that we now turn.

3. Baur's Challenges to Biblical Theology

If classical conceptions of biblical theology depended upon a robust sense of the unity of Scripture, in some sense, and upon the significance of the canon, Baur can be seen as offering a disturbing challenge to both of these foundational assumptions.[13]

A. Challenge to the Unity of Scripture

Baur was of course not the first to call into question the unity of Scripture. He follows on, for example, from the arguments of J. S. Semler (himself the heir to the English deists) in emphasizing the plurality and

---

10. Ibid., 34.

11. Balla, in his *Challenges to New Testament Theology*, 23–25, suggests that Baur should have (but did not) come under Wrede's censure for his use of *Lehrbegriffe*, but (*pace* Balla) the *Totalanschauung* in Baur's works casts his use of the doctrinal concepts model in a different light than the others whom Wrede criticizes in his essay, "Task and Methods".

12. Baur, *Vorlesungen*, 38.

13. By "classical conceptions of biblical theology" I have in mind especially approaches that depend on privileging the divine authorship of Scripture over human authorship, and so seek a unified message (or salvation history) across the different constituent books of the Bible.

disagreement in early Christianity.[14] But with reference to biblical theology, Baur's challenge to the unity of Scripture takes two forms. First, he follows and radicalizes a tendency in some predecessors to prefer specificity rather than commonality in assessing the contribution of individual authors or corpora to the whole of Scripture. This is first expressed in an emphasis on historical periodization that has as its first effect the severing of the Old Testament from the New. While G. L. Bauer had earlier treated the Old and New Testaments in separate works,[15] it is especially W. M. L. de Wette whom Baur praises for his concern with the individuality and historical particularity of the biblical writings, noting how proper it is for him to have divided Old Testament from the New, and to have further periodized each of these. The substantial step forward in de Wette's work, according to Baur, lies precisely in the attempt to distinguish between different periods according to their characteristics. De Wette "not only presents the religion of the Old and the New as separate, but also distinguishes in the former between Hebraism and Judaism, and in the latter between the teaching of Jesus and that of the apostles, and seeks to determine the basic character of the one as of the other."[16]

It is striking that Baur nowhere feels the need to argue for the division between Old and New Testaments, but can take this as an assured result. A major rift, then, in the attempt to construct a pan-biblical theology already comes to Baur as a *fait accompli*. When one surveys Baur's work as a whole, it is striking how little engagement with the Old Testament can be found. This may be, in part, because Baur taught New Testament exegesis, Christian ethics, Church history, and the history of dogma, but not Old Testament in Tübingen.[17] But while Baur recognizes the significance the Old Testament has for early Christianity, there is still a sense in which the Old Testament is particularistic and so stands in strong contrast to the movement of Christianity, belonging, with Judaism, to a past movement of the Spirit realizing itself within history.[18]

14. For details of one strand of this tradition, see Lincicum, "Baur's Place." For Semler's influence on Baur, see Hilgenfeld, "Ferdinand Christian Baur," 223, 232; Baur discusses Semler in his 1852 published version of lectures delivered in the previous decade (in Hodgson, *Baur on the Writing of Church History*, 153–62).

15. On G. L. Bauer and his influence on F. C. Baur, see Merk, *Biblische Theologie*, 205–36.

16. Baur, *Vorlesungen*, 12. Cf. de Wette, *Biblische Dogmatik*, 27–28, cited in Merk, *Biblische Theologie*, 211.

17. See Harris, *Tübingen School*, 22.

18. See his comments in *The Church History of the First Three Centuries*, 1.17–18.

But even within the New Testament, Baur prefers to emphasize diversity and specificity rather than commonality. Like G. L. Bauer and de Wette before him, Baur famously constructed a periodization and division of New Testament writings based precisely on their differences, their "tendencies." While de Wette wanted to place the individual writings of the New Testament into historical relationship with one another, and divided them into three classes (Jewish-Christian; Alexandrian or Hellenistic; and Pauline), Baur progressed beyond this by linking the classes of writings to a particular schema of historical development. Using as one of his main criteria a judgment as to whether a given writing reflects the struggle between a Judaizing particularism and a Pauline universalizing impulse, he summarized his three periods in this way:

> In the first [period] stand the doctrinal concepts of the apostle Paul and John the Apocalyptist over against one another, in the second belong the doctrinal concepts of the letter to the Hebrews, the shorter Pauline letters, the Petrine letters and James, the synoptic gospels and Acts, in the third period, those of the Pastoral Epistles and the Johannine writings.[19]

Though Baur has often been accused of imposing a crass Hegelian dialectic of thesis, antithesis, synthesis on the diverse picture of early Christianity, scholars such as Robert Morgan and Peter Hodgson have shown that Baur came to some of his fundamental insights before having read Hegel,[20] and was as much influenced by Schelling, Schleiermacher, and (especially later in his life) Kant as Hegel. But Baur does, for a significant portion of his career, find in Hegel's conception of history a vehicle for his own insights concerning the process of historical development of early Christianity. While Baur's arguments about the precise nature of the oppositions in early Christianity have been drastically qualified since his time, he did not force the history of the early church into a Procrustean bed the way his student Albert Schwegler did, in his massive *Das nachapostolische Zeitalter in den Hauptmomenten seiner Entwicklung*.[21] Many of those who criticized Baur's reconstruction did so with the very

---

19. Baur, *Vorlesungen*, 42; cf. 39-42; also the scheme followed in his *Church History of the First Three Centuries* and elsewhere.

20. Especially in his 1831 essay, "Christuspartei"; see the discussion in Lincicum, "Baur's Place." See further Morgan, "Ferdinand Christian Baur," and "Non Angli sed Angeli"; Hodgson, *Formation of Historical Theology*.

21. On Schwegler, see Harris, *Tübingen School*, 78-88; Krämer, "Bewährung,"; Matzerath, "Historische Kritik".

historical-critical method Baur championed, and so their criticisms can be taken as modifications in degree rather than in kind to the picture Baur suggests.

In so opting for the diversity of the New Testament doctrinal conceptions, Baur is opposing not simply harmonizing reconstructions of early Christian thought that treat all of the New Testament as a quarry for *dicta probantia*, but also more subtle approaches. In particular, Baur contests the great Berlin church historian, August Neander, and his suggestion that one could describe the contours of New Testament theology by means of *Mannigfaltigkeit und Einheit*, or "Variety and Unity." Rather, Baur thinks *Mannigfaltigkeit* is a dishonest euphemism for *Verschiedenheit*—which in Baur's usage implies substantial diversity of theological conviction—and it is the latter that Baur champions.[22] The results of Baur's critical research on the New Testament are clearly germane to his New Testament theology, as we shall see, and here it is worth noting that he suggests that the larger the time frame encompassed by New Testament history, the larger will be the differences and contradictions.[23]

So Baur's first major challenge to the possibility of biblical theology comprises his unyielding insistence on the individuality of biblical writings and the need to separate them accordingly. A pan-biblical theology is not an option Baur considers seriously, since for him the Old Testament belongs fundamentally to another time. Nor does he want to suggest a *"biblische Theologie des Neuen Testaments"* approach, in which one might place significant weight on the reception of the Old Testament in the New or on tradition history as a way of getting at the unity of Scripture (one thinks recently of the works, as different as they are, by Hans Hübner, Peter Stuhlmacher, or G. K. Beale).[24] Rather, Baur's emphasis lies squarely on the differences, the contradictions, the tensions in the New Testament, these writings now seen as bound together by historical context rather than doctrinal agreement or subject matter. While Baur was not the first to question the unity of Scripture in this way, his comprehensive alterna-

22. On Neander's "Mannigfaltigkeit und Einheit", see Baur *Vorlesungen*, 26–29, 43; cf. Merk, *Biblische Theologie*, 218–19. In Hahn's *Theologie des Neuen Testaments*, 1.1–28, he mentions Gabler, Bauer, Baur, and Wrede as foundational in the nineteenth century, but does not mention Neander, which is interesting given his own Einheit-Vielfalt schema. For Baur's estimation of Neander as a church historian, see his *Epochs* (ET Hodgson), 207–29.

23. Baur, *Vorlesungen*, 38–39.

24. Hübner, *Biblische Theologie*; Stuhlmacher, *Biblische Theologie*; Beale, *New Testament Biblical Theology*.

tive formulation of early Christianity was one of the most far-reaching and significant, and the influence of such a conception of the dis-unity of Scripture is only too readily seen in twentieth- and twenty-first century exegesis. One might here simply recall Bultmann's opting for the *Verschiedenheit* of the New Testament rather than the *Einheit* with which we began.[25]

B. Challenge to the Canon of Scripture

Baur's second major challenge is closely related to the first. In addition to questioning the unity of Scripture, he also effectively problematizes the status of the canon and its importance for New Testament theology. We observe this challenge by considering how Baur locates New Testament theology with regard to the history of dogma on the one hand, and the task of New Testament criticism on the other.

First, Baur effectively subsumes New Testament theology under the history of dogma (*Dogmengeschichte*). He suggests that, given the focus of New Testament theology on *Lehrbegriffe* or doctrinal concepts, the discipline is closer to the history of dogma than to church history per se.[26] In the preface to his *Lectures on the History of Dogma*, Baur rejects the view that the New Testament could be sealed off from the history of dogma and made the immutable foundation for the latter: "the content of the New Testament cannot merely be made the presupposition of the history of dogma; that content in itself is already the beginning of historical movement."[27] Baur does go on to attempt a rationale for treating New Testament theology separately from the history of dogma. He suggests that, "[s]ince . . . this beginning of the historical movement is delimited by having its sphere consist of the writings of the New Testament, it can be detached as an autonomous whole from history of dogma proper," appealing more or less to pragmatic considerations than to any inherent difference between canonical and non-canonical writings.[28] Indeed, as he says, "[t]he formative concept of a history of dogma—that it regards its

---

25. Samuel Davidson can describe Baur's achievement as having "disturbed an organic unity of the New Testament which had been merely *assumed* by traditionalists". See Davidson, *Canon of the Bible*, 250.

26. Baur, *Vorlesungen*, 30; cf. 33. Note Wallraff, "Evangelium und Dogma," esp. 274–76 on Baur.

27. ET in Hodgson, *Baur on the Writing of Church History*, 275.

28. Ibid., 275; cf. 276.

object from the point of view of a historical development—also constitutes the authentic concept of New Testament theology."[29]

Thus it appears that the decision to focus on the New Testament as distinct from non-canonical literature is more or less arbitrary, ascribed to the nature of these documents as proximate historical sources rather than Scripture with a divine origin or possessing any particular authority in and of themselves. Although Baur does not explicitly include non-canonical writings in his lectures on New Testament theology, arguably it would be consistent with his program to do so—and in fact it is precisely this program that has come to mature fruition in the past century. Baur himself, in speaking of the so-called Apostolic Fathers, had suggested that "The idea that these writings are separated from the whole body of the canonical books by as wide a gulf as that which divides from each other two wholly different periods of Church history, is only possible to those who hold the most extravagant view of the inspiration of the whole canonical collection."[30] One is not surprised to find Helmut Koester explicitly appealing to Baur in his criticism of those who want to hold to a discipline of New Testament, rather than simply early Christianity.[31] And here, of course, Koester speaks for a large proportion of those who currently undertake academic work on the writings of the New Testament.

Second, Baur calls the significance of the New Testament canon into question by the task he envisages critical questions of New Testament introduction or *Einleitung* to play. In his *Lectures on New Testament Theology*, Baur speaks of the "close connection" between the results of New Testament criticism and New Testament theology.[32] The precise nature of this connection can be seen in Baur's important essay from 1850 to 1851 on "Die Einleitung in das Neue Testament als theologische Wissenschaft" ("Introduction to the New Testament as a theological task"). Baur argues that the question theological science has above all to decide, is "which writings in the canon are canonical and which are not, with what right does each book of the canon take its place in the same, and whether all those concepts that one usually binds to the canon can also be historically justified?"[33] The task of New Testament Introduction, in other words, is

29. Ibid., 275.
30. *Church History*, 1.137.
31. See Koester, "New Testament Introduction".
32. Baur, *Vorlesungen*, 20–21; 42. Cf. Morgan, "Baur's Lectures," esp. 203; Merk, *Biblische Theologie*, 230, 235.
33. "Einleitung in das neue Testament." Here, see Part I (1850) 466–67.

criticism of the canon, "*Kritik des Kanons*."³⁴ Non-apostolic authorship is enough to call into question the legitimacy of a writing's place in the canon.³⁵ Parenthetically, one may note that there is some circularity in Baur's logic, since one of the means by which one might judge the authorship of a writing to be non-apostolic is precisely the *Tendenzkritik* that Baur has developed as a way to discern the true conflicts in the apostolic church. By these means he famously reduced the number of authentic Pauline letters to the four *Hauptbriefe*. But this process is effectively the substitution of one guiding holistic construct (a certain picture of early Christian history) for the normative holistic construct of the canon. We will return to this point momentarily.

It is interesting that in Baur's *Lectures on New Testament Theology* he does retain the focus on the twenty-seven writings of the New Testament, but this retention has no clear justification in Baur's thought and appears to be a concession to normal practice. If one should, as Baur suggests, attempt an *Entwicklungsgeschichte der neutestamentlichen Theologie* (a history of the development of New Testament theology),³⁶ rather than a static homogenizing picture of New Testament doctrine, and if it is possible to judge, paradoxically, some canonical writings to be non-canonical, then it seems to make more sense for Baur's project to be a *Theologiegeschichte des Urchristentums* ("a history of early Christian theology") rather than a New Testament theology per se.³⁷ In the next section I will suggest that something along these lines is, in fact, the more important of Baur's exegetical legacies.

C. Sola Scriptura?

But first, these critical questions about the unity and canon of Scripture raise further questions about the Protestant principle of *sola scriptura*. Baur himself was certainly not unaware of the challenges his critical work had for traditional Protestant dogmatics. In this sense, it is important to note that Baur's formative exegetical work in the 1830s took place

---

34. Ibid., 474–75; similar phraseology was already used by F. Lücke in the Vorrede to Schleiermacher, *Einleitung*, xi–xiv.

35. "Einleitung in das neue Testament," (1850) 472, 478, etc.; in criticism, see Kümmel, *New Testament*, 131–32, though for a strangely similar judgment, coming from an opposite starting point, note Porter, "Pauline Authorship".

36. Baur, *Vorlesungen*, 24.

37. Merk, *Biblische Theologie*, 235.

alongside his intense conflict with the Catholic theologian J. A. Moehler, in which Baur defended Protestantism.[38] But as Jörg Lauster has convincingly shown, Baur transposes the true principle of Protestantism from *sola scriptura* to the principle of criticism or autonomy.[39] Baur even inverts the traditional scripture principle and suggests that "an absolute authority of Scripture" stands "in the clearest contradiction with the protestant principle, the free right of scriptural research".[40] That is to say, an appeal to Scripture as authoritative in itself is decidedly *un*-Protestant. The roots of this reversal are complex, and Lauster offers an insightful telling of the story. For our purposes, we can simply note that Baur's rejection of the Scripture principle coheres well with his questions to the unity and canon of Scripture. And one can readily hear echoes of Baur's voice at this point in his great twentieth-century successor in Tübingen, Ernst Käsemann.[41]

4. Biblical Theology as the History of Early Christianity

But if Baur's works do form a multi-faceted challenge to some traditional conceptions of biblical theology, it would be a mistake to assume that Baur's program is essentially negative in character. Rather, as I have already hinted, he has a positive alternative to substitute in its place, and this "positive criticism" sets him apart from some of his forebears like Semler or contemporaries like Strauss.[42] The challenge Baur lodges against a certain conception of biblical theology is the flipside of his own constructive proposal to recover a sort of unity of a different order.

---

38. On which see Fitzer, *Moehler and Baur*.

39. Lauster, *Prinzip und Methode*, 111–22.

40. From the Vorrede of Baur's *Die christliche Lehre*, vii, cited in Lauster, *Prinzip und Methode*, 120.

41. E.g., in Käsemann's "Einleitung"; note the anecdote recalled by Harrisville and Sundberg (*Bible in Modern Culture*, 130): "On the wall in Käsemann's living room study hangs a copy of the University of Tübingen's portrait of Baur, a gift to the New Testament scholar upon his retirement. Once outside Baur's direct influence, the one-time pupil of Bultmann finally came to write of Baur as the true 'progenitor' of a criticism at the root, a criticism conceived not merely as scientific method but as a presupposition for the life of the spirit. One summer day he pointed to that portrait on his study wall and said, 'greater even than Bultmann.'"

42. Note Baur's explicit reflections about the "negative criticism" of Strauss in his "Abgenötigte Erklärung". See also the introduction to his *Die sogennanten Pastoralbriefe*.

Recall that for Baur one of the tasks of a New Testament theology, especially when conceived in a purely historical manner, must be not simply "to distinguish several doctrines and set them . . . side by side," but rather, "progress of development must be shown."[43] This progress of development entails a holistic construal of the theological development of earliest Christianity from its origins to the time of the last composed New Testament documents—for Baur some time in the latter part of the second century. This then requires a circular movement by which the whole is grasped as a context for interpreting the details, and the details are interpreted as a way of ascertaining the whole. Baur's innovation lies precisely in pressing the need for what he sometimes calls the "*Totalanschauung*," the view of the totality of early Christian history.[44] Baur himself never despised the details of history, but he did prioritize, in a certain sense, the whole over the parts. In his book on Paul, he writes,

> what alone in the final analysis can tip the scales in favor of a view put forward in a wider perspective is, indeed, only the general, on which also the detail is again and again dependent, the consequence of the whole, the convincing inner probability and necessity of the matter which comes to the fore of itself and before which sooner or later the party interests of the day must be struck dumb.[45]

The way in which this concern for a differentiated whole expressed itself in Baur's exegetical work is well known. Ernst Käsemann summarises Baur's total picture well:

> If the early catholic church [*frühkatholische Kirche*] arose out of an antithesis and, viewed radically, grew out of the two different origins of Jewish Christianity and of Paulinism, then inevitably a dogmatic-historical program followed which had to reach far beyond the bounds of the New Testament. At the same time there was found a hermeneutical key to the New Testament writings which allowed them to be ordered in highly differentiated ways and with varying proximity to the two poles. It compelled

---

43. Baur, *Vorlesungen*, ET as in Kümmel, *History*, 140.

44. For the idea of the 'Totalanschauung,' see e.g., *Kritische Untersuchungen*, iv, vi; cf. also "Die evangelisch-theologische Fakultät," 408. Compare Zachhuber, "Albrecht Ritschl," who highlights especially Baur's ideational historicism and the way in which he flattens details by his big picture. For broader context, see Rollmann, "From Baur to Wrede."

45. ET in Kümmel, *History*, 136, from Baur's *Paulus*, 520.

one to determine the respective "tendencies" of each individual within the early Christian or New Testament field of tension so that historical criticism now obtained a dogmatic-historical depth in tendency criticism [*Tendenzkritik*]. The dogmatic debate about the real driving force of early Christian history had to be explained from such a perspective and the relationship of the various "concepts of doctrine" to the central object of historical-theological research had to be undertaken.[46]

Stefan Alkier thus suggests that it is first with Baur that one can speak of an exegetical discipline of "the history of early Christianity" (*Geschichte des Urchristentums*).[47] Indeed, the concept of *Urchristentum* is a means, among other things, of allowing contradictions and differences to stand without resolution.[48] It is the concept of "context" or "connection" (*Zusammenhang*) that enables Baur to achieve a form of wholeness without succumbing to what he took to be the temptation to *Einheit* on the one hand (with the orthodox), or to unexplained plurality on the other (as in Semler).[49] That this historical context should be determined and achieved by the historical critical method rather than in a theological sense having to do with a canonical context is a conviction that Baur has bequeathed to the discipline of New Testament studies as a whole. One might here again recall Bultmann's statement that to focus on writings in their historical individuality can then enable them to be understood "as members of a historical context." Baur's positive alternative to biblical theology is the consideration of theological concepts in their historical connection to one another, including a full appreciation of their diversity without regard for the significance of the canon. In this sense, his convictions, while radical at the time, have now come to represent something like mainstream study of the New Testament. Even if his critical positions on, for example, the date and authenticity of certain writings have been corrected, these corrections have been carried out by means of the method which Baur refines and under the overarching program which Baur transposed into a new key. In today's New Testament guild, there is a sense in which we are all Baur's children. Noting how many of Baur's concrete results have been corrected, James Carleton Paget also argues that Baur's foundational importance must be grasped:

46. Käsemann, "Einleitung," xi. Compare also Merk, *Biblische Theologie*, 229.
47. Alkier, *Urchristentum*, 254; cf. 174.
48. Ibid., 254.
49. Cf. Ibid., 201, 203, 227.

Baur's is the first thorough-going historical account of early Christianity, whose presuppositions were to influence many of those who followed him, whether in agreement or disagreement; and . . . his views about the relationship between John and the Synoptics, the question of the authenticity of many New Testament books, the theological tendency of individual New Testament writings, and the role of conflict in the creation of early Christian ideas, while disputed, continue to be standard topics of discussion in any account of New Testament and later history. If we accept these points, then Baur will appear as the central and most influential figure in the history of the study of Christian origins. Indeed, seen against this broader canvas, it may only be a slight exaggeration, here adapting the words of A. N. Whitehead on Plato, to state that the study of Christian origins after Baur is no more than a series of corrective footnotes.[50]

A major shift has occurred, however, in that while Baur maintained a broadly idealist concept of history, in which history as such had a theological meaning in the way it revealed the Spirit's action in the world, contemporary biblical scholarship has largely rejected his Hegelian metaphysics, while retaining the historicizing elements of Baur's thought. Baur's critical method remains, while the broader philosophical framework which imbued his results with *meaning* has largely been left aside.

5. Conclusion

According to Otto Merk, "[w]ith F. C. Baur's adaptation of New Testament theology the end and high point of the discipline inaugurated by J. P. Gabler and G. L. Bauer is reached."[51] Like Paul's *telos tou nomou* in Rom 10:4, one would like to interrogate Merk's ambiguous *Endpunkt*: does Baur perfect or destroy the discipline of biblical theology? The evidence of this paper admittedly portrays Baur as a problematizer rather than a perfecter of the discipline. He lodges far-reaching challenges to the attempt to read Scripture as a whole, at least on historical grounds, in the service of a pan-biblical theology, and poses trenchant questions about the nature of the canon of the New Testament in particular. Moreover, he substitutes a critical construct of early Christian history for the canonical context that had for so long been the broader setting in which

---

50. Carleton Paget, "Reception of Baur," 336–37.
51. Merk, *Biblische Theologie*, 235.

individual documents or statements were interpreted. In all these cases, the new perspectives Baur opened up have proven to be incredibly fruitful over the past two centuries.[52] That said, although it is a task not here undertaken, there is room to criticize Baur's idealist historicism and the theological convictions with which he operated. Baur himself has a theological superstructure in which his critical historical work is situated, and it would be naïve to attempt, as so often in Anglophone engagement with Baur, merely to squabble with Baur's historical details without also engaging the broader theological and philosophical concerns he harbors. That is a task for another day, but any contemporary restatement of biblical theology will need to take seriously the challenges posed by Baur and his heirs, doing justice to the historical particularity he rightly highlighted, but perhaps seeking alternative theological resources to discern a unity of Scripture that is not reducible to mere univocity or untroubled story line and yet refuses to succumb to unexplained diffusion and plurality.

Bibliography

Alkier, Stefan. *Urchristentum: Zur Geschichte und Theologie einer exegetischen Disziplin.* BHT 83. Tübingen: Mohr Siebeck, 1993.

Balla, Peter. *Challenges to New Testament Theology: An Attempt to Justify the Enterprise.* WUNT 2.95. Tübingen: Mohr Siebeck, 1997. Reprint. Peabody, MA: Hendrickson, 1998.

Baur, Ferdinand Christian. "Abgenötigte Erklärung gegen einen Artikel der Evangelischen Kirchenzeitung, herausgegeben von D. E. W. Hengstenberg, Prof. der Theol. an der Universität zu Berlin. Mai 1836." *Tübinger Zeitschrift für Theologie* Heft III (1836) 179–232.

———. *Die christliche Lehre von der Dreieinigkeit und Menschwerdung Gottes in ihrer geschichtlichen Entwicklung.* Erster Theil. Tübingen: Osiander, 1841.

———. "Die Christuspartei in der korinthischen Gemeinde, der Gegensatz des petrinischen und paulinischen Christenthums in der ältesten Kirche, der Apostel Petrus in Rom." *Tübinger Zeitschrift für Theologie* Heft IV (1831) 61–206.

———. *The Church History of the First Three Centuries.* Translated by Allan Menzies. 2 vols. Theological Translation Fund Library. London: Williams and Norgate, 1878.

———. "Die Einleiting in das neue Testament als theologische Wissenschaft. Ihr Begriff und ihre Aufgabe, ihr Entwicklungsgang und ihr innerer Organismus." *Theologische Jahrbücher* Part I (1850) 463–566; Part II (1851) 70–94, 222–53, 291–329.

---

52. Note, for example, the role assigned to Baur in Räisänen, *Beyond New Testament Theology*, 16–17.

———. *Die Epochen der kirchlichen Geschichtschreibung.* In *Ferdinand Christian Baur on the Writing of Church History,* edited by Peter C. Hodgson, 41–257. New York: Oxford University Press, 1968.

———. "Die evangelisch-theologische Fakultät vom Jahr 1812 bis 1848." In *Geschichte und Beschreibung der Universität Tübingen,* edited by K. Klüpfel, 389–428. Tübingen: L. F. Fues, 1849.

———. *Kritische Untersuchungen über die kanonischen Evangelien, ihr Verhältnis zu einander, ihren Charakter und Ursprung.* Tübingen: L. F. Fues, 1847.

———. Review of *Die biblische Theologie,* by Gottlob Philipp Christian Kaiser. *Archiv für die Theologie und ihre neueste Literatur* II.3 (1818) 656–717.

———. *Die sogennanten Pastoralbriefe des Apostels Paulus, aufs Neue kritisch untersucht.* Stuttgart: J. G. Cotta, 1835.

———. *Vorlesungen über neutestamentliche Theologie.* Edited by F. F. Baur. Leipzig: Fues, 1864.

Beale, G. K. *A New Testament Biblical Theology.* Grand Rapids: Baker, 2011.

Bultmann, Rudolf. *Theologie des Neuen Testaments.* 8. Aufl. Tübingen: Mohr Siebeck, 1980.

———. *Theology of the New Testament.* 2 vols. Translated by K. Grobel. New York: Charles Scribner's Sons, 1951–1955.

Carleton Paget, James. "The Reception of Baur in Britain." In *Ferdinand Christian Baur und die Geschichte des Urchristentums,* edited by Martin Bauspiess, Christof Landmesser and David Lincicum, 335–86. WUNT 333. Tübingen: Mohr Siebeck, 2014.

Davidson, Samuel. *The Canon of the Bible: Its Formation, History and Fluctuations.* 3rd ed. London: C. Kegan Paul, 1880.

de Wette, W. M. L. *Biblische Dogmatik Alten und Neuen Testaments. Oder kritische Darstellung der Religionslehre des Hebraismus, des Judenthums und Urchristentums. Zum Gebrauch akademischer Vorlesungen.* Berlin: G. Reimer, 1813.

Fitzer, Joseph. *Moehler and Baur in Controversy, 1832–38: Romantic-Idealist Assessment of the Reformation and Counter-Reformation.* AAR Studies in Religion 7. Tallahasse, FL: American Academy of Religion, 1974.

Hahn, Ferdinand. *Theologie des Neuen Testaments.* 2 vols. 2nd ed. Tübingen: Mohr Siebeck, 2005.

Harris, Horton. *The Tübingen School: A Historical and Theological Investigation of the School of F. C. Baur.* Oxford: Oxford University Press, 1975. Reprint, Leicester: Apollos, 1990.

Harrisville, Roy A., and Walter Sundberg. *The Bible in Modern Culture: Theology and Historical-Critical Method from Spinoza to Käsemann.* Grand Rapids: Eerdmans, 1995.

Hilgenfeld, Adolf. "Ferdinand Christian Baur nach seiner wissenschaftlichen Entwickelung und Bedeutung." *ZWT* 36.1 (1893) 222–44.

Hodgson, Peter C. *The Formation of Historical Theology: A Study of Ferdinand Christian Baur.* New York: Harper & Row, 1966.

Hopper, Matthew T. "Historical Theology as the Crossroads of Faith and Reason: The Contribution of Ferdinand Christian Baur." MA thesis, University of Georgia, 2008.

Hübner, Hans. *Biblische Theologie des Neuen Testaments.* 3 vols. Göttingen: Vandenhoeck & Ruprecht, 1990–1995.

Kaiser, Gottlob Philipp Christian. *Die biblische Theologie, oder Judaismus und Christianismus nach der grammatisch-historischen Interpretation und nach einer freymütigen Stellung in die kritisch-vergleichende Universalgeschichte der Religionen, und die universale Religion.* 3 vols. Erlangen: n.p., 1813–1821.
Käsemann, Ernst. "Einleitung." In *Ausgewählte Werke: Historisch-kritische Untersuchungen zum Neuen Testament*, edited by Klaus Scholder, 1.viii–xxv. Stuttgart-Bad Cannstatt: Fromann, 1963.
Koester, Helmut. "New Testament Introduction: A Critique of a Discipline." In *Christianity, Judaism, and Other Greco-Roman Cults. Studies for Morton Smith at Sixty*, edited by Morton Smith and Jacob Neusner, 1–20. Part One: New Testament. SJLA 12. Leiden: Brill, 1975.
Krämer, Hans. "Die Bewährung der historischen Kritik an der Geschichte der antiken Philosophie: Eduard Zeller und Albert Schwegler." In *Historisch-kritische Geschichtsbetrachtung: Ferdinand Christian Baur und seine Schüler. 8. Blaubeurer Symposion*, edited by U. Köpf, 141–52. Contubernium 40. Sigmaringen: Jan Thorbecke, 1994.
Kümmel, Werner Georg. *The New Testament: The History of the Investigation of its Problems.* London: SCM, 1973.
Lauster, Jörg. *Prinzip und Methode: die Transformation des protestantischen Schriftprinzips durch die historische Kritik von Schleiermacher bis zur Gegenwart.* HUT 46. Tübingen, Mohr Siebeck, 2004.
Lincicum, David. "F. C. Baur's Place in the Study of Jewish Christianity." In *The Rediscovery of Jewish Christianity: From Toland to Baur*, edited by F. Stanley Jones, 137–66. History of Biblical Studies. Atlanta: Society of Biblical Literature, 2012.
Matzerath, Josef. "Historische Kritik in der Alten Geschichte—Albert Schwegler." In *Historisch-kritische Geschichtsbetrachtung: Ferdinand Christian Baur und seine Schüler. 8. Blaubeurer Symposion*, edited by U. Köpf, 153–64. Contubernium 40. Sigmaringen: Jan Thorbecke, 1994.
Merk, Otto. *Biblische Theologie des Neuen Testaments in ihrer Anfangszeit: Ihre methodischen Probleme bei Johann Philipp Gabler und Georg Lorenz Bauer und deren Nachwirkungen.* Marburger Theologische Studien 9. Marburg: N. G. Elwert, 1972.
Morgan, Robert. "F. C. Baur's Lectures on New Testament Theology." *ExpTim* 88 (1977) 202–6.
———. "Ferdinand Christian Baur." In *Nineteenth Century Religious Thought in the West*, edited by N. Smart et al., 1.261–89. Cambridge: Cambridge University Press, 1985.
———. "Non Angli sed Angeli: Some Anglican Reactions to German Gospel Criticism." In *New Studies in Theology*, edited by S. Sykes and D. Holmes, 1.1–30. London: Duckworth, 1980.
Porter, Stanley E. "Pauline Authorship and the Pastoral Epistles: Implications for Canon." *BBR* 5 (1995) 105–24.
Räisänen, Heikki. *Beyond New Testament Theology: A Story and a Programme.* 2nd ed. London: SCM, 2000.
Rollmann, Hans. "From Baur to Wrede: The Quest for a Historical Method." *Studies In Religion/Sciences Religieuses* 17 (1988) 443–54.
Schleiermacher, F. D. E. *Einleitung ins neue Testament.* Edited by G. Wolde. Friedrich Schleiermachers Sammtliche Werke 1.3. Berlin: G. Reimer, 1845.

Schwegler, Albert. *Das nachapostolische Zeitalter in den Hauptmomenten seiner Entwicklung.* 2 vols. Tübingen: L. F. Fues, 1846.
Stuhlmacher, Peter. *Biblische Theologie des Neuen Testaments.* 2 vols. Göttingen: Vandenhoeck & Ruprecht, 1992.
Wallraff, Martin. "Evangelium und Dogma: zu den Anfängen der Gattung Dogmengeschichte (bis 1850)." In *Biblische Theologie und historisches Denken. Wissenschaftsgeschichtliche Studien,* edited by M. Kessler and M. Wallraff, 256–78. Basel: Schwabe, 2008.
Wrede, William. "The Task and Methods of 'New Testament Theology.'" In *The Nature of New Testament Theology: The Contribution of William Wrede and Adolf Schlatter,* edited and translated by Robert Morgan, 68–116. London: SCM, 1973.
Zachhuber, Johannes. "Albrecht Ritschl and the Tübingen School: A Neglected Link in the History of Nineteenth-Century Theology." *Zeitschrift für neuere Theologiegeschichte* 18 (2011) 51–70.

Seeing with One Eye

Biblical Interpretation in the Seventeenth and Eighteenth Centuries[1]

Michael C. Legaspi

THIS ARTICLE CONTAINS A review of the third section of volume two of Magne Sæbø's *Hebrew Bible / Old Testament: The History of Its Interpretation*. Volume two of Sæbø's authoritative collection covers the period from the Renaissance to the Enlightenment, and the third section of this volume contains eighteen chapters on interpreters and interpretive traditions in the seventeenth and eighteenth centuries, on topics ranging from the scientific revolution to the aftermath of the French Revolution. Contributors include biblical scholars, historical theologians, scholars of religion, and intellectual historians from a variety of backgrounds. We have, for example, an article from Moshe Idel on Hasidic hermeneutics, one from Stephen Prickett on English literature, and a piece by Steven Nadler on Spinoza, along with articles from familiar "history of interpretation" luminaries: Hayes, Rogerson, Bultmann, Reventlow, and many others. It is hard to say something coherent about such a deep and wide array of excellent pieces in the space of a brief article. What I propose to

---

1. This article was presented to the Biblical Theology Section of the International Meeting of the Society of Biblical Literature in Vienna, Austria on July 10, 2014. The purview of this paper is Magne Sæbø's *Hebrew Bible / Old Testament: The History of Its Interpretation*. Volume II: From Renaissance to Enlightenment; Part C. "Scriptural Interpretation between Orthodoxy and Rationalism and the Establishing of a Historical-Critical Study of the Hebrew Bible / Old Testament in the Seventeenth and Eighteenth Centuries" (Göttingen: Vandenhoeck & Ruprecht, 2008; chs. 27 to 44). In footnotes that follow, references to this volume will include the abbreviation *HB/OT*, followed by the name of the author of the article and the page number.

do is to lift a theme from Sæbø's introduction to the volume and trace it through some of the various topics covered by many of the contributors.

In the volume's opening essay, Sæbø examines three broad historiographic terms that structure the volume: 1) Renaissance; 2) Humanism (in which he also discusses the Reformation); and 3) Enlightenment. Having nuanced and qualified these periodizations in all the appropriate ways, Sæbø offers, if not quite a "scarlet thread of redemption," then at least a consistent theme, a unifying idea in all three epochs: individualism. This term, to be sure, does not exhaust the meaning or intellectual-historical significance of these time periods for Sæbø, but he does return repeatedly to the idea that each period was characterized by a distinctive mentality. He says, further, that this mentality included an elevated view of human creativity and reason—along with a sharper focus on the particularity and concreteness of the human situation. In the final paragraph of the essay, Sæbø identifies this outlook with humanism: both the philological humanism of the Renaissance and the later scientific humanism of philosophers like René Descartes. He then goes on to say that "despite many historical and ideological changes and differences, there was a certain consistency throughout the long and variegated period of time that is covered by the present volume. This seems, above all, to be due to the phenomenon of humanism, at the core of which there was an increasingly strong individualism."[2]

I take as my starting point, then, Sæbø's suggestion—really, his conclusion—that individualism unifies intellectual culture across the early modern period in a way that is relevant to the history of biblical interpretation. But I would like to alter the vocabulary slightly and substitute "subjectivity" for individualism. The term "individualism" has, in my mind at least, a narrow scope. It suggests a conscious effort to be oneself in the face of pressures to conform or rely on others; or it refers to a designed social arrangement in which particular persons function as irreducible, self-contained units. We may speak in this vein, for example, of Emersonian individualism or of the "rugged individualism" of the American West. I recommend instead the term "subjectivity" because it captures not only one's conscious activity but also one's underlying stance toward the world. More specifically, it evokes the primacy of one's position in the world, above all, as a knowing, acting self. In early modern epistemological debates, for example, we recognize the emergence of

---

2. *HB/OT*, Sæbø, 45.

subjectivity as a pressing concern; we might also do the same in the history of art and literature as well. The point here, though, is to see subjectivity not only in its cognitive and aesthetic dimensions but in its ethical aspect as well. Early modern interpreters were not all individualists in a cultural or political sense (though, as Jon Levenson has argued, there is a close correspondence between Enlightenment biblical criticism and the liberal political ideal).[3] Yet, a heightened sense of subjectivity exercised profound influence on interpreters in this period. Subjectivity suggests a kind of hermeneutic virtue-ethical ideal: namely, that the good interpreter is a fully integrated self. Subjectivity demands that experience, belief, and judgment cohere without remainder in the confines of the self. On this view, one must not be, according to the German expression, *ein zwei Seelen Mensch*, a double-souled man. Yet the point is not only to have "one soul" but also to see, as it were, with one eye: that is, to constrict and unify one's vision so as to see clearly for oneself. Sociologist Philip Rieff associated this clarity of vision with modern self-possession. Here a quote from Rieff: "I, too, aspire to see clearly, like a rifleman, with one eye shut; I, too, aspire to think without assent. . . . I, too, share the modern desire not to be deceived."[4] The rifleman sees clearly and sharply; he is involved but detached. The modern interpreter desires, above all, the dignity of believing the truth, but, specifically, one that corresponds fully to his experience and understanding.

For the sake of convenience, I will divide interpreters discussed in this volume into two groups: those who identified hermeneutic virtue with aggressive criticism of tradition and those who saw the same possibility for virtue in a critical repossession of tradition. For the first group, subjectivity was expressed largely in terms of the effort to free interpretation from the interference of confessional dogma, church authority, and the legacy of patristic and medieval theologians. In weakening the hold of tradition on what might be said about the Bible, they sought to leave the interpreter alone with a Bible whose *true message* might be endorsed by a moral, rational, and tasteful human being. Most in this group came round to a critical understanding of the Bible that aligned it, at least in part, with sound philosophy. (There were some exceptions, of course. Of the interpreters discussed in this volume, a few such as Thomas Paine and Voltaire perhaps did not think that the Bible was ultimately salvageable.)

3. Levenson, *Hebrew Bible*, 106–126.
4. Rieff, *Triumph of the Therapeutic*, 10.

In the second group we meet interpreters who share the subjectivistic sensibilities of the first group, the same aspiration toward hermeneutical integrity. But these interpreters were inclined for various reasons to see in tradition fresh possibilities for the same kind of moral and intellectual integration of the self. They shared with the first group a sense of disjuncture with the past, a recognition that they were living, somehow, in a new era discontinuous with what came before. But they negotiated their relationship with tradition differently, ultimately finding that it too could be subjectively reappropriated. The division between these two groups is by no means absolute; nor is it meant to mark some deep ontological or political difference. It is simply a convenient way to mark characteristic emphases and organize this review. Whether one pursues a critical or constructive engagement with the tradition, the goal in this period is still to see with one eye or, perhaps, one set of eyes.

Perhaps no one better exemplifies the drive toward oneness or singularity of understanding than Baruch Spinoza. His monism and thoroughgoing naturalism enclosed everything within a single substantial reality and prevented him from crediting the metaphysical claims of the Bible (for example, that there is a transcendent personal God or that the Jews are a divinely chosen people). He saw religion as an essentially human phenomenon: religion is good insofar as it contributes to true morality; bad religion is simply a form of political control. Steven Nadler provides an excellent account of the reflexes of these beliefs for biblical interpretation, specifically Spinoza's use of historical criticism to identify what the biblical authors really believed and to thereby create separation between those beliefs and beliefs befitting a just and rational person. As described by Nadler, Spinoza's project is to bring the Bible and religions based on the Bible into line with principled inquiry, political rule that respects individual freedom of conscience and intellect, and a moralistic understanding of religion.

Though other figures in this volume did not formulate an explicit metaphysical doctrine in the way Spinoza did, we see the same monistic tendency, the same two-step maneuver to begin with a single, integrated understanding of reality in its moral and metaphysical aspects—one that the subject may hold without embarrassment—and to measure the Bible against that understanding. Christoph Bultmann in his article on Lessing, Voltaire, and Reimarus notes that these three entered the interpretive fray from positions outside the academic guild and engaged scholarship with a decidedly "more aggressive tone." What gave their criticisms clarity and force was not an antagonism toward religion but, interestingly, a firm commitment to it. Theirs, however, was a philosophically respectable religion, which was also designated variously as rational, natural, universal, and moral religion. It was a conception of religion characterized by singularity. As Bultmann says of Voltaire's deism: "deists worship one single god . . . inculcate virtue . . . respect political authority . . . respect all human beings as their brothers and sisters."[5] Thus there is one transcendent being: God; one moral demand: virtue; one earthly authority: the political; and one category for people: universal humanity. In a more sophisticated way, Lessing argued that the "contingent truths of history can never become the proof of necessary truths of reason."[6] If the Bible is to be believed, it must compel belief on philosophical grounds: neither its antiquity nor its traditional authority is sufficient. By subordinating historical truths to philosophical truths, Lessing disposes of the Bible's ancient venerability and isolates the single frame of reference within which the modern subject may appropriate or decline to appropriate the Bible.

In this first group, we may also include some British interpreters: the English Deists (discussed by H. G. Reventlow) and, from the late eighteenth-century, Robert Lowth and Alexander Geddes (discussed by William McKane). Like Lessing, Reimarus, and Voltaire, the English Deists approached biblical interpretation with a philosophical understanding of religion in hand (in this case, influenced by the epistemology of John Locke). Their philosophical framework brought morality into sharp focus while rendering traditional modes of interpretation dark, obscure, and incoherent. Reventlow discusses, for example, Anthony Collins's influential criticism of claims that Jesus fulfilled Old Testament prophecies. Hans Frei explains helpfully: "For Collins, following Locke, historical statements were simply and solely empirical, demanding a strength of assent which is suited to the persuasiveness of the evidence."[7] That is, the meaning of statements is confined to one relationship: the relation of the speaker to "the single, external reference of the words."[8] The meanings of prophetic statements (for example the Immanuel prophecy in Isaiah 7), then, were exhausted by reference to empirical conditions in the prophet's own time and place. It is therefore on this view nonsensical

---

5. *HB/OT*, Bultmann, 888.
6. Ibid., 897.
7. Frei, *Eclipse of Biblical Narrative*, 78.
8. Ibid., 79.

to speak of additional meanings beyond this original context. Collins's demand for a single semantic framework that corresponds to his own experience of language is, I believe, a clear instance of seeing with one hermeneutical eye.

We learn from William McKane that Alexander Geddes, arriving on the scene a generation or two after Locke, Collins, and company, was far more learned than they. An accomplished translator and commentator, Geddes was well-apprised of developments in German scholarship (influenced especially by Michaelis) and of textual research spurred on by Kennicott's variorum edition of the Hebrew Bible (1776, 1780). But as McKane points out, Geddes did not only seek a critical reconstruction of the Hebrew text; he also sought a renovation of the Christian religion. By the time he published his final work, the *Critical Remarks* of 1800, he was, as McKane says, isolated from Catholics and Protestants alike, having completely lost faith in institutional Christianity: "He was now nursing an elitist hope of a gathering of thoughtful Christians from all sects to embrace a new Christianity in a temple of reason, where only religious belief recommended by reason would have currency."[9] Though a Catholic priest, Geddes refused to align his own view with that of the Church and to participate in Church life. Geddes's case is among the most dramatic in the volume: his subjectivity, his rationalistic pursuit of hermeneutical integrity culminated in actual isolation.

I turn now to the second group. It is a great credit to this volume that it contains articles about interpreters and interpretive movements from outside the critical, scholarly mainstream and which, even today, figure only marginally in disciplinary accounts of the history of biblical interpretation. These figures and movements are marked by a greater degree of continuity with traditional forms of Judaism and Christianity.

The finest contribution in this group comes from Johann Anselm Steiger, who reviews the era of Protestant Orthodoxy. Steiger is conscious of the fact that Protestant Orthodoxy, as he says, has been "ignored by scholarship" and "regarded as lifeless, fossilized and one-sidedly doctrinaire."[10] Citing Gottlob Wilhelm Mayer, Hans-Joachim Kraus, and Henning Graf Reventlow, Steiger also notes that Protestant Orthodoxy has served as a foil to critical precursors in modern histories of interpretation and has frequently been dismissed as retrograde or "pre-critical."

---

9. *HB/OT*, McKane, 970.
10. *HB/OT*, Steiger, 697.

Yet he is surely right to insist that this approach does not do justice to the period and that Protestant Orthodoxy should therefore be understood on its own terms. Though it is possible to discern in the article a slightly apologetic tone, Steiger makes a compelling case for Protestant Orthodoxy as a self-conscious program designed to strike a difficult set of balances: as he says, between "doctrine and piety, learning and the praxis of faith, inwardness and the world, Christian faith and pagan antiquity, Athens and Jerusalem, Reformation and Humanism."[11] To refute the view, for example, that Protestant Orthodox reappropriation of Aristotelian philosophy in the wake of the Reformation was an unfortunate vestige of medieval heteronomy, Steiger describes the usefulness of Aristotle in summarizing, transmitting, and formalizing Protestant theology, and in carrying on high-level debate with Roman Catholics (as in the dispute between Johann Gerhard and Cardinal Bellarmine). Steiger argues that Protestant Orthodox, instead of holding nostalgically to a static view of inspiration, were motivated by their high view of Scripture to investigate the literary styles of biblical authors and to break new ground in Hebrew philology, rabbinics, and even Kabbalah. And without the "high esteem" of the biblical text and the disciplined cultivation of philological competencies and sensibilities associated with Protestant Orthodoxy, Steiger argues, later critical scholarship would have been unthinkable. But, considered on its own terms, Protestant Orthodoxy should be credited with the stabilization of the Protestant theological tradition and the establishment of a deep and rich Christian culture. Think Bach not Mozart.

I would like to make one final point about Steiger's article that is relevant to the theme of this review. In our first group of interpreters, we encountered a monistic version of subjectivity that seeks conformity between the subject as rational and moral agent and the world as a single reality that corresponds without remainder to the subject. Steiger's article does not venture into this philosophical background, but he brings up a relevant point in a discussion of the importance of Chalcedonian Christology for Protestant Orthodox views of biblical inspiration. Against the view (held by Hermann Rahtmann) that it compromises the freedom of the Holy Spirit to say that the He is somehow identifiable with the actual words of Scripture, Johann Gerhard maintained that just as the two natures of Christ, human and divine, coexist and cooperate without confusion or diminishment, so the Spirit allows the human speech that

---

11. Ibid., 703.

makes up the Bible to be the very Word of God. What I find interesting here is the use of a traditional theological formulation to explain the nature of scripture. If Steiger is correct in saying that Protestant Orthodoxy anticipated the Enlightenment in seeking a synthesis of faith and critical reason, then we may see in Protestant Orthodoxy a version of subjectivity that seeks integrity not in the denigration of tradition but in the principled rearticulation of it.

Next: Pietism, which is the subject of an article by Johannes Wallmann. Despite strong objections to the spiritual condition of the Protestant Orthodox churches, Pietists shared with Orthodox counterparts a desire to strengthen their Reformational inheritance. Under the leadership of Philipp Jakob Spener, author of *Pia Desideria*, and August Hermann Francke, the energetic leader of the Halle movement, Pietists emphasized conversion and personal holiness and promoted Bible reading and study in lay conventicles. This interest in the Bible yielded academic fruit as well: the textual researches of J. A. Bengel in New Testament and J. H. Michaelis in Old Testament; the massive eight-volume Berleburger Bible, with its fresh translations and commentary; and, importantly, the founding of the Collegium Orientale Theologicum at the University of Halle. It is surprising, in light of this, that Wallmann describes "Pietism's contribution to biblical scholarship" as "negligible."[12] The school of grammatical-historical interpretation that developed at Halle, for example, may have been oriented toward spiritual reading and application, but the process that Wallmann describes of interpreting the Bible by moving from an external, philological "husk" to an authentic, inner "kernel" is the same image employed later by Semler and Gabler.

Moshe Idel, in his article on Hasidism, does not connect this eighteenth-century movement to other attempts, elsewhere, to recover from within existing traditions a "religion of the heart": for example, Jansenism in France, Wesleyanism in England, and, as we have seen, Pietism among the Lutheran and Reformed on the Continent. Yet Hasidism shares affinities with these other movements: a focus on inwardness, a connection between the validity of interpretation and the personal righteousness of the interpreter, and certain mystical tendencies. Idel speaks of "linguistic immanence" in Hasidism, the idea that God is present in the words of the Torah and even in the spaces between letters—so-called "white letters" that may be "read" by the spiritually prepared. The ultimate goal of

---

12. *HB/OT*, Wallmann, 920.

interpretation is mystical union with God. Idel states: "Letters are conceived of as consisting of an external aspect, understood as a palace or box, within which the luminous, vital, spiritual or even divine aspect is present."[13] Like Pietism, Hasidism affords the interpreter a heightened sense of subjectivity—not in the form of rational control of the biblical text—but in transformative personal experience of divine realities to which older traditions bear witness.

I turn next to Edward Breuer's fine article on the *Haskalah*, the Jewish Enlightenment. Prior to the eighteenth century, Breuer notes, early modern Jewish scholarship focused largely on the study of the Talmud and legal codes. There was a neglect of medieval commentators and grammarians, and a preference instead for homiletic interpretation. In Berlin and Königsberg, though, members of these Prussian Jewish communities came into contact with the German Enlightenment. Naftali Hirz Wessely and, preeminently, Moses Mendelssohn emerged as leaders of a movement to forge a synthesis between modern culture and rabbinic Judaism. Engaging the biblical scholarship of the time, Mendelssohn was especially concerned to defend the validity of polysemous interpretation, or interpretation that recognizes multiple meanings for the same passage. He also produced a new edition of the Pentateuch that defended the Masoretic Text at a time when general esteem for the consonantal text and the vocalization of the rabbinic Bible was at a very low level. The stakes were high for Jewish interpreters. As Breuer points out, "rabbinic traditions of interpretation, after all, were formally anchored in the precise lettering and vocalization of the Hebrew Bible, and the slightest change to the text would ostensibly appear to undermine this ancient structure."[14] Thus, Mendelssohn used the tools of scholarship to defend rabbinic interpretation and to demonstrate that critical analysis of the biblical text, far from weakening Jewish tradition, provided it with ample support. As Breuer notes, the Jewish Enlightenment set a conservative precedent for engagement with biblical scholarship: "the nineteenth-century inheritors of this cultural movement remained cautious with regard to the developments of European biblical scholarship, and internalized it only in modest and measured degrees."[15]

---

13. *HB/OT*, Idel, 947.
14. *HB/OT*, Breuer, 1016.
15. Ibid., 1023.

The last member of this second group, Stephen Prickett's article on John Milton and John Bunyan, presents yet another example of constructive engagement with tradition that nevertheless brings subjectivity into view. Prickett's analysis demonstrates how both Milton and Bunyan used traditional forms, the book of Genesis and the long-standing tradition of Christian allegory, to structure and furnish accounts of modern religious experience. Adam's fall in *Paradise Lost*, for example, is not simply a sinful violation of divine commandment but a complicated, difficult decision to remain loyal to Eve after she sinned. He chose her over God. His decision in the moments after the Fall to give in to his desire for Eve was, perhaps, a little less difficult. Beneath Milton's negative description of their sexual union as "lascivious" and "wanton," Prickett detects a certain ambivalence on Milton's part as Adam is made to lie with Eve on a "shady bank," where "flowers were the couch," taking their "fill of love and love's disport . . . till dewey sleep oppressed them, wearied with their amorous play."[16] The psychological, not to mention physical realism of the two great works, *Paradise Lost* and *Pilgrim's Progress*, adds depth and complexity to the traditional forms by drawing the reader into the drama of deliberation, uncertainty, and internal conflict.

CONCLUSION

I am sorry to say that I have left several articles out of this review. Rather than rush through summaries of them, I would like to return to the idea of individualism or subjectivity. In discussing the development of biblical criticism in the early modern period, we are accustomed to speaking, not of subjectivity but of *objectivity*. We point to the development in this period of textual criticism associated with humanism, which put the textual disorder of manuscript traditions at the front of scholarly research agendas. With the rise of the new science of Copernicus, Galileo, and Newton, we witness the detachment of cosmology from the literal sense of Genesis and Joshua and a shift in the status of the Bible as something that explains the world to something that must itself be explained. The seventeenth and eighteenth centuries were also politically momentous. In this era, the Bible endured, to a great degree, as a contested inheritance, a matter of dispute, a source of authority to be managed in new social and political arrangements. All of these things contributed, no doubt, to

---

16. *HB/OT*, Prickett, 930.

methods and modes of interpretation oriented toward objectivity: both the objectivity of the Bible—its status as a thing, a text, and an artifact to be understood with reference to other objects—and the objectivity of the interpreter, the ability to put aside prejudices and theological commitments, gain an impartial understanding of everything that pertains to the Bible, and provide reasonable solutions to interpretive problems of various types. Those inclined to see biblical scholarship in terms of critically reconstructed knowledge about the language, text, and history of the Bible are apt to recognize the early modern period as advancing the cause of objectivity.

There is nothing wrong with this view, of course, or with the influential corollary to this view: namely, that the essential features of the early modern period and the Enlightenment may be discerned in their contributions to the rise of historicism. Historical thinking guides the interpreter in two ways: as a basic principle aimed toward explicating the influence of culture and language on authors, and as a strategy for making sense of biblical texts that have come to appear, for many reasons, increasingly alien. Historicism allows us to say, "that was then, this is now." In the final essay of the volume, H. G. Reventlow discusses several figures on the cusp of the transition from the eighteenth century to the nineteenth century: J. G. Herder, J. G. Eichhorn, and J. P. Gabler. Reventlow sees them as transitional figures, men who were at once committed to the universalism of the Enlightenment and sensitive to "history" and "historical development" as principles of method. Herder, for example, feels his way into ancient Hebrew poetry; Eichhorn transforms biblical scholarship into something resembling a critical history of Israelite literature; and Gabler insists on a clear separation between what pertained merely to the cultural context of biblical authors and what had enduring value for theology. What I find most interesting about Reventlow's article, though, is his discussion of Immanuel Kant. Reventlow notes there that both Eichhorn and Gabler were highly critical of Kant's attempt in *Religion within the Bounds of Reason* to derive a moral philosophy from the early chapters of Genesis. Kant investigated there the nature and origin of evil, identifying evil with the conscious adoption of an immoral maxim and thus tracing evil to human free will. Eichhorn and Gabler both accused Kant of backsliding into allegorical interpretation, of using the biblical stories to clothe philosophical arguments in the manner of Philo or even Leibniz. For this reason, Reventlow says that despite Kant's great influence on philosophy and theology of the nineteenth century, "his impact on Biblical hermeneutics and exegesis in a strict sense remained minimal."[17]

This is, in one sense, quite true. If we think of nineteenth-century criticism in terms of German historicism (as Reventlow does) or in terms of minutely researched scholarship characterized by scientific objectivity, then it is hard not to see Kant as a dead end, an example of a rationalistic, universalistic moralism that had lost its hold on intellectual culture. But I am inclined to see Kant's legacy differently. Kant succeeded in grasping and formalizing what philosophers for a century and a half had been groping toward and stumbling over. The heightened sense of subjectivity that we find both in opponents and advocates of tradition—the same drive to inhabit a world fully proportionate to human faculties—finds masterful expression in Kant. For Kant, it is not only our claims to knowledge that grow out of human subjectivity. Our experience of beauty, our reverence for the divine, our inexplicable aspirations toward goodness are also to be found in the inner recesses of the self. And it is by means of the self that these cohere. From this conception of selfhood, then, emerges an ideal of hermeneutical integrity, one that is expressed in the chasteness of interpretive method, in impatience with religious hypocrisy, and in the urgent pursuit of exegetical programs suited to us in the present moment—programs, in other words, that are modern. This ideal did not fade away at the close of the Enlightenment; it endured and is still very much with us.

Bibliography

Frei, Hans. *The Eclipse of Biblical Narrative: A Study in Eighteenth and Nineteenth Century Hermeneutics*. New Haven, CT: Yale University Press, 1974.
Legaspi, Michael C. *The Death of Scripture and the Rise of Biblical Studies*. Oxford Studies in Historical Theology. New York: Oxford University Press, 2010.
Levenson, Jon. *The Hebrew Bible, the Old Testament, and Historical Criticism*. Louisville, KY: WJK, 1993.
Rieff, Philip. *The Triumph of the Therapeutic: Uses of Faith After Freud*. Wilmington, DE: ISI, 2006.
Sæbø, Magne. *Hebrew Bible / Old Testament: The History of Its Interpretation*. Vol 2. Göttingen: Vandenhoeck & Ruprecht, 2008.

---

17. *HB/OT*, Reventlow, 1040.

Reality, History, and the Old Testament in the Nineteenth Century[1]

Philip Sumpter

ONE CAN APPROACH A book on the history of the interpretation of the Old Testament from a number of perspectives. For example, one can draw upon the analysis in order to gain insight into the intellectual and spiritual culture of a particular era, or one can look in detail at the evolution of particular approaches and theories concerning the Bible throughout the period in question. Volume three, part one of Magne Sæbø's series on the history of Hebrew Bible/Old Testament interpretation certainly provides a wealth of information as regards these questions. The various contributors provide careful discussions of key scholars, methods, and fields of research, often pointing out the broader ideological background as well as the implications of these developments for ongoing biblical research in the present. For this, the book can be highly recommended. In this review, however, I will be taking a different approach, asking questions informed by my own position as a Biblical scholar concerned with the ongoing capacity of the Old Testament to speak in the present.

My own understanding of this issue has been heavily influenced by the work of Brevard S. Childs (1923–2007),[2] and so from the outset I assumed that a key contribution a book on *past* interpretation can offer to ongoing exegesis in the *present* is its ability to display the various in-

---

1. This article was presented to the Biblical Theology Section of the International Meeting of the Society of Biblical Literature in Vienna, Austria on July 10, 2014. It constitutes a review of Magne Sæbø's *Hebrew Bible/Old Testament: The History of Its Interpretation.* Volume III/1: The Nineteenth Century—a Century of Modernism and Historicism (Göttingen: Vandenhoeck & Ruprecht, 2013).

2. See Sumpter, *Psalm 24*.

terpretive categories through which the text has been appropriated over the centuries. The critical question for the contemporary exegete is this: which categories are most commensurate with the material at hand? Or to put it more concretely—and this is the question I have posed to Sæbø's volume: *how did interpreters of this particular season of Biblical exegesis wrestle with both the nature of the text as well as the nature of the broader reality out of which it emerged, within which it cohered, and to which it witnessed?* The question of "reality," so central to Childs's "canonical approach,"[3] is central to my review of this book.

I made this interpretive decision before I started my review, so, as you can imagine, I was delighted to discover that a similar concern for the "reality" of the text appears to have been shared both by the editor of the volume as a whole as well as many individual contributors. Indeed, it almost appears to structure the book as a whole. I will point out this dimension shortly. Before I start, however, it is best to turn to the editor's introductory chapter, for it most helpfully summarizes the central concerns of the book and provides a framework for interpreting what follows.

Sæbø's title indicates what was at stake in the nineteenth century: "Fascination with 'History'—Biblical Interpretation in a Century of Modernism and Historicism." For this period, it was the concept of "history" that provided the dominant framework for understanding both the nature of the Bible and the broader reality within which it cohered. And yet, as Sæbø's use of scare quotes for the word "history" indicates, this broader phenomenon was itself a contested concept, undergoing developments throughout the century and raising a host of insights, possibilities, as well as challenges along the way. So the more specific questions that are raised for reading this volume are these: just what was the nature of this substance called "history," and how should it shape our reading of the Bible? Conversely, is there any indication of how our reading of the Bible should shape our understanding of "history"?

Sæbø divides his article into three sections, briefly sketching out the content (i.e., the "reality") of the terms "history" and "historicism" during this age, their impact upon the reading of the Bible, and the challenges that they precipitated for those who promulgated them. In short, "history" referenced an essentially human sphere of activity within which the Bible had its being. Over time, this reality became understood in terms

---

3. See especially Childs, "Interpretation in Faith"; *Biblical Theology*; "Jesus Christ?"

of 1) *distance*—the past is *different* to the present and structured according to a chronologically unfolding sequence of relatively self-contained epochs, each shaped by its own inner causal and cultural relationships; 2) *individual human agency;* and 3) *empiricism*—i.e., the idea that human agents are situated within the "world" (another term Sæbø puts in scare quotes), understood as something that could be analyzed objectively in light of experience.

The positive effect of this apprehension of the specifically human and contingent nature of Scripture was that it led to increased attention to the details of that dimension of its context—now understood to be the primary and determinative context within which the Bible was to render its meaning. As a result of this new perspective, the nineteenth century saw an explosion of research into the broader linguistic and cultural environment within which the tradents of Israel's tradition operated. The gradual realization that Israel's canonical representation of history was only obliquely related to actual "historical" facts led to the creation of the genre of "histories of Israel," which not only traced the development of the nation but also provided the proper contexts within which to re-situate Israel's traditions (the most significant shift being the placement of the book of Deuteronomy in the monarchic or exilic period, rather than with Moses on the eve of the conquest). Finally, towards the end of the century, as the ever shifting and contingent nature of human history became increasingly apparent, that which was once considered "eternal," namely the religious truth claims of the people of Israel, were also dissolved in the same processes of evolution and changed that had engulfed every other aspect of the Bible. Old Testament "theology" was replaced with the "history of its religion."

Sæbø goes on to note how this gradual awareness of the historical contingency of all human events raised a challenge, not only to modernity's appropriation of the Bible in particular but also of the human past in general. In short, the past was atomized and relativized, making it increasingly difficult to turn to it as a source of instruction and guidance. Attempts were made to bridge the widening gap by construing a particular "world view" or "philosophy of life" within which to encompass the past and the present, but these abstract construals were consistently judged wanting at the bar of empirical history.

With this final observation, Sæbø has helpfully set the stage for approaching the various contributions that follow. In short, each chapter documents to one degree or another a deep tension in the nineteenth century between rigorous historical empiricism on the one hand, which sought to measure every construal in light of the facts, and the need to situate these perceived "facts" within a broader frame of reference that also encompassed the present.

We will now take a brief look at the way the details of this tension are played out in the rest of the book. Before looking at key individual chapters, we will first turn to Sæbø's editorial arrangement of these chapters into a coherent whole. The material is divided into three subsections bearing the following titles: "A. The General Cultural Context of Nineteenth Century's Biblical Interpretation," "B. Main regional and Confessional Areas of the Nineteenth Century's Biblical Scholarship," and "C. Special Fields and Different Approaches in the Interpretation of the Hebrew Bible/Old Testament." In terms the key concerns mentioned above, one could perhaps see these sections as moving progressively from theories concerning the broader reality within which the Bible was understood to subsist towards interpretations of the concrete realia of the Bible itself.

Section A ("general cultural context") represents the broadest horizon in which the Bible was situated. The articles contained therein can be further subdivided into two categories: the first two articles outline and analyse the broader philosophical/theological construals of *reality* within which the most influential thinkers of this period situated the Bible. These thinkers are almost entirely influenced by German Enlightenment philosophy. The remaining three articles deal with those elements of the Bible's context that these construals of reality made it imperative to study further, namely the Bible's historical, linguistic, and socio-religious contexts.

Section B narrows the focus a bit further by looking at a number of local variations of these two themes, both geographically (i.e., North America, the British Isles and the European Continent, and Northern Europe), or confessionally (i.e., the Catholic Church and Judaism—Protestants do not receive their own chapter, as they were the key players in the development of theory in this period, although Jan Rohl's opening article does have a special section on "Old Testament Studies and Protestant Theology at German Universities").

Finally, section C ("Special Fields and Different Approaches") turns to the concrete details of the Biblical text, as understood by key thinkers of the period, the vast majority of whom were German. The thirteen articles in this section treat issues of method ("lower" and "higher criticism") and areas of study, whether blocks of canonical material (the Pentateuch, the Former Prophets, Latter Prophets, the Writings, the canon as a whole), or particular dimensions of the historical nature of the material (i.e., its compositional nature or its rootedness in broader ancient Near Eastern cultural patterns), or its context within the history or the theology of Israel.

I now turn to each section in turn. Given the limitations of space, I will only focus on those elements of each chapter that contribute to the question of the relation between *reality* and *text* raised above (and selection is necessary, given the large amount of overlap in subject matter between the various chapters).

In the first article, Jahn Rohls provides a broad overview of the ideological content of much thought in this period, particularly as it relates to the Bible. The first thinker of significance is Immanuel Kant (1724–1804) with his moralistic interpretation of religion and rejection of historical facts as the basis of salvation. In light of that kind of faith, the Bible merely functions as a guideline to moral faith in reason, the authority of which must be grounded by philosophy. Interestingly, this has the implication that that philological-historical exegesis must be replaced by a philosophical-doctrinal exegesis emphasizing the Bible's moral value. Here we see that the Enlightenment's legacy did not immediately lead to historical inquiry but rather to a form of "allegory," for the text's meaning lies within the moral-symbolic sphere and not in its literal sense.

For the theologian Friedrich Schleiermacher (1768–1834), on the other hand, the essence of the Christian religion consisted in the emotional experience of the infinite. This experience must remain dynamic, so that for Schleiermacher, it was inevitable that earlier expressions of faith become outdated. Along this line of thought, the closing of the biblical canon represented a contradiction of Christianity's true spirit. G. F. W. Hegel (1770–1831) had an historical rather than moralistic or emotional focus. For him, all history is constituted by a dialectical movement towards unification, the overcoming of the subject and object in what Hegel termed "love." Within this "world view," the Old Testament is neither a cypher for a higher morality nor an expression of an emotion but rather a witness to Israel's and Judaism's religious evolution.

Rohls provides us with a wealth of examples of the various attitudes to the Old Testament in the Protestant faculties of this period, but I will just mention two key Old Testament scholars here who were clearly indebted to these aforementioned philosophies. Wilhelm Martin

Leberecht de Wette (1780–1849) was inspired by the moralism of Kant and the emotional emphasis found, for example, in his colleague Schleiermacher, although it goes back to the work of J. G. Herder (1744–1803). This commitment liberated him from having to care much about the historical veracity of the Old Testament. Instead, the Old Testament largely contained "myth," which was de Wette's label for a particular kind of literature that grew out of an encounter between a finite human and the infinite. This experience of the ultimate essence of things is anchored in emotion and can only be represented by means of figurative language. Its ultimate focal point is the moral notion of the one God. De Wette thus understood exegesis to consist in seeking for "ideas" understood in their original historical setting which were the bases of symbols and myths. An example of a scholar influenced by Hegel, on the other hand, is Wilhelm Vatkte (1806–1882), who interpreted Israel's religion within Hegel's speculative categories. Accordingly, he saw in the Old Testament a developmental process taking part in three moments: 1) universality and immediacy, which extended from Moses to the oldest prophets; 2) the externalization of this self-awareness in pubic ritual and ideology, as can be found in most of the Pentateuch; and 3) the return to the immediate self-awareness of the inspired prophets, after it had been given concrete institutional expression, thereby reconciling the subject with the object.

Rohls's essay overlaps to a degree and the following essay by Gunter Scholtz, which is dedicated to "The Phenomenon of 'Historicism' as a Backcloth of Biblical Scholarship." Scholtz provides additional interesting insight into some of the metaphysical assumptions undergirding a lot of nineteenth-century emphasis on human cultural particularity, such as Herder's theory that every manifestation of nature and history is a "revelation" of the divine being, thus transforming revelation into a dynamic metaphysic. In relation to Rohls's essay, however, Scholtz's primary contribution is his tracing of the conundrum touched upon in Sæbø's opening article, namely the corrosive effect that a rigorous historicism has upon all attempts to bridge history by means of philosophy and/or theology. The tension arises because, Scholtz argues, historical study cannot actually be done without some kind of philosophical framework. He notes how the growing awareness of plurality and variability in the human world and the relativism it engendered undermined attempts to establish universal norms by which to judge and evaluate the past. This was a crisis not only felt in the field of theology but also in law, economics, and cultural analysis. In this context of growing historical awareness,

Hegel's philosophy of history was attractive because his system integrated the results of historical evolution, on the one hand, with an interpretation of that evolution in terms of a reasoned progress, on the other. With the ongoing increase in historical knowledge, however, this mixture of philosophy, theology and history cracked until it burst and was eventually judged illusory. And yet, even though historians tended as a result to turn away from philosophical approaches to history and focus on empirical description instead, it was recognized that the human nature of the subject matter—particularly the fact that it is ideas that make history—required from the interpreter aesthetic capacities that involved developing an intuition about the whole context within which these developments took place.

Scholtz provides illustrations of the philosophical and theological underpinnings of Old Testament scholarship that went under the name of "neutral" and "objective," for which I have already provided the examples of de Wette and Vatke above. The loss of cultural orientation brought about by historicism led, by the end of the nineteenth century, to a "dissonance between the richness of historical knowledge on the one hand and the open question of their significance for life on the other" (72). Scholtz summarizes the situation with this wonderful metaphor: "At the end of the . . . so-called 'historical century,' many scholars had the feeling of sitting hungry at a table full with food of all centuries and nations" (73).

Scholtz's description of the "richness of historical knowledge" bequeathed to us by the nineteenth century takes us to the final three chapters of this opening section, all of which deal with the various spheres of knowledge that, in light of the new historical focus, required investigation. These spheres are the Bible's historical, linguistic, and socio-cultural contexts and the articles treating them provide us with a wealth of insights into the way these disciplines developed as well as the impact they have had on all further study of the Bible. Given my overarching interest in the interrelation between concepts of reality and concepts of the text, I will limit my observations to this dimension.

In the article on the Bible's broader historical context, Holloway illustrates how it was a quest to prove the historicity of the Bible that lead to industrious work in digging up the archaeological sites of the region. He describes, for example, the production of Biblical maps as a form of "geopiety" in which "the Bible maps themselves became episodes in sacramental history alongside the Bibles they complemented" (105). Holloway also points out the economic and political factors that drove research. He goes on to describe the eventual undermining of the quest for Israel's uniqueness, as discoveries of texts from other ancient Near Eastern cultures demonstrated that Israel was very much a part of its broader cultural milieu.

In the article on socio-religious context, J. W. Rogerson notes how Biblical scholars were dependent on the work of non-theological folklorists and philologists for reconstructing the cultural history of mankind as a whole within which to situate the Bible, whether Jakob Grimm's theory of "primal religion" or Sir James George Frazer's religious evolutionism. In time, focus shifted to the new discoveries from the ancient Near East. Whether the focus was universal humanity or the ancient "Semites," these theories also began to dissolve previous assumptions about Israel's specialness. Finally, in the realm of language, Holger Gzella documents how the new comparative approach to linguistics ultimately led to the dethronement of the Hebrew language, both as a unique language of revelation as well as an object worthy of much study, particularly considering the richer resources found in other ancient Near Eastern languages. In sum, each chapter tells a similar story: growth in historical knowledge led to a reduction in historians' ability to appreciate Israel's abiding significance. To use Scholtz's metaphor, these chapters document the production of a rich buffet offering little spiritual nourishment.

The second section sketches the ways in which discrete geographical and confessional communities wrestled with their Bibles in this period. Interestingly, whereas one might expect a lot of overlap between these chapters, each country seems to have a sufficiently distinct profile as to make its own contribution to our theme. Thus, in the chapter on North America, James P. Byrd notes that until late in the century the general American public approached the Bible with a "democratic hermeneutic" (175) in which each individual was considered perfectly able to understand the Bible on his or her own without the need of extensive research. This was because the Bible was understood to reveal universal truth that is available to all through pure reason and common sense reflection. Biblical interpretation thus involved a "Baconian search for evidence, assembling the facts of Scripture and classifying them to understand biblical truth" (176).

As one can imagine, Americans were quite content with this approach until Germany's historicism, fueled by its idealism, gradually permeated American society by means of its universities. J. W. Rogerson's article on the scholarship of the British Isles and the Continent presents the development of Biblical criticism as a conflict between what he considers to be enlightened and reasonable thinkers with their home base in Germany, on the one hand, and the overwhelming resistance to these clear insights by irrational traditionalists in Britain, who used all kinds of political means to stem the tide of critical scholarship or, as Rogerson puts it, "any approach to the Bible which allowed for the use of human reason." Eventually, however, the newer approach also made headway in Britain.

Scholarship in northern Europe, according to Jesper Høgenhaven's account, appears to have been more tuned into the theological needs of the church while still wrestling with the new historical consciousness. This led to the development of what he calls "historical 'Biblicism.'" In this approach, the Bible was not taken to be an infallible text, but it did witness to divine revelation, understood in processual terms as the unfolding of the kingdom of God in history, with Jesus as its final expression. The Old Testament is prophecy in that it contains stages of God's revelation pointing forward to full revelation in Jesus. As Høgenhaven points out, this approach made historical study central to the theological task of understanding the biblical message. Perhaps we can find in this conservative synthesis the impact of historical consciousness in its strong focus on the "economic" dimension of the divine economy rather than the "ontic"? And yet it is also in this region that we have one of the most interesting exceptions to this development, namely the work of the Danish philosopher Søren Kierkegaard (1813–1855). Rather than read the Bible "horizontally," as it were, he claimed that the Biblical stories should be read paradigmatically. He remained an exception, however, and in Northern Europe, too, historical criticism was eventually to win the day.

The final two chapters of the section are dedicated to two faith communities, Catholics and Jews, and it is interesting to read them in unison in order to see how these two communities' differing visions of reality shaped their approaches to the text, particularly in light of the century's historicizing focus. According to Gerald Fogarty, for Catholics, the primary concern was the purity of doctrine. This shaped the initial vigorous rejection of all forms of "higher criticism," with its theories and, as we have seen, assumptions often so profoundly seeming to undermine basic tenants of Christian faith. It also explains the more relaxed attitude towards "lower criticism," which was simply concerned with issues of text and thus the better clarification of the message of the canonical documents.

The situation was different within Judaism, however. According to Edward Breuer and Chanan Gafni, the religious commitments of Jews meant that they could not be so open towards textual criticism. Rather than seeing the text as "a source for ancient history or a primer on God's providential ways" (266), Jews were committed to the text as a *mitzvah* to be studied, taught, observed, and performed. In this Halakhic approach to the text, the exact lettering matters. As such, those Jews who did venture into textual criticism tended to be conservative in their approach.

This latter observation brings us to the third and final section of the book, which treats specific areas of study. Its second article deals with the "lower criticism" of the Bible, overlapping to a degree with the chapter on Jewish approaches, for one of the most important contributors to this field was the Reform Rabbi Abraham Geiger (1810–1874), a figure who was also discussed in the chapter on Judaism. In this chapter, Richard Weis provides a detailed overview of the theories of the period and he ultimately endorses Geiger's approach as the one closest to the truth, now vindicated by the finds in Qumran. In light of the previous article's description of Geiger's religious commitments to Judaism, it seems clear that it was these commitments that shaped his interpretation. In short, he asserts that the Masoretic text developed in connection with its religious use by a community of faith, who cherished it as sacred Scripture and thus shape it in line with their religious norms. This contrasts with the view of Paul de Lagarde (1827–1891), who argued that the Masoretic (i.e., traditional Jewish) manuscripts in our possession today are simply the distorted results of accumulated arbitrary and mechanical distortions from an originally pure archetype. (Interestingly, Weis makes the point that, a particular view of reality was at work for de Lagarde as well; he saw modernity and contemporary German society as degraded and he believed the solution to this situation was to reach back through the centuries of decline and corruption to reach the purity of the origins [361].)

The remaining chapters of this final section tend to be largely descriptive in nature, dealing with nuances in the development of historical critical approaches and historical critical interpretations of various portions of the Hebrew Bible/Old Testament. Given limitations of space, I will just briefly touch on a number of salient points, which will in turn lead to some general conclusions.

For a start, given my conviction that Childs's "canonical approach" provides a way forward out of the historicist impasse, my attention was immediately drawn to the concluding essay of the collection by Stephen

Chapman, which is dedicated to "canon." It is fascinating that a book that opens by describing both the possibilities as well the challenges of "historicism" should end with a chapter on precisely this subject. As many will know, it is largely in the realm of "canon" that Childs developed his response to historicism.[4] Is it the hermeneutical significance of "canon" that guided the editor's choice to place this chapter here? Chapman is in fact indebted to Childs in his own way and an initial glance at the title of the essay does indeed seem to indicate that this is how the author understood the function of his contribution: "Modernity's Canonical Crisis: Historiography and Theology in Collision." The genitive of the main title can be understood in both directions and my initial hope was that it would primarily indicate the challenge posed to modernity by the canon rather than the other way round.

Chapman does very tentatively touch on this dimension, though primarily by means of negation by noting the *failure* of nineteenth century Catholic and Protestant scholars to think about the *nature* of tradition and history on a deeper, more *theological* level. He does tantalizingly mention the post-war Barthian emphasis on revelation taking place within the witness of the text itself, but he does not follow that lead and instead dedicates the rest of his article to describing the various theories concerning the constitution of the final form of the canon by key German, American, and British thinkers. Only someone tuned into Childs's ideas will see those ideas shimmering through the lines of Chapman's analysis.

The same reserve is found in the contribution on the "prophets" by another scholar closely associated with Childs: Christopher Seitz. His essay too, has nothing of the brilliant hermeneutical insights on the nature of time, referentiality, and literary association that can be found in his book *Prophecy and Hermeneutics*, a lack that is also surprising because in that book he has some fascinating things to say about the "godly exegetical instincts" of one of the nineteenth century's most important Old Testament scholars: George Adam Smith. Instead, we are simply provided with this period's critical re-contextualization of biblical prophecy within an alternative "dispensation" informed by the categories of chronological sequence and original authorial intentionality.

---

4. In addition to the publications mentioned in footnote 2, I recommend Childs, *Introduction to the Old Testament* and *New Testament as Canon*. For an exhaustive bibliography of Childs's publications, see the bibliography at the end of Driver, *Brevard Childs*.

Is it unfair of me to have hoped for more? I think more explicit critical engagement with the assumptions of historicism in light of hermeneutical developments that properly belong in the twentieth century (though lines can be traced back to the likes of, e.g., Martin Kähler and Søren Kierkegaard) would not have been out of place in this volume, not only because other articles do in fact trace developments into the twentieth century (especially the treatment on textual criticism and Catholic theology), but because other contributors are quite transparent in their affirmation of the perceive to be the essential adequacy of historicism's victory.

This comes out clearly in Joachim Schaper's excellent chapter on what he judges to be the rightful replacement of the discipline of Biblical Theology with the History of Religion. However, I thought that the most fascinating example of advocacy for the *spiritual* superiority of a historicist approach was Erhard Gerstenberger's chapter on the History of Religions approach (Gerstenberger was, incidentally, a life-long close friend of Childs). According to Gerstenberger, seeing history as a "manmade retrospective construct" (465), rather than simply as consisting in the "framing [of] eternally given gold-nuggets of divine revelation with ornamental design" (457–458), has the advantage of undermining hegemonic systems which ground their authority in transcendental truths, as well as shifting confessional Biblical scholars' concerns towards the real life processes of normal parishioners and members of other religions.

It is clear that contributors to this volume (Chapman; Seitz) would consider Gerstenberger's sharp dichotomy between transcendent revelation and human agency to be sub-Christian and misrepresentative, but why couldn't these scholars have been more assertive in articulating their own standpoint? It would have highlighted the genuine tension between relativism and truth unearthed in Scholtz's excellent essay and it would have made the volume more fruitful for contemporary appropriation by Biblical scholars attempting to grasp their subject matter in its fullest dimensions.

As a whole, then, we can say that this installment of the *Hebrew Bible/Old Testament: The History of Its Interpretation* series provides its readers with a good indication of the hermeneutical issues at stake in the historicism of this century, but the bulk of the material, particularly in the third and largest section, emphasizes the textual side of the tension between text and reality. Perhaps that is the greatest legacy of the nineteenth century. I look forward to seeing whether the forthcoming final volume in the series, which will necessarily cover the confessional revival in scholarship in the first half of the twentieth century, will complement this picture and point ways forward out of the impasse.

Bibliography

Childs, Brevard. *Biblical Theology of the Old and New Testaments: Theological Reflection on the Christian Bible*. Minneapolis: Fortress, 1993.

———. "Does the Old Testament Witness to Jesus Christ?" In *Evangelium, Schriftauslegung, Kirche: Festschrift für Peter Stuhlmacher zum 65. Geburtstag*, edited by Jostein Adna and Scott J. Hafemann, 57–64. Göttingen: Vandenhoeck & Ruprecht, 1997.

———. "Interpretation in Faith: The Theological Responsibility of an Old Testament Commentary." *Interpretation* 18.40 (1962) 432–49.

———. *Introduction to the Old Testament as Scripture*. Philadelphia: Fortress, 1979.

———. *The New Testament as Canon: An Introduction*. Philadelphia: Fortress, 1984.

Driver, Daniel. *Brevard Childs, Biblical Theologian: For the Church's One Bible*. Grand Rapids: Baker Academic, 2012.a

Sæbø, Magne, ed. *Hebrew Bible/Old Testament: The History of Its Interpretation*. Volume III/1: The Nineteenth Century—A Century of Modernism and Historicism. Göttingen: Vandenhoeck & Ruprecht, 2013.

Seitz, Christopher. *Prophecy and Hermeneutics: Toward a New Introduction to the Prophets*. Grand Rapids: Baker Academic, 2007.

Sumpter, Philip. *The Substance of Psalm 24: An Attempt to Read the Bible after Brevard S. Childs*. Library of Hebrew Bible/Old Testament Series 600. London: T. & T. Clark, 2015.

II. PRESENT: METHODOLOGICAL CONSIDERATIONS FOR BIBLICAL THEOLOGY NOW

Biblical Theology in Transition

An Overview of Recent Works, and a Look Ahead at How to Proceed

Georg Fischer

A GOOD FIFTY YEARS have passed since the seminal work of Gerhard von Rad's *Theologie des Alten Testaments*,[1] and many things have changed in OT research. He was confident in his ability to outline a history of OT faith, and tried to do so by a description of the historical and prophetic traditions. At this time he did not consider the possibility of later origins of the biblical books; nowadays we assume that most of them came into being in their final redaction only in postexilic times. In addition to that, archeological evidence has dramatically altered our understanding of Israel's history. These are two of the main reasons why von Rad's "Theology," although brilliant in its day, can no longer be considered relevant.

For this short article,[2] I have to pass over many other theologies that followed his lead; Manfred Oeming,[3] Jörg Jeremias,[4] and especially Hen-

---

1. von Rad, *Theologie des Alten Testaments. Band 1* and *Band 2*.

2. This contribution is based on a paper which was read at the ISBL conference in Amsterdam, on July 25 of 2012, on the invitation of Mark Elliott, chair of the session on Biblical Theology. I thank him for the opportunity to present my research in this field. Given the date of the original delivery, this "overview" only covers books published earlier; however, I will occasionally refer to more recent works.

3. Oeming, "Ermitteln und Vermitteln," esp. 18–38, offers an overview of forty different theologies of the Old Testament, starting with Walter Eichrodt (1933–1939) and ending with Jack Miles (2002).

4. Jeremias, "Neuere Entwürfe," 29–58, too, presents various concepts for OT theologies. He does it more systematically, with greater focus on recent times.

ning Graf Reventlow[5] have presented helpful overviews which may make up for what cannot be offered here. Instead, I wish to concentrate on *some specific theologies of the past twenty years* and analyze briefly their characteristics. It is my aim to achieve thus some insights that might indicate directions for future "biblical theologies."

Major Studies of the Past Twenty Years

I start with Horst Dietrich Preuss who published his two volumes on *Theologie des Alten Testaments* in 1991 and 1992.[6] As the subtitle of his first volume indicates, one of his basic ideas concerns Yhwh's *election* of Israel, and from this he deduces the people's obligations; his approach can be termed "systematic,"[7] and he devotes large portions to Israel's conduct. In fact, almost the entire second volume deals with the people's response and institutions, aspects that primarily belong to social and ethical areas.

Preuss grasped correctly a major aspect of the biblical God, with his emphasis on "election." Nevertheless, today it seems difficult to base on just one main motif, the rich, multifaceted manner in which God is spoken of in the OT. A second point of discussion is the extent to which affairs that predominantly touch people may be dealt with in a "theology."

In the same year as Preuss's second volume, Brevard S. Childs's *Biblical Theology of the Old and New Testaments* came out.[8] It has become extraordinarily influential. His *canonical approach* takes into account the whole of the biblical scriptures and has heavily influenced German exegesis, too.[9] Childs succeeds in showing the interrelatedness and unity

---

5. Reventlow, "Biblische," reviews all relevant publications from the years 1995 to 2004 in four major contributions, dealing also with related fields like the connection with "Religionsgeschichte," or with special theological topics, like creation, or prayer.

6. Preuss, *Theologie des Alten Testaments. Band 1* and *Band 2*.

7. This is the classification attributed to him by Jeremias, "Neuere Entwürfe," 42 and 46.

8. Childs, *Biblical Theology*; the edition I quote is London: Xpress Reprints, 1996.

9. Childs's impact can be grasped in the most influential German introduction to the OT, where Erich Zenger pleads for a "Hermeneutik des kanonischen Diskurses": Erich Zenger et al., *Einleitung in das Alte Testament*, 21; on the following pages (till 36) he exemplifies this concept with regard to the various canons of the Hebrew (Tanak) and the Christian Bible. Other important authors taking up Childs's canonical approach in German exegesis are Christoph Dohmen, *Vom Umgang mit dem Alten Testament*, 53-57, and Georg Steins, *Die "Bindung Isaaks" im Kanon (Gen 22)*.

of the OT and the NT, and the importance of interpreting biblical texts within the range of the canon.

Whereas from a Christian perspective his approach of viewing the Bible from "the one scope of scripture, which is Jesus Christ"[10] can be more easily accepted, this is hardly an adequate stance from which to interpret OT texts in their own right.[11] Furthermore, the attention given to the "canon" does not answer in itself theological issues.[12]

Another outstanding and prolific scholar is Walter Brueggemann, whose *Theology of the Old Testament* appeared in 1997.[13] Therein he concentrates on the motif of "testimony," in the various modes of "core, counter, unsolicited and embodied testimonies." The first two aspects are especially helpful and illuminating. On the one hand, there is a kernel ("core") in the way in which the OT speaks about God. On the other, these basic concepts are disputed by moments of "hiddenness, ambiguity and negativity." The central notion of "*testimony*," too, deserves appreciation. All we know about the God of the Bible comes from what others have said and written about him.

Certainly, the books of Brueggemann are in many ways illuminating and inspiring. However, there are questions raised about them, too. In his own article[14] he answers the issues raised against him regarding "historicity" and "ontology," though, in my estimation, not completely convincingly. He should distinguish more clearly between God's "existence" and our way of speaking about him, and also perceive more clearly where the OT itself is marked by ideology.[15]

---

10. Childs, *Biblical Theology*, 725.

11. Ibid. ". . . the New Testament's use of the Old Testament cannot be easily rconciled with the Old Testament's own witness."

12. In the largest part 6 of his book Childs covers ten themes, offering "theological reflection on the Christian Bible." This means that the canonical approach does not *per se* proffer a theology; an extra step is needed for it. For a critique of Childs's approach see also Jeremias, "Neuere Entwürfe," 37–38, and Elliott, *Reality of Biblical Theology*, 55–64.

13. Brueggemann, *Theology of the Old Testament*. See also idem, *Old Testament Theology. An Introduction*, and idem, *An Unsettling God*.

14. Brueggemann, "Theology of the Old Testament".

15. Eric A. Seibert, in his review of Brueggemann's *An Unsettling God*, 4, criticizes: "I found his brief discussion of the genocidal commands in Deuteronomy (104–5) unsatisfying and wished he would have dealt with these texts—and others like them—more extensively. What do such divine decrees suggest about God's partnership with the nations?"

Maybe less well-known, yet nonetheless interesting, is the Old Testament Theology by Paul R. House.[16] It is primarily intended as a textbook for students and has features of an "Introduction to the OT," but provides also an informed overview of the history and methodology of OT theology,[17] and at the end an appendix with an analysis of the most recent works which have appeared since 1993.[18] He pleads in favor of following the order of the Hebrew Bible and wants to show for each book "its unique theological contribution to the OT."[19]

House's book is very useful, and he is generally sound in his hermeneutical positions, especially in his orientation towards the single books of the OT and their texts. One difficulty may lie in his desire to present "what the OT says about God as a coherent whole."[20] The emphasis on "theological unity" can sometimes obscure the perception of the differences in the various theologies of the biblical books.[21]

Turning again to German studies, the very title of the book of Erhard S. Gerstenberger bears distinctive features: *Theologien im Alten Testament. Pluralität und Synkretismus alttestamentlichen Gottesglaubens.*[22] He uses the plural "theologies," changes the normal genitive construction to *im* (= within) and indicates by the subtitle the alterations and variety of OT faith. Gerstenberger thus takes seriously the *diversity* of concepts and presentations of the biblical God. He attributes them to historical developments and various social groups and settings. They are in his eyes responsible for the inner contradictions within the OT.

Gerstenberger perceives correctly the rootedness of theology in society, and he is aware of the differences among the many theologies of the OT. He focuses very much on historical issues and changes in Israel; this implies a shift in attention from God towards the people. Therefore his

---

16. House, *Old Testament Theology.*

17. Ibid., 11–57.

18. Ibid., 548–59. Similarly, Robin Routledge, *Old Testament Theology*, starting with page 27, also gives an overview on Old Testament theologies, from page 50 onwards especially on more recent ones.

19. House, *Old Testament Theology*, 55 and 57.

20. Ibid., 53, where he refers for that to Walter Zimmerli.

21. This is especially valid for House's treatment of the Twelve Prophets, 346–401, or of the Psalms, 402–23.

22. Published in 2001.

book is less a "theology," and more a "*Sozialgeschichte.*"[23] In addition to this, some of his textual and historical assumptions are also questionable.

Equally distinctive is the work of Bernhard Lang, *Jahwe der biblische Gott. Ein Porträt.*[24] He follows the lead of Georges Dumézil[25] and conceives the biblical God as "Herr der drei Gaben,"[26] namely wisdom, victory (war), and life. He emphasizes that God grants countless good things, and summarizes many motifs within these three main aspects.

Once again, as with Preuss, we find a central motif, this time split up into three main areas. This helps to organize a lot of the material, yet it has its limitations. Henning Graf Reventlow, in his review,[27] criticizes further the "weitgehende Einebnung des vorexilischen Israel in die altorientalische Umwelt." Lang seems to neglect the peculiarities of the biblical God. Central motifs like covenant, relationship, mercy, and forgiveness do not receive adequate treatment.

The most recent "theology" comes from Reinhard Feldmeier and Hermann Spieckermann and is entitled *Der Gott der Lebendigen. Eine biblische Gotteslehre.*[28] It is the fruit of the collaboration of a New and an Old Testament scholar, both professors in Göttingen. The first main section, "Grundlegung" (= basics, essentials), deals with God's "essence / being," in German "Gottes Wesen"; the second one, "Entfaltung" (= unfolding, display), concentrates on God's actions, "Gottes Wirken."[29] Their work presents systematically many major aspects of the biblical God, e.g., his name(s), love, omnipotence . . . , always dealing with both parts of the Bible.

---

23. Gerstenberger, *Theologien*, chapter 3. There he argues for the social history of Israel as a base for an "inductive" approach to OT theology.

24. It came out in 2002.

25. Dumézil, *La Religion romaine archaïque.*

26. I.e., "Lord of the three gifts," Lang, *Jahwe*, 10. He develops this concept in five "Bildern" (= images), attributing to the third element, God as the giver of life, the three aspects: "Herr der Tiere," "Herr des Einzelnen und der 'persönliche' Gott." and "Herr der Ernte."

27. Reventlow, "Theologie und Hermeneutik," 427.

28. "Recent" at the beginning of the phrase refers to the delivery of the paper in July 2012. Meanwhile other books on Old Testament Theology have appeared; some of them will briefly be mentioned in part B.

29. See, for a similar combination, the recent programmatic article of Hartenstein, "JHWHs Wesen im Wandel," 12–13. There he develops further these two aspects of the biblical God.

Feldmeier and Spieckermann have produced the most up-to-date biblical theology in the sense that two specialists have contributed to the best of their knowledge from their respective fields and have found a good balance. Their concentration on the aspect of God giving life ("Gott der *Lebendigen*") is also appropriate for the biblical God. Questions have been raised regarding the existence of literary strata, and also concerning their dating.[30] The single books of the Bible and their messages also tend to disappear before the detailed treatment of particular motifs and related texts, so that it is sometimes difficult to perceive the respective contexts.

This short overview of some major "Biblical / Old Testament Theologies" paints an impressive picture. A good number of prominent scholars have addressed this topic, showing that it is regarded as important and relevant for the present time, and that there is a renewed interest in the biblical God. We can detect a "flowering" of biblical theologies. The overview also indicates a shift in recent exegetical studies. Apart from detailed investigations into specific texts, many colleagues feel the desire or perceive the need to incorporate their findings into a theological framework, and they try to connect them with the Bible's portrayal(s) of God.

Reflections and Further Avenues

We could have dealt with many more "biblical theologies,"[31] yet already some traits of their development in the past twenty years have become clear, and we can now reflect more deeply on them, summing up, in a systematic way, a few results. The overview allows us to perceive strengths and weaknesses in the various approaches, to consider their consequences and thus to recognize debated themes and issues. I want to address five of them here.

The Relationship between the Old and New Testaments

All the "Biblical theologies" mentioned above were written by Christians, and mostly from a Christian perspective. This is a point of dispute,

---

30. Walter Klaiber, in his review of their book (654), noted this as a critical issue. He also desired more of a systematic reflection on the *one* God of the entire Bible.

31. Cf. the many other works cited in Reventlow's review article in five parts.

especially for the dialogue with Jewish scholars.[32] From a Christian viewpoint, the canon of the Bible includes the New Testament, and "Biblical" theology therefore requires that we take into account the whole of the Bible, including the New Testament. Feldmeier and Spieckermann have solved this in an ideal way by their collaboration, giving the Old Testament its own rightful place.[33] Childs, on the other hand, seems to relativize the value and importance of the Old Testament from a Christian perspective.

These two examples show a fundamental issue to be resolved right at the start: May one's faith orientation influence the interpretation of biblical texts? And, more specifically: Is it permissible to view the Hebrew Bible with "New Testament eyes"?[34]

Just as it would be unfair to evaluate Edison's light bulb only from experience with modern LED lamps, or to assess others only from one's own viewpoint, so it is not just to judge texts of the Hebrew Bible only from the perspective of the later, different books of the New Testament. This implies that any biblical theology, no matter whether Jewish or Christian, should take seriously God's primary revelation in the Old Testament, as standing in its own right, and develop its message without qualifying it from the beginning by New Testament standards. In a second step, however, it may also show the relationship, cohesion, and the differences between the two parts of the Bible.[35]

---

32. Sweeney (*Tanak*) insists in his introduction very much on the difference between "Christian Old Testament Theology" and "Jewish Biblical Theology" (5–20). In a similar vein, Dalit Rom-Shiloni, in her papers read at the SBL-congresses in Vienna (July 2014) and San Diego (November 2014), also stresses the disparity between a Jewish and a Christian approach to biblical theology.

33. Elliott, *Reality*, 271–303, also pleads for respecting the Old Testament's specific message about faith in its own right and distinct from the experience of the New Testament. Routledge, *Theology*, 17–18, addresses the question by discussing the implications of the terms "Old Testament" and "Hebrew Bible".

34. Moberly (*Old Testament Theology*) tries to combine both perspectives, presenting eight larger motifs as case studies.

35. Interestingly, but not surprising, there is a far-reaching coincidence between the way the Old Testament talks about God and the life and message of Jesus: Fischer, *Theologien des Alten Testaments*, 295–98.

A Variety of "Theologies" within the Bible

Gerstenberger is one of the few who talks of theologies in the plural. This does not mean that there are various Gods in the Bible, but that the portrayal of God in the individual books differs markedly. For this reason, "systematic" approaches concentrating on one main aspect[36] hardly do justice to the richness of the way in which the Bible speaks of God.

Reading the various books of the Old Testament, one can hardly escape the impression that many of them show different profiles in their description of God and in their use of metaphors for him/her. Isaiah compares Yhwh's consoling to that of a mother (Isa 66:13); shortly before, a prayer addresses God thrice as "our father" (Isa 63:16; 64:7). Deuteronomy 32 is the starting point for talking about God as "rock,"[37] Jer 2:13, on the contrary, calls God "the fountain of living water"—both images are taken from nature and deviate very much from the parental vocabulary of Isaiah. In contrast to the water image, God himself promises in Zech 2:9 to be a "wall of fire" around Jerusalem. These are only a few examples of how biblical texts talk very differently about God.

Biblical theology should bring to light the great variety of ways in which Yhwh is seen and described,[38] and at the same time demonstrate that he is the same, one God to whom all these different portrayals refer. This requires a delicate balance of diversity and unity,[39] bringing together the many different features and relating them to a "core," to what is characteristic and essential for God.[40]

---

36. Examples for such approaches are the concentration on "election," by Horst Dietrich Preuss, or on the "Lord of the three gifts," by Bernhard Lang (for both see above).

37. Deut 32:4; all together "rock" is used seven times theologically in the Song of Moses; for this trait in the portrayal of God see Georg Fischer, "Der Fels."

38. Good examples are the works of House, *Old Testament Theology*; Mills, *Images of God in the Old Testament*; and Vanhoozer, ed., *Theological Interpretation of the Old Testament*.

39. Jeremias, "Neuere Entwürfe," 57–58.

40. Oeming, "Viele Wege zu dem Einen," 105, compares our perception of God with coming to know a human person, as a process involving many facets and changes. On the relationship between God's essential characteristics and his varying appearance, and on the tension between his supposed "immutability" and "alteration" or development in God see Fischer, *Theologien*, 251–85.

Focus on God

Some "theologies" do not really deserve this name, as they deal with many other, mostly social or ethical, issues.[41] On the other hand, Brueggemann, Lang, and Feldmeier and Spieckermann are positive examples of a concentration on the biblical God.[42] This orientation corresponds to the original meaning of "theology," in the sense of "word (about) God."

Yhwh is the main character in the Old Testament, is mentioned the most and is described as acting, with few exceptions, throughout all books.[43] At the same time, for Christians he is, as the "father" of Jesus, also the most important "figure" of the New Testament. It is only appropriate to comply with that divine dominance in both parts of the Bible by laying the emphasis in biblical theology on him and his characteristics. Reventlow and Oeming, too, demand such an orientation in their articles.[44]

How to Approach Biblical Theology?

The "systematic" approaches of Preuss, Lang, Feldmeier, and Spieckermann and others allow us to grasp main features of God, but have the side effect of "hopping" around in the Bible. Mostly they quote, for a particular aspect, e.g. God's justice, strength, or love . . . several texts distributed over a wide range throughout the Bible, and with very different contexts.[45] This makes it difficult to perceive the peculiarities of

---

41. See, e.g., the theologies of Preuss, Gerstenberger, Josef Schreiner, *Theologie des Alten Testaments*; McConville, *God and Earthly Power*, and others.

42. The focus on God is also noticeable in Hartenstein's programmatic article "JHWHs Wesen".

43. The Book of Esther never mentions God; however, it speaks in a veiled form in Est 4:14 about help "from another place". A disputed case is the Book of the Song of Songs: The end of Cant 8:6 may be translated either as "a most vehement flame" (so NRSV), or as "a flame of Jah"—for the latter see Fischer, *Theologien*, 197–99.

44. Reventlow, "Theologie," 442; Oeming, "Viele Wege," 92. This focus on God himself marks also the difference from "history of religion" as well as from "science of religion", as they both deal more with the human expressions of faith.

45. For example Spieckermann, *Gott*, in dealing with "Der Allmächtige" (the Almighty), adduces as texts Psalms 93; 24; 46; 84; 139; the motif of "Yhwh of hosts" in the Twelve Prophets, esp. Amos 9:1–6, and several passages from the Book of Job (153–75). However, many other parts of this large book also refer to Psalms, Prophets, and Job, so that the nexus of the various facets of God's portrayal within a specific biblical book can hardly be seen.

the single books, their focal points, and the evolution/development of biblical thinking about God.

Another difficulty has shown up with respect to the assumptions regarding Israel's "history" and literary layers.[46] Many of these theses are speculative, and such hypotheses may change rapidly, as the example of von Rad's work demonstrates.

A more suitable path is to deal with entire biblical books on their own, first synchronically, without entering—at least not at the beginning—into historical-critical issues,[47] and concentrate on their theological profiles. They are often connected with key texts, e.g. Deut 4; 32, and particularly condensed in prayers, like Exod 15; Isa 63:7—64:11; Neh 9, etc. Further it seems useful for the Old Testament to follow (more or less) the sequence of the Hebrew Bible,[48] because it corresponds largely to an order in the development of the canon.

The Need to Reflect on the Procedural and Hermeneutical Issues

The above themes show the complexity of "biblical theology." Anyone writing or speaking about God as portrayed in the Bible has to address many questions and problems. Brueggemann himself, responding to criticism, is an example of awareness of these issues connected with biblical theology.[49] A new book by John Kessler is particularly sensitive and helpful for questions of biblical hermeneutics.[50]

---

46. Gerstenberger, *Theologien*, traces in chapters 3—7 a development reaching from "family and clan" via "dörfliche Wohngemeinschaften" and "Stammesverband" to "Reichstheologien"; this model may be partially appropriate, but is also debatable, as the concept of "tribes" ("Stämme") is very much discussed, and as the idea of an official "theology" in the time of the monarchy still cannot be proved. In a similar way, the attribution of texts to literary strata often remains uncertain; for this see also above (n. 30) the review by Walter Klaiber of Feldmeier and Spieckermann's *Der Gott der Lebendigen*.

47. Examples for such a procedure are House, *Old Testament Theology*; Mills, *Images*; McConville, *God*, etc. My own book, *Theologien*, follows this approach, too.

48. This is also the suggestion of House, *Old Testament Theology*, 55, and Oeming, "Viele Wege," 94.

49. Brueggemann, "Theology . . . Revisited." In my view, he could have made even clearer the distinction between human speaking about God and God's "being".

50. Kessler, *Old Testament Theology*. The first three chapters of his book address the problems of a theological reading and interpretation of the Old Testament in a profoundly reflected, very nuanced and balanced way.

Besides the aspects mentioned above, it is necessary to reflect on and make decisions regarding: Israel's history; the relationship with the "history of religion," especially of the Ancient Near East; the status of religious language; the aspect of "ideology" in the Bible, among others. Because of these many connected issues it is clear that any study of biblical theology requires not only exegetical analysis, but also philosophical reflection, an intimate acquaintance with large parts of the Bible, if not all of it, and the ability to evaluate, and combine the results appropriately. These requirements would seem to be met by God alone, not by humans. Nevertheless, it is my hope that this short article may contribute to a more accurate perception of the task, and also of the beauty, of doing research into the God of the Bible.

Bibliography

Brueggemann, Walter. *Theology of the Old Testament: Testimony, Dispute, Advocacy.* Minneapolis: Fortress 1997.

———. "Theology of the Old Testament: Testimony, Dispute, Advocacy Revisited." *Catholic Biblical Quarterly* 74 (2012) 28–38.

———. *An Unsettling God. The Heart of the Hebrew Bible.* Minneapolis: Fortress 2009.

Childs, Brevard S. *Biblical Theology of the Old and New Testaments.* London: SCM, 1992.

Dohmen, Christoph, *Vom Umgang mit dem Alten Testament.* NSK-AT 27. Stuttgart: Katholisches Bibelwerk, 1995.

Dumézil, Georges, *La Religion romaine archaïque, avec un appendice sur la religion des Étrusques.* Paris: Payot 1966.

Elliott, Mark W. *The Reality of Biblical Theology.* Religions in Discourse. Oxford: Lang 2007.

Feldmeier, Reinhard, and Hermann Spieckermann. *Der Gott der Lebendigen. Eine biblische Gotteslehre.* Tübingen: Mohr 2011.

Fischer, Georg. "'Der Fels.' Beobachtungen im Umfeld einer theologischen Metapher." In *Sprachen—Bilder—Klänge,* edited by Christiane Karrer-Grube et al., 23–33. Münster: Ugarit-Verlag 2009.

———. *Theologien des Alten Testaments.* NSK-AT 31. Stuttgart: Katholisches Bibelwerk, 2012.

Gerstenberger, Erhard S. *Theologien im Alten Testament. Pluralität und Synkretismus alttestamentlichen Gottesglaubens.* Stuttgart: Kohlhammer, 2001.

Hartenstein, Friedhelm. "JHWHs Wesen im Wandel. Vorüberlegungen zu einer Theologie des Alten Testaments." *Theologische Literaturzeitung* 137 (2012) 4–20.

House, Paul R. *Old Testament Theology.* Downers Grove, IL: InterVarsity, 1998.

Jeremias, Jörg. "Neuere Entwürfe zu einer 'Theologie des Alten Testaments.'" *Verkündigung und Forschung* 48 (2003) 29–58.

Kessler, John. *Old Testament Theology. Divine Call and Human Response.* Waco: Baylor University Press, 2013.

Klaiber, Walter. Review of Feldmeier and Spieckermann, *Der Gott der Lebendigen*. *Theologische Literaturzeitung* 137 (1012) 651–54.
Lang, Bernhard. *Jahwe der biblische Gott. Ein Porträt*. München: Beck, 2002.
McConville, J. Gordon. *God and Earthly Power. An Old Testament Political Theology*. New York: T. & T. Clark, 2006.
Mills, Mary E. *Images of God in the Old Testament*. London: Michael Glazer, 1998.
Moberly, R. Walter L. *Old Testament Theology. Reading the Hebrew Bible as Christian Scripture*. Grand Rapids: Baker, 2013.
Oeming, Manfred. "Ermitteln und Vermitteln. Grundentscheidungen bei der Konzeption einer Theologie des Alten Testaments." *Verstehen und Glauben* 142 (2003) 9–48.
———. "Viele Wege zu dem Einen. Die transzendente Mitte einer Theologie des Alten Testaments im Spannungsfeld von Vielheit und Einheit." In *Viele Wege zu dem Einen*, edited by Stefan Beyerle, Axel Graupner, and Udo Rütersworden, 83–108. Biblisch-theologische Studien 121. Neukirchen: Neukirchener Verlag, 2012.
Preuss, Horst Dietrich. *Theologie des Alten Testaments. Band 1: JHWHs erwählendes und verpflichtendes Handeln*. Stuttgart: Kohlhammer, 1991.
———. *Theologie des Alten Testaments. Band 2: Israels Weg mit JHWH*. Stuttgart: Kohlhammer, 1992.
Reventlow, Henning Graf. "Biblische, besonders alttestamentliche Theologie und Hermeneutik." *Theologische Rundschau* 70 (2005) 1–43; 137–73; 279–337, and *Theologische Rundschau* 71 (2006) 1–59.
Routledge, Robin. *Old Testament Theology. A Thematic Approach*. Downers Grove, IL: InterVarsity, 2008.
Schreiner, Josef. *Theologie des Alten Testaments*. NEB Ergänzungsband 1. Würzburg: Echter, 1995.
Seibert, Eric A. "Review of Walter Brueggemann's *An Unsettling God.*" *Review of Biblical Literature* 8/2010.
Steins, Georg. *Die "Bindung Isaaks" im Kanon (Gen 22). Grundlagen und Programm einer kanonisch-intertextuellen Lektüre*. HBS 20. Freiburg: Herder 1999.
Sweeney, Marvin A. *Tanak. A Theological and Critical Introduction to the Jewish Bible*. Minneapolis: Fortress 2012.
Vanhoozer, Kevin J., ed., *Theological Interpretation of the Old Testament. A Book-by-Book Survey*. Grand Rapids: Baker, 2008.
von Rad, Gerhard, *Theologie des Alten Testaments. Band 1: Die Theologie der geschichtlichen Überlieferungen Israels*. München: Kaiser, 1960.
———. *Theologie des Alten Testaments. Band 2: Die Theologie der prophetischen Überlieferungen Israels*. München: Kaiser, 1960.
Zenger, Erich, et al. *Einleitung in das Alte Testament*. Stuttgart: Kohlhammer, 1995.

Some Ways of "Doing" Biblical Theology
Assessments and a Proposal

Darian Lockett

CONSCIOUSLY OR UNCONSCIOUSLY THE reader of the two Testaments of the Christian Bible operates with some understanding of theology in its relation to the biblical tradition. In this regard, Brevard Childs rightly noted, "The real question is not whether to do Biblical Theology or not, but rather what kind of Biblical Theology does one have!"[1] Even claiming that the individual texts of the Old and New Testaments are so diverse in historical circumstances, genre, and content such that it is impossible to speak meaningfully about a biblical theology, *is itself* a way of doing biblical theology.[2] Often implicit and unarticulated, one's judgment of how the Old and New Testaments go together undergirds biblical interpretation, and such a judgment regarding the Bible's unity (or disunity) is a fundamental element in biblical theology. The problem is that there is little agreement on what biblical theology actually *is* let alone how to *do* it. Even when cognizant of Childs's point above interpreters talk past each other working with different notions of or approaches to biblical theology.

As an anthropologist would seek to offer a thick description of the varieties of tribes and people groups with whom she wishes to speak, so here, in an effort to describe the varieties of biblical theology, this essay

---

1. Childs, *Biblical Theology in Crisis*, 95.
2. The charge of radical diversity within the biblical witness is itself a biblical-theological judgment. What cannot be endorsed is the claim that such a judgment regarding diversity is non- or pre-theological for even the conviction that canonical texts be read in isolation from one another due to their different historical contexts is itself a kind of *theological* commitment which shapes exegesis.

offers a five-fold taxonomy clarifying various types of biblical theology as they are currently practiced. These types were worked out initially (and more fully) in *Understanding Biblical Theology*.³ This essay unfolds in two sections: the first section is comprised of a précis of each of the five types supplemented by a brief section considering each approach's weakness. Second, in light of these weaknesses, the essay offers two constructive points articulating the best way forward for biblical theology. A recurring theme in these suggestions is the need to consider the concept of canon as *the* foundational criterion for biblical theology. This snapshot of the discipline of biblical theology, along with the suggestions for its future, are offered in the hope of avoiding misunderstanding and promoting a robust dialogue focusing on the goals and methods for biblical theology.

Five Ways of Doing Biblical Theology

History and theology constitute the terminal points on what essentially is a spectrum of five types of biblical theology. To be clear, this taxonomy is a heuristic construct enabling a wide-angle view of the field. It must be noted that a) these types are not mutually exclusive as there are elements common among each approach, b) several of the types could be further sub-categorized (e.g., BT2 or BT3) for sake of greater clarity, and c) though the views are roughly arranged sequentially, from more historical to more theological, this is not intended to imply that the taxonomy is necessarily progressive or developmental. That is, if one were to move from BT2 to BT4 it is not necessary to progress through BT3.

Biblical Theology as Historical Description (BT1)

BT1 is the most historical. In this view, biblical theology is separated from doctrinal or confessional concerns and focuses on description. While theologians are concerned with "what it means," BT1, always careful to guard against anachronism, is only concerned with "what it meant." Biblical theology is "biblical" because it is the theology believed by ancient peoples; it is the theology of the Bible as it existed within the times, languages, and cultures of the ancient world. For this reason biblical theology for BT1 is a rather diverse set of convictions held by different authors in different times and in different contexts.

3. See Klink and Lockett, *Understanding Biblical Theology*.

For BT1, theologically connecting the OT with the New Testament is to do a disservice to both. One can appreciate a degree of historical development from OT to NT, but even this historical connection must not obscure the distinctive character of each Testament on its own terms. BT1 is dependent, therefore, on contemporary research done within the academy, and further, is in no way bound to the so-called Christian "canon" as its source. The theology of the confessing church has already moved beyond the context of the ancient texts by translating their theology into a new social-historical context. These concerns were articulated by Krister Stendahl in his article on biblical theology in the *Interpreters Dictionary of the Bible*.[4] Describing the desired approach to biblical theology, Stendahl noted:

> It became a scholarly ideal to creep out of one's Western and twentieth-century skin and identify oneself with the feelings and thought patterns of the past. The distance between biblical times and modern times was stressed. . . . What emerged was a descriptive study of biblical thought . . . .[5]

Stendahl calls this new phenomenon a "mature outgrowth of the historical and critical study of the Scriptures."[6] Stated succinctly, *the task of BT1 is to affirm the exegetical or descriptive nature of biblical theology and deny the theological or normative nature of biblical theology.*

Weakness of BT1

This approach has a tendency to reduce biblical theology to mere historical description with little to no normative force for contemporary readers, thus rendering biblical theology purely of antiquarian interest. Thomas Schreiner tersely notes that "Stendahl limits biblical theology to mere description."[7]

BT1 ends up relativizing the literary and theological role of canon. For scholars of BT1, such as James Barr, the canon (whether Jewish or Christian) is an anachronistic distortion of the texts' original meaning. Rather than a "theologically motivated" canon, it is in the events and concepts behind the text where theology is to be found. Because these

---

4. Stendahl, "Biblical Theology," 1:418–32.
5. Ibid., 418.
6. Ibid.
7. Schreiner, *New Testament Theology*, 871.

pre-textual realities constitute theological meaning, extra-canonical literature is as authoritative for theology as any other literature. For BT1 the Dead Sea Scrolls are as important as the Minor Prophets or the four Gospels. However, the fact that no modern community has defended the Dead Sea Scrolls as part of their canon must sound a cautionary note. There is historical as well as theological warrant for limiting biblical theology to the Christian canon, even if the parameters of such a canon are contested.

Furthermore, BT1 emphasizes academic scholarship at the expense of religious devotion. The high goal of scholarly objectivity and dispassionate historical discovery led scholars like James Barr to bracket out their own personal faith. Of course as faith commitments are bracketed out other commitments inevitably move in and take their place. Stendahl's vision of creeping "out of one's . . . twentieth-century skin" ends up being impossible if not undesirable. Whereas a degree of scholarly objectivity is a virtue, neutrality toward the subject is not. For biblical theology, academic objectivity often appears in the dressing of suspicion toward divine claims and expresses no interest in "putting the biblical texts together under the conviction that one Mind finally stands behind all of Scripture."[8] In the end BT1 primarily reads the Bible as an historical artifact describing what ancient peoples believed about God.

Biblical Theology as History of Redemption (BT2)

BT2 is similarly framed by history, but rather a special history that is derived from theological criteria. The Bible reveals a history of redemption progressing chronologically through its various narratives. The unitary meaning of Christian Scripture *is* its reference to one special sequence of events, from creation to the end of history with Christ as its center. Thus biblical theology is a special "salvation history" which understands the continuity of Old and New Testaments as they refer to the historical progression of God's providential acts in and through time. This redemptive history is visible by tracing the progressively unfolding patterns of fulfillment of God's will by means of major themes as they develop through Old and New Testaments (e.g., covenant, kingdom, promise and fulfillment).

---

8. Carson, "Theological Interpretation of Scripture," 189.

This special history, structured sequentially, is then transparently equated with the actual events of world history. Redemptive history is most clear when tracing various themes through the biblical narrative which, in turn, serve as connecting fibers between the Old and New Testaments. While the historical nature of BT2 is directly parallel to the work of the academy, the goal is a biblical theology for the church. Such historically defined theology remains within the orbit of a "what it meant/what it means" hermeneutic. Stated succinctly, *the task of BT2 is to discern the historical progression of God's work of redemption through an inductive analysis of key themes developing through both discrete corpora and the whole of Scripture. Major themes such as covenant or kingdom constitute the theological connecting fibers between the Old and New Testaments and these themes necessarily run along a historical trajectory giving fundamental structure to the theology of the Bible.*

In English-speaking scholarship, this approach to biblical theology has developed into three distinct "schools" rooted in different ecclesial and academic traditions. First, the "Dallas School," is characterized by a dispensational and progressive dispensational hermeneutical framework, understands redemptive history as a sequence of well defined and, to various degrees, separate dispensations within which God uniquely accomplishes his will. Though Old and New are linked historically, this approach stresses the discontinuity between the two. Second, the "Chicago School" stresses the overall historical continuity between Old and New Testaments through central themes within Scripture, especially stressing typology as a key interpretive tool. Finally, the "Philadelphia School" is rooted in traditional covenant (or federal) theology, which reads Scripture with a salvation-historical sequence characterized by God's relationship with his people through a progression of covenants. Stressing even greater continuity between Old and New Testaments, this approach to redemptive history sees the whole as greater than the sum of the thematic parts of Scripture.

Weakness of BT2

This approach has a tendency to reduce biblical theology to the Bible's reference to a special history. In other words biblical theology is the Bible's reference to one special sequence of events, rather than to the person of Jesus Christ; biblical theology ultimately refers to *what* rather than *whom*. Richard Gaffin notes,

> [T]he proper focus of interpretation [for BT2] is the subject matter of the text, that is, the *history* with Christ at its center that lies in back of the text. . . . The context that ultimately controls the understanding of a given text is not a literary framework or pattern of relationships but the *historical structure of the revelation process itself*.[9]

The problem with such a redemptive historical understanding of biblical theology is that rather than viewing Christ as the subject matter of both testaments it is the temporally distinct and ordered stages of the history of salvation that serves as the subject of both Testaments. Christopher Seitz argues, "The OT has a salvation-historical dimension, but that dimension is by no means the chief way to understand the Scriptures of Israel as a Christian witness." He continues,

> If one incautiously combines historical accounts of the use of the OT in the NT with a salvation-historical framework for assessing a two-testament Bible, the result is deep confusion about how the early church might have used a rule of faith, and how the character of Christian Scripture might otherwise be grasped. . . . Stated differently, the character of Christian Scripture, Old and New, involves thinking of their temporal relationship in terms other than salvation-historical only. It entails thinking about the OT figurally as well as predictively. . . . The dimension of use of the OT in the NT would enormously cramp and foreshorten the capacity of the OT both to speak of God in Christ and to be heard in relationship to the NT in ways the NT need not have contemplated or set forth in its own material form.[10]

Seitz points out the problematic emphasis upon a redemptive history pressed into service as a method. Setting such ground rules as the only way for reading and interpreting Scripture, in Seitz's words, will "cramp and foreshorten the capacity" of the OT to speak of Christ on its own without first being heard in and through the NT. Scripture's ability "to refer" to its subject matter is sequential and chronological, but ought not be limited to only these. The subject matter of Scripture is accurately

---

9. Gaffin, "Systematic and Biblical Theology," 293–94 (emphasis added).
10. Seitz, *Character of Christian Scripture*, 21–22.

described from within this sequential chronology yet that very description points beyond itself to God's transcendence.

Furthermore, BT2 defines biblical theology as a "bridge" discipline between exegesis and systematic theology. This image of biblical theology as a "bridge" discipline has the potential to distort the relationship between biblical and systematic theology. This image suggests that biblical theology is closer to the text because it is more historical whereas systematic theology, at one remove from the text, must rely upon biblical theology to bridge the gap. This image obscures the fact that both biblical and systematic theology work from the text of Scripture, yet rely on differing means of retrieval or abstraction; namely, historical or philosophical instruments of analysis. Either abstraction need not be maliciously distorting, for as the abstraction of space in a city map actually helps one navigate, so too the abstraction unique to either biblical or systematic theology have potential to help navigate interpretation of the text. It is better to avoid claiming that either biblical or systematic theology is closer to the text of Scripture. BT2 has the tendency to claim that redemptive history *is* the subject matter of Scripture, and, consequently, biblical theology constitutes a one-way "bridge" from exegesis to systematic theology. BT2 has difficulty in acknowledging the abstracting quality of history and equates the subject matter of Scripture to a special history of God's saving acts.

Biblical Theology as Worldview-Story (BT3)

BT3 represents the middle of the spectrum and is strongly framed by the literary and philosophical category of "narrative." Rather than a special history, BT3 is shaped by the overarching narrative connections between the Old and New Testaments and originates from an academic desire to read Scripture without historical-criticism functioning as the primary methodology. One distinct trajectory within BT3 focuses on reconstructing the historical world of the author and audience which then informs the overarching narrative unity of the Bible (N. T. Wright's stress on the worldview of the authors). A second trajectory focuses on the literary coherence of the narrative itself with less concern for how that narrative refers to events of history outside the text itself (Richard Hays's stress on the narrative substructure). Both of these trajectories use the category of narrative to balance literary, historical, and theological elements in the text.

Attempting a balance of both history and theology, BT3 seeks the "worldview-story" either residing in the mind of the authors or in the intertextual connections within the text itself. While the historical approach to the biblical narrative of BT3 is directly parallel to the work of the academy, the guidance provided by the resources of theology has much to commend it to the church. BT3 begins from the claim that the Bible's unity is fundamentally a quality of its narrative structure and thus works to understand the relationship between the Testaments through the lens of narrative analysis and seeks to discern the theological world that flows out of this coherent "story-shaped" reading of the Bible.

Stated succinctly, *using the category of narrative to broker a balance between history and theology, the task of BT3 directs readers to understand the individual episodes or passages of Scripture in light of its overarching storyline. Instead of progressing from the smallest bits and pieces of the narrative to the larger whole, BT3 starts with the larger narrative portions of text through which individual units are read.*

Weakness of BT3

This approach has a tendency to reduce biblical theology to an "appreciation of the theological use made by the New of the Old."[11] Richard Hays' version of BT3 appeals to the "narrative world" of Paul, that is, a reconstruction of Paul's reading and theological appropriation of the OT story, which, in turn, he argues should fund a theological reading of Scripture today.

Seitz worries that the appeal to "narrative world" is subject to various construals. Is the "narrative world" of the OT constructed via Paul's reception of the OT? Or, perhaps, it is Peter's reception? If, as Hays suggests, modern readers should do likewise, then could not the "narrative world" of the OT actually be constructed via any number of subsequent moments of reception? Even if limited to Paul's reception, Seitz notes,

> The problem is that . . . the OT threatens to be swallowed up into Paul's confessions and construals about it (or in an imaginative reconstruction of a narrative world said to be influencing him, by deduction). This narrative world is an abstraction derived by

11. Seitz, *Character of Christian Scripture*, 54.

recourse to historical tools, and it exists apart from the canonical form of the Pauline Letter collection and the influence this form has on interpretation.

Thus Seitz asks, "Why should [Paul's] 'narrative world' (as reconstructed by Hays) speak over the manifold witness of the OT said to be generating it?"[12]

On the other hand, N. T. Wrights' worldview-story version of the narrative is actually constructed of essentially historical background material. Describing his magisterial *Jesus and the Victory of God*, Wright notes, "the book was basically about the mindset of Jesus as he went to the cross."[13] It is through reading the texts of Second Temple Judaism and early Christianity in their historical contexts with an eye for the overarching worldview narrative contained in them with which Jesus' self-understanding is reconstructed. It is with this mindset of Jesus firmly in place that one may appreciate the relationship between the two Testaments. C. Stephen Evans notes: "It seems remarkable that Wright can know not only what Jesus believed about himself but the manner in which the knowledge was obtained and the degree of certainty he possessed."[14] With an appreciative skepticism, Evans further notes how Wright works with an implicit "methodological naturalism."[15] Within the scholarly discussion of the biblical texts, such "methodological naturalism" serves Wright well as he wishes to articulate both the unity and theological subject matter of the Bible in the context of the secular historian. However, even Evans notes the cost involved: "there are times when Wright appears to go beyond using this historical method to suggest a much stronger claim: that such a method is the best or even the only means of ascertaining the historical truth about Jesus of Nazareth."[16] Either stressing a "reconstructed narrative world" or the historically driven reconstruction of Jesus' self-understanding, BT3 runs the risk of over-constructing the overarching "narrative" at the expense of the text of Scripture—both are ways of going behind the text.

---

12. Ibid., 84–85.
13. Wright, "A Response," 268.
14. Evans, "Methodological Naturalism," 195.
15. Ibid., 180–205.
16. Ibid., 201.

BIBLICAL THEOLOGY | II. PRESENT

Biblical Theology as Canonical Approach (BT4)

BT4 is strongly framed by the category of the Christian canon. Key to BT4 is the conviction that biblical theology is a theological-historical project that is necessarily defined by the boundaries of the biblical canon and the final (canonical) form of the biblical texts. A basic presupposition undergirding BT4 is that the significance of canon is not limited to the listing of received books (canon as a fixed collection), but also involves the process by which these texts were received, collected, transmitted, and shaped in the early apostolic period (canon as a ruled process). The development of canon as a fixed list of books is directly connected to a process of canonization shaped by the "rule of faith," and this process, according to BT4 is hermeneutically significant and should guide biblical theology.

The process of canonization was like a path that from composition to canonization has been traversed by many apostolic travelers ("tradents"), each of whom has left footprints. Specific elements of this shaping process include editing, collection, and arrangement of the apostolically authored texts into a final canonical form. These remnants of canonical shaping discovered in the text itself become the biblical theological context within which to balance history and theology. Such an approach allows biblical theology to be both descriptive and prescriptive. BT4 contains elements of both academy and church: the academy is needed to explore the textual traditions that have been received, collected, transmitted, and shaped throughout different times, cultures, and languages; the confessing church is needed as the audience to whom the texts speak a clarifying word regarding identity and obedience. Ultimately BT4's stress on canon establishes Scripture as a witness that refers to the Bible's true subject matter; namely, Jesus Christ.

Stated succinctly, *the task of BT4 is to affirm the exegetical form and function of the canon for biblical theology, embracing both the descriptive (historical) and prescriptive (theological) nature of scripture and its confessional community.*

WEAKNESS OF BT4

This approach has a tendency to reduce biblical theology to an ill-defined notion of canon, which to some, is anachronistic to the biblical texts themselves. The greatest area of confusion is the use of the term "canon" or "canonical." Is it a process, a product, or a theological principle? Perhaps "canon" contains elements of each of these? Along with the lack of terminological clarity, even those sympathetic toward the canonical approach have not been able to articulate the steps in a "canonical" approach. For some, this is because Childs's never argued for the canonical approach as a new or alternative method—even so, for many it is unclear how one should do biblical theology within a canonical approach.

Another weakness is the question of whether the canon's history and tradents (collectors/editors) can be located and defined in a manner suggested by Childs. John Barton argues that Childs was inconsistent, desiring on the one hand to honor the text's historical dimension—the complexity of the sources and traditions behind the final form of the canon—and on the other, insisting some how that the sum—final form of the canon—is greater than the parts. Barton argues that if the final redactors were so skilled in producing a seamless text from the disparate sources, why were they there in the first place.[17] In other words, Barton notes Childs's inconsistency in both finding fault with historical reconstruction behind the text while at the same time arguing such historical reconstruction is necessary at the level of the canonical tradents. For many this highlights Childs's (and BT4's) ambivalence toward using historical criticism.

Biblical Theological as Theological Construction (BT5)

BT5 is strongly framed by theological concerns. Critiquing the abuses of historical criticism, BT5 positions itself within the concerns of the church and is associated with a growing interest in a theological interpretation of Scripture.[18] BT5 intentionally resists the academy's departmentalization of biblical studies and systematic theology with the concomitant bifurcation between ancient text and contemporary Scripture. This leads to the claim that the Bible properly belongs to the church and not the academy. For this reason the task of biblical theology is an integrated exegetical-hermeneutical discipline with overriding theological concerns, incorporating biblical scholarship into the larger enterprise of dogmatic theology.

---

17. Barton, *Reading the Old Testament*, 56–58.
18. See Treier, *Introducing Theological Interpretation*.

Because BT5 is located in the church it must incorporate and be ruled by faith commitments or theological presuppositions. Stephen Fowl gives a helpful explanation of this distinction:

> [T]o identify oneself as a Christian is . . . to bring oneself into a particular sort of relationship to the Bible in which the Bible functions as a normative standard for faith and practice. For the professional biblical scholar, the Bible is simply one (among many) texts upon which scholars might bring their interpretive interests and practices to bear. Christians stand in a different relationship to the Bible. The Bible, for Christians, is their Scripture . . . .[19]

In this way the posture and presuppositions of the Christian church are given primary authority over the practice of biblical theology. Stated succinctly, *the task of BT5 is to affirm the integrated nature of biblical theology as a theological, hermeneutical, and exegetical discipline with overriding theological concerns, incorporating biblical scholarship into the larger enterprise of Christian theology.*

Weakness of BT5

This approach has a tendency to reduce biblical theology to a theological tribalism of competing agendas in reading Scripture for the church. In other words, because BT5 tends toward a functional definition of Scripture, it often overemphasizes the community's use and performance of the text.

Fowl's version of BT5 focuses on the use to which Scripture is put in the community's performance of the text. The Bible serves as a normative standard shaping and directing a community in its journey of discipleship. The use or performance of Scripture within the believing community is founded upon the church's discernment of the canon via the Spirit's leading. As theological issues are at the forefront, such discernment is focused not on the identity of a text's author, audience, or general historical setting, but rather on Scripture's use and function in the faith community. The trouble is that use and function are often emphasized at the expense of historical concerns that are necessary for understanding the text.

---

19. Fowl, *Engaging Scripture*, 3.

BT5 risks detachment from the questions of history especially when it limits the reading of Scripture merely to an internal closed literary system that "renders a world" not clearly connected to the events of history. Though this move relieves the pressure of historical questions, it cuts the tie between the text and historical event. Theological models of biblical theology that lose sight of history all together are in danger of a "docetic" (disembodied) notion of the text.

A final weakness appears in BT5's emphasis on pre-critical exegesis. Calling attention to the hubris of dismissing exegesis before the rise of historical criticism is welcome. However, two problems often arise at this moment. First pre-critical exegesis is given greater credibility over against modern, historical exegesis, but this badly misunderstands pre-critical exegesis as theological and modern exegesis as historical—an assessment completely lacking nuance. Second, when preference is shown toward pre-critical exegesis it is almost always selective. Stressing examples of pre-critical exegesis of one's own liking reinforces the theological tribalism mentioned above—crying "I am of Calvin," "I am of Aquinas," or "I am of Irenaeus."

Proposal: Canon as the Way Forward for Biblical Theology

The above taxonomy highlights the abiding challenge for biblical theology, namely the relationship between history and theology in reading the Old and New Testaments as Christian Scripture. Whereas BT1 is prone to historical reduction, BT5 risks the opposite danger, untethering the church's theological appropriation of Scripture from both the historical events to which it points and the historical moment of its composition. The insights of BT2 and BT3 have promise; however, neither looking to a "special history" nor relying on the category of "narrative" will strike the right balance between history and theology as both focus on a subject "behind the text." Rather, Stephen B. Chapman rightly notes, "The church's concept of a canon lay precisely at the fault line between history and theology."[20] The historical and theological characteristics of canon constitute a crucial way forward for biblical theology. Aided by the conceptual clarity of the above taxonomy, the essay concludes with two brief implications for the role of canon in biblical theology.

---

20. Chapman, "Reclaiming Inspiration for the Bible," 167.

First, emphasizing canon will lead to a rejection of the long-held and academically perpetuated dichotomy between historical-critical analysis of New and Old Testaments and reception-historical (theological) study of their importance in early Christianity. Historical reconstruction and theological significance have been isolated from one another as they are usually assigned completely different disciplines within the academy—namely, Biblical Studies and Patristics—with practitioners rarely accounting for the results of each other's work.

Such isolation stems from the key question of whether subsequent judgments regarding the Christian canon *clarify* or *obscure* the meaning of these texts. Famously, Harnack argued that "Canonization works like whitewash; it hides the original colors and obliterates all the contours," hiding "the true origin and significance of the works."[21] The historical-critical approach to biblical studies rejects later judgments regarding the collecting and ordering of the canon as anachronistic to their right interpretation. Thus the text's situation in *history* is set over against its situation in the *canon*.

However, Jens Schröter is correct to argue that "historical-critical interpretation of the New Testament texts and a theology of the New Testament do *not* exclude each other—and neither should they be dissolved into each other—but stand in a tension-filled dynamic in relation to each other . . ."[22] Rather than pitting historical description against theological significance, it is actually the fundamental role of canon that allows for taking up both together. Again, Schröter notes,

> the emergence of the NT canon is—in contrast to what Wrede [and Harnack] thought—not an arbitrary establishment of ancient church bishops and theologians that through historical criticism has become antiquated in the meantime and therefore unimportant. Rather, the formation of the New Testament belongs to those developments of the early church in which fundamental characteristics of Christian faith manifest themselves.[23]

As was a central focus in Childs's canonical approach, taking the canon seriously in one's interpretation challenges "the widespread assumption of the NT guild that the issue of canon lies in the field of

---

21. Harnack, *Origins of the New Testament*, 140–41.
22. Schröter, *From Jesus to the New Testament*, 330 (emphasis original).
23. Ibid., 337–38.

subsequent church history and is irrelevant to the study of [the NT itself]."[24] Canon itself incorporates a historical process and theological judgment at the same time.

A second implication of canon for biblical theology is to resist the separation between the descriptive and constructive movements in biblical interpretation. Leander Keck noted this element as a key characteristic of Childs's canonical approach. According to Keck, Childs sought

> to hold together dialectically ... historical analysis and theological insight instead of *separating* them sequentially (first history, then interpretation . . .) as in much liberal theology, or *fusing* them materially (and therefore also methodologically . . .), as is common in defensive conservatism and fundamentalism. . . . To avoid both pitfalls, Childs developed the "canonical approach" as a hermeneutical alternative.[25]

Thus, description and construction must be distinguished but never separated. Herein lies the balance between history and theology at the level of biblical theological analysis.

The key terms of "witness" and "subject matter" help to navigate the distinct-but-never-separate relationship between description (history) and construction (theology). For Childs, the "witness" refers to the text, the words, sentences, paragraphs, and entire books of the Bible. The "witness" comes to us in a final form, the canon of Christian Scripture. The "subject matter" (the *res* or *die Sache*) is the concept or conclusion to which the "witness" refers. Simply, it is the content of the Bible. Not merely the sum total of all the words, sentences, paragraphs, and stories of Scripture, but rather the very thing it seeks to convey. Words are signs that signify reality, "Nobody, after all, uses words except for the sake of signifying something."[26] Reflecting on Augustine, Paul McGlasson notes, "there is a dialectical relation of the biblical witness (sign) and the reality of which it speaks (thing). Augustine would never allow the two to be separated, but neither would he ever allow the two simply to be collapsed."[27] The "dialectic" relationship between witness (descriptive) and subject matter (constructive) need not imply Hegelian subsumption

---

24. Childs, *Church's Guide for Reading Paul*, 253.
25. Keck, "Faith Seeking Canonical Understanding," 104.
26. *Teaching Christianity*, I.2.
27. McGlasson, *Invitation to Dogmatic Theology*, 111.

and progress, rather it denotes "distinction in relationship and ongoing dynamic tension."[28]

Using the example of the economic versus immanent Trinity, Childs illustrates how the witness relates to the subject matter.

> It is constitutive of Biblical Theology that it takes seriously the historical forms of the biblical witnesses which are registered in the two testaments. Yet it was a fatal mistake of some forms of Biblical Theology when dealing with the identity of God to feel that it could reflect on the subject *only* in terms of its historical sequence.[29]

The "historical sequence" of God's acts (economic Trinity) put forth in the "witness" point to the being of God (immanent Trinity). Childs insists that the "subject matter . . . requires that proper theological understanding move from the biblical witness to the reality itself. . . ."[30]

A canonical approach insists that witness and subject matter not be collapsed (as in BT2) nor separated (as in BT1 and potentially in BT5). Furthermore, the dynamic relationship between witness (description) and subject matter (construction) cannot be maintained by the literary/philosophical concept of "narrative," because as implied above, BT3 will either stress the historical over the theological (Wright) or the theological over the historical (Hays). Canon is a more helpful way forward in maintaining the dialectical relationship between description and construction. Avoiding both conflation and separation, emphasizing the role of the canon in biblical theology provides a way forward for the discipline of reading the two Testaments of Christian Scripture as a single witness to Jesus Christ.

Bibliography

Augustine. *Teaching Christianity (On Christian Doctrine)*. New York: New City, 1996.
Barton, John. *Reading the Old Testament: Method in Biblical Studies*. 2nd ed. London: Darton, Longman & Todd, 1996.
Carson, D. A. "Theological Interpretation of Scripture: Yes, But . . . ." In *Theological Commentary: Evangelical Perspectives*, edited by R. Michael Allen, 187–207. London: T. & T. Clark, 2011.

---

28. Finn, "Reflections on the Rule of Faith," 234 n.53.
29. Childs, *Biblical Theology of the Old and New Testaments*, 370 (emphasis added).
30. Ibid.

Chapman, Stephen B. "Reclaiming Inspiration for the Bible." In *Canon and Biblical Interpretation*, edited by Craig G. Bartholomew, et al., 167–99. Scripture and Hermeneutics Series 7. Grand Rapids: Zondervan, 2006.

Childs, Brevard S. *Biblical Theology in Crisis*. Philadelphia: Westminster, 1970.

———. *Biblical Theology of the Old and New Testaments: Theological Reflection on the Christian Bible*. Minneapolis: Fortress, 1993.

———. *The Church's Guide for Reading Paul: The Canonical Shaping of the Pauline Corpus*. Grand Rapids: Eerdmans, 2008.

Evans, C. Stephen. "Methodological Naturalism in Historical Biblical Scholarship." In *Jesus and the Restoration of Israel*, edited by Carey C. Newman, 180–205. Downers Grove, IL: InterVarsity, 1999.

Finn, Leonard G. "Reflections on the Rule of Faith." In *The Bible as Scripture: The Work of Brevard S. Childs*, edited by Christopher R. Seitz and Kent H. Richards, 221–42. Atlanta: Society of Biblical Literature, 2013.

Fowl, Stephen E. *Engaging Scripture: A Model for Theological Interpretation*. Challenges in Contemporary Theology. Malden, MA: Blackwell, 1998.

Gaffin, Richard. "Systematic and Biblical Theology." *Westminster Theological Journal* 38 (1976) 293–94.

Harnack, Adolf von. *Origins of the New Testament and the Important Consequences of the New Creation*. Translated by R. Wilkinson Jr. 1925. Reprint. New Testament Studies 6. Eugene, OR: Wipf and Stock, 2004.

Keck, "Faith Seeking Canonical Understanding: Childs's Guide to the Pauline Letters." In *The Bible as Scripture: The Work of Brevard S. Childs*, edited by Christopher R. Seitz and Kent H. Richards, 103–18. Atlanta: Society of Biblical Literature, 2013.

Klink, Edward W., and Darian R. Lockett. *Understanding Biblical Theology: A Comparison of Theory and Practice*. Grand Rapids: Zondervan, 2012.

McGlasson, Paul C. *Invitation to Dogmatic Theology: A Canonical Approach*. Grand Rapids: Brazos, 2006.

Seitz, Christopher. *The Character of Christian Scripture: The Significance of a Two-Testament Bible*. Grand Rapids: Baker Academic, 2011.

Schreiner, Thomas R. *New Testament Theology: Magnifying God in Christ*. Grand Rapids: Baker Academic, 2008.

Schröter, Jens. *From Jesus to the New Testament: Early Christian Theology and the Origin of the New Testament Canon*. Baylor-Mohr Siebeck Studies in Early Christianity 1. Waco, TX: Baylor University Press, 2013.

Stendahl, Krister. "Biblical Theology, Contemporary." In *The Interpreter's Dictionary of the Bible* 1:418–32.

Treier, Daniel J. *Introducing Theological Interpretation of Scripture: Recovering a Christian Practice*. Grand Rapids: Baker Academic, 2008.

Wright, N. T. "In Grateful Dialogue: A Response." In *Jesus and the Restoration of Israel*, edited by Carey C. Newman, 244–80. Downers Grove, IL: InterVarsity, 1999.

What's the Point of Biblical Theology?

Reflections Prompted by Brevard Childs[1]

Scott Hafemann

> Some of us might think that biblical theology is as dead as the dodo, or that if it still splutters on, then it should be. Others might think there is more to it than a myth, a piously confessional "retreat," and that it might be salutary for helping to defragment the discipline of theology. — Mark Elliott

IT IS EASY TO understand such mixed responses to the project of a two-testament biblical theology at the start of the new millennium. Even its strong proponents do not know exactly what to say methodologically about how to do a "whole-Bible theology" that seeks conceptual unity at the level of the Bible's own interpretation of the realities it reports. For example, James Mead begins his recent treatment of the "issues, methods, and themes" of biblical theology with the exciting announcement that "the field of biblical theology has entered a new century with a tremendous surge of interest and vitality."[2] He then lets the air out of his own sails when he observes that in the last century there has been a "relative lack of scholarly works devoted to a biblical theology of the entire Christian Scriptures," though "many scholars continue to work from this perspective."[3] Lots of work, little results. Even Charles H. H. Scobie remained perplexed after finishing his massive compendium of biblical-theological data organized around the basic framework of inaugurated

---

1. This revised essay was first published in the Indian journal *DTJ* 11.1 (2014) 41–54, and, with appreciation, is presented here with permission.
2. Mead, *Biblical Theology*, 1.
3. Ibid., 63.

eschatology. He lamented that the development of "a broader framework or structure of some kind for understanding the canonical material as a whole," "some kind of overall structure for understanding the complex and diverse mass of biblical material," is "in fact the greatest single challenge facing biblical scholarship at the present time."[4]

The Dogma of Diversity

Despite the felt need to move forward, Mead rightly attributes this dearth of results to what I would call the now-reigning, ecumenical dogma of diversity. Mead details this dogma by pointing to the Reformed scholar Brevard Childs's summary of the Lutheran theologian Gerhard Ebeling's evaluation of the situation.[5] As Childs puts it, "The theological unity of the Old and New Testaments has become extremely fragile and it seems now impossible to combine the testaments on the same level in order to produce a unified theology."[6]

Mead himself continues in response:

> It remains to be seen what, if anything, might happen to change this fact of biblical studies. The rigorous treatment of and sensitivity to the historical contexts of each testament has resulted in Old and New Testament theology remaining distinct from each other. Perhaps the pendulum of scholarship has swung too far away from the treatment of the whole Bible, or perhaps the burden of proof still lies with those who would bring the two testaments together in one theological analysis.[7]

---

4. Scobie, *Ways of Our God*, 79–80.

5. For all of Childs's emphasis on the fact that the OT has received "a unifying theological redaction in characterizing Israel's relationship to God under the categories of a Deuteronomic formulation," in the end it is a diversity of covenants that wins out in Childs's theology. At times, Childs's emphasis on "divine initiative" and "the unity of law and covenant" leads to covenant conceived of as "a unilateral act of divine grace, a complete act of divine mercy (Gen 17:1ff.)"; at other times, the covenant is "conceived of as conditional and its maintenance dependent upon Israel's obedient response (Exod 24:3–8)"; see Childs, *Biblical Theology of the Old and New Testaments*, 420. Indeed, in concluding his work, Childs warns that the first of the "threats of mishearing" the Bible is "to turn gospel into law . . ." (726).

6. Mead, *Biblical Theology*, 29, quoting Childs, *Biblical Theology of the Old and New Testaments*, 7.

7. Ibid.

Mead says this in spite of what many would consider Childs's own large-scale attempt to bring the testaments together in his now (in)famous canonical approach to biblical theology. But Mead is right. In the end, the emphasis of Childs's work is not on the unity of the Bible, but on its diversity. Childs's entire project is set up as a comparison of the "discrete" witnesses of the Old and New Testaments, which only come together at the end of the process with a Christian reading of the canon, a reading which itself has as its hallmark this same discreet diversity.[8] And at the heart of Childs's attempt to create a unity out of diversity remains the *theological* polarity inherited from the Reformation. Childs thus embeds Ebeling's dialectical, existential understanding of the law/gospel contrast as a description of universal human experience into the particular story of Israel, Jesus, and the church, which, when taken together, are seen to express a contrast between conditional and unconditional covenants. As a result, the Lutheran concern with the individual's "vertical" relationship with God is transposed into the Reformed concern for mapping out a "horizontal" history of redemption. Nevertheless, the essential "conflict" theory of reading the Bible remains intact.

Moreover, as in all paradigms where diversity reigns, for Childs too this is because, contrary to the way he is often characterized, the emphasis on diversity is grounded in an emphasis on the particularity, or, we would say now, on the determinative and disparate social locations of all human history (all the more so when matched with the closed continuum of cause and effect characteristic of rationalism). For this reason, Childs rejects Hans Frei's attempt to recover from "the eclipse of biblical narrative" by reading the Bible as a history-like "realistic novel" that was "basically non-referential"; he likewise renounces George Lindbeck's attempt to do theology as the result of a "cultural-linguistic" model that lives completely within the "fictive" world created by the Bible's own, self-contained "'intratextuality.'"[9] The problem with both approaches is the "evident" reference to history in the Bible—that is, its "concrete, earthly quality," climaxing in "the wonder of the gospel message . . . that into this real world of flesh and blood God has entered, and the call of Christian discipleship is to follow faithfully into this same world."[10]

---

8. See the structure of Childs's *Biblical Theology of the Old and New Testaments*, vi–xiv, and 74: "The simple juxtaposition of the two testaments as the two parts of the one Bible continued to allow for a rich theological diversity."

9. Ibid., 19, 21.

10. Ibid., 21–22.

The Problem of History

The problem of biblical theology, based on the canonical collection of historically discrete and genre-distinct documents, all of which are related to a history of a people that is interpreted theologically, is therefore the problem of history itself. Childs recognizes this clearly. "The once-for-all quality (*Einmaligkeit*) of historical events within a chronological sequence is a fundamental characteristic of the entire Old Testament witness."[11] Yet, for Childs, biblical theology is still possible, if we accept von Rad's approach to recognizing Israel's own theological appraisal of redemptive history, without falling prey to the attempt to reconstruct traditions *behind* the text as the locus of this theology:

> It would seem to be a fundamental task of biblical theology which is done in accord with the canonical structuring carefully to describe the theological functions of the great revelatory events in Israel's history and their subsequent appropriation by the tradition. This enterprise would share, for example, with von Rad the conviction that a fruitful avenue into Old Testament theology is in terms of Israel's continual reflection on the great redemptive events of her history. Yet it would differ from von Rad in hearing the voice of Israel, not in the form of scientifically reconstructed streams of tradition, but in the canonically shaped literature of the Old Testament as the vehicle of Israel's *Heilsgeschichte*.[12]

Here again, however, even when following the canonically shaped literature of a Christian Bible, diversity reigns:

> the gospel of Jesus Christ is understood by means of a *transformed* Old Testament. The writers of the New Testament began from their experience with Jesus Christ from whom they received a *radically new* understanding of the Jewish Scriptures. Then on the basis of this *transformed* Old Testament, the New Testament writers interpreted the theological significance of Jesus Christ to the Christian church by means of the Old.[13]

Once "transformation" is the key hermeneutical concept for construing a whole-Bible biblical theology, the always-central role of the interpreter now becomes dominant as the one who is perceptive enough

---

11. Ibid., 91.
12. Ibid., 92.
13. Ibid., 93, emphases mine.

theologically to recognize this transformation. And, of course, here is where the determinative role of tradition merges with that of the interpreter. This is what troubles James Barr so much about Childs's work. Barr agrees with and applauds the evaluation that Childs is not a fundamentalist in the "traditional" sense of one who holds to the historical accuracy and inerrancy of the Bible. What he viciously attacks is Childs's "theological fundamentalism" in which historical criticism can be tolerated, but "theological criticism is virtually or totally excluded," "a kind of theological inerrancy" based on an ideological commitment to Barth's theology that allowed Childs to dismiss other viewpoints out of hand, just as Barth had done.[14] In Barr's contrasting ideology, practically any viewpoint can be held, as long as it is held lightly in recognition of the validity of opposing perspectives. Barr consequently concludes his extensive survey of the concepts of biblical theology employed throughout the discipline of OT theology by pointing to his own "final form exegesis" (another jab at Childs?) in which he argues that Genesis 1 and 2 were "intended to be read together," only to add immediately, "But I do not believe that such exercises necessarily produce a better theology, or a better interpretation, than that which we had when the two sources were perceived as separate."[15] Under the dogma of diversity, Barr seems to do theological exegesis merely for the sake of the intrinsically interesting and, one senses, entertaining value of doing such exegesis. For Barr, all teleological motivation in doing theology is both naïve and suspicious.

The Death of Biblical Theology

Although both the dialectical, "Lutheran" and transformational, "Reformed" approaches to biblical theology continue to remain vibrant,[16] these reflections from the end of the last millenium once again raise the larger, age-old question of the worldview needed to do biblical theology, and to do it in this new century. Faced with this question in the past, biblical theology as a discipline within the Protestant church, where it largely had its home, died twice. First, the Reformation demand for a

---

14. Barr, *Concept of Biblical Theology*, 437, in view of the critique of Childs on 436–37; for Barr's critique of Barth's superior attitude toward exegesis, see 72.

15. Ibid., 605–6.

16. For the former, see Spiekermann and Feldmeier, *Der lebendige Gott*; for the latter, see Beale, *A New Testament Biblical Theology*.

biblical theology that could challenge the medieval consensus by showing that its new synthesis could be based solely on Scripture collapsed under the weight of the Enlightenment's emphasis on the Bible's distant historicity, irreconcilable diversity of theological affirmations, and embarrisingly outdated supernaturalism. Within a modernist worldview, how can biblical theology incorporate a supernaturalism that expresses itself in everything from walking on water, and water turned into blood and wine, to a floating axehead and the raising of a sleeply listener from a death caused by a long-winded preacher, not to mention a still sun, raptured individuals, a virgin birth, and the bodily resurrection. Then add to this the biblical concept of divine election, the affirmations that the biblical narratives themselves are divinely-directed, and God's active sovereignty over the histories of all nations (cf. Acts 17:26–27). Even if factual, the attempt to isolate timeless truths from such time-bound accidents of history simply led back to the primacy of tradition over the Bible, whether ecclesiastical or scientific.[17] So by the time we move from F. C. Baur's (1792–1860) non-supernatural revision of the biblical text as the corollary to Schleiermacher's (1768–1834) dogmatics of religious self-consciousness to William Wrede's (1859–1906) rediscovery of Jewish apocalyptic as the key to the thought of the early Christians, we find biblical theology largely supplanted within the university by the history of religion and the "academic Bible," with the power of "unaided reason" leading to historical positivism.[18]

Second, the subsequent rise of the "biblical theology movement" in the middle of the twentieth century, which attempted to counter this modernist hegemony by applying a "neo-orthodox" reading of the Bible as God's unified Word *to* us from *outside* of us, likewise collapsed by its inability to sustain momentum in the face of historical criticism. It was Childs himself who showed that it was impossible to steer a course between fundamentalism and liberalism without crashing.[19] The move-

17. For the principle that "the accidental truths of history can never become the proof of necessary truths of reason," see G. E. Lessing's (1729–1781) tract, "On the Proof of the Spirit and of Power" (1777), quoted by Chadwick, *Lessing's Theological Writings*, 31. For Lessing, this was "the ugly, broad ditch which I cannot get across, however often and however earnestly I have tried to make the leap" (quoted, ibid., 31).

18. On this transition within the university, see now Legaspi, *Death of Scripture*.

19. On this attempt to forge a middle way, see Childs, *Biblical Theology in Crisis*, 15–22. Childs observes that the UK neither felt the need for this middle way, nor had the same enthusiasm for Barth and Brunner that the US did, due to the fact that the modernist-fundamentalist controversy in the US bypassed it (22).

ment's own conflicting theologies could not be adjudicated, since they were the result of the traditionalisms and/or creativities of its interpreters (with aspects of the biblical witness silenced under the principle of the "analogy of Scripture"), of its growing divorce of revelation from history, and of its turn to an ecclesiastical experientialism and/or soft-creedalism. The marriage between the neo-orthodoxy of the biblical theology movement and the rationalism of its liberal social location within the university was subsequently short lived. As Childs himself observed, the issue of authority in theology was never resolved, since the biblical theology movement could not, in the end, integrate Scripture and experience. As a result, the demise of the biblical theology movement has prompted a return to the hermeneutical priority of the faith-experience of the believer or of the believing church as the key to doing biblical theology.[20]

By the end of the twentieth century, experience won out over history partly due to the fact that experience is easier to come by than linguistic and exegetical skills. The priority of experience also reflected the wider cultural shift to experientialism ever since the 1960s. It is no surprise, then, that interest in the historical study of the Bible in universities and most seminaries has simply died out. Indeed, as James Smart argued already in 1979, to call "biblical theology" a "movement" was itself "the kiss of death," since movements, by cultural definition, are temporary answers to abiding issues that come and go.[21] Far from being a "movement," Smart stressed that the Bible is not witnessing to events or ideas outside of itself, but is an expression of theological activity itself, so that biblical theology "is simply an enlargement of the dimensions of biblical science to make its character and methodology commensurate with the contents of the documents which it is its task to interpret."[22] Smart's own approach, however, was essentially also that of neo-orthodoxy, so that he too pitted revelation against the Scriptures, placing the locus of divine revelation ultimately in human experience.[23] It is not too much to say, then, by way of comparison with the Englightenment, that as we look

---

20. To give just one example, see Graf Reventlow, *Problems of Biblical Theology*, 14, who argues that since the Christ-event is not a direct continuation or development of an OT event, only the experience of faith, in view of Christ, can discover the historical dimension of that same faith in the OT witnesses.

21. Smart, *Past, Present, and Future*, 11.

22. Ibid., 11.

23. Ibid., 42.

back at the last century, revelation is to postmodernism what miracles were to modernism.

Life after Death?

If history is the problem of biblical theology, and the attempt to separate revelation from history a solution that has not worked, might the way forward be the way back to the "salvation-history" approach of those who did not separate revelation from history, while at the same time resisting all the attempts even within this approach to reconstruct a history behind the text? Robert Yarbrough has reminded us that for the last one hundred fifty years there has persisted a much-neglected school of thought that, instead of privileging "the reflex of the subjectivity of the authors," has sought to overcome the Kantian "epistemological dualism" in which faith (theological assertions) and facts (cognitive knowledge) lie in two different realms.[24] Under the dominance of critical orthodoxy, however, it became an assumed impossibility to maintain "that a particular trajectory within the historical nexus somehow took on normative significance for all history due to God's unique saving presence in and through it" and that this could be pursued as a "viable historiographical possibility," not merely as a matter of ahistorical "believing self-understanding."[25] Hence, the concept of "salvation history" came to be regarded as a "precritical myth" and therefore "a methodological fallacy."[26] Indeed, salvation history approaches were declared at the close of the last century to be "irretrievably *passé*."[27]

Nevertheless, though banished from the guild and "buried beneath the kind of triumphalist historiography that has tended to characterize accounts of New Testament scholarship over the last few hundred years," "salvation history" continued to exist as a resistance movement against the Baur-Wrede-Bultmann–led hegemony within academic scholarship.[28] As diverse examples of this minority voice, Yarbrough focuses on

---

24. Yarbrough, *Salvation Historical Fallacy?*, 10, 328. For my review of his work, see *TJ* 29 (2008) 153–56.

25. Ibid., 3.

26. Ibid., 4; cf. 294.

27. Ibid., 340, responding to the judgments of Hinze and Hodgson that salvation history was over as part of the larger death of "'macro-historical ideas'" (G. Trompf).

28. Ibid., 343.

"a rediscovery of significant labor unjustly forgotten," from that of J. C. K. von Hofmann (1810–1877) to the work of A. Schlatter (1852–1938), M. Albertz (1882–1956), L. Goppelt (1911–1973), and O. Cullmann (1902–1998).

Against this dominant subjectivism, which ironically is to be found at the center of liberalism, neo-orthodoxy, and pietism, "salvation history . . . interprets ostensibly immanent phenomena as the historically visible expression of God's personal sovereign purpose."[29] Hence, "a broader and deeper concept of truth . . . is sought. A merging of openness to the transcendent and careful observation of the phenomenal is attempted."[30] To be part of this heritage is thus to share a "concern to avoid an exaggerated faith/fact or theology/history split and to let critical methods be adapted to the subject matter, as well as (an) overt advocacy of a salvation-historical reading of the New Testament."[31] Even though the guild has disparaged the salvation-history school as "antiquated and unscientific," it is striking that all ten-volumes of *TDNT* are dedicated to Adolf Schlatter as the one who set the standard for modern scholarship with his magisterial work, *Der Glaube im Neuen Testament* (1885), which by 1927 had already reached its fourth edition before Schlatter's influence was eclipsed by the rise of the Bultmannian paradigm.[32]

Perhaps we can do no better than to turn to Oscar Cullmann, Yarbrough's "prophet without honor," whose method may provide a bridge from the past to the future of biblical theology. Or at least, by doing so, we can assert minority rights. For Cullmann, Christianity makes the "offensive assertion" that as the climax and central point of all divine self-revelation God "entered so completely into history that this unique entrance can be designated by dates just as can every other historical event: the emperor Augustus (Luke 2:1); under the emperor Tiberius (Luke 3:1)."[33] So, in accordance with the conviction of the New Testament writers,

> the "Biblical history," which we . . . can also designate as "revelatory history" or—since indeed all revelation is God's love—as "redemptive history," is the heart of all New Testament theology.

---

29. Ibid., 113.

30. Ibid., 115.

31. Ibid., 207. For a recent example of these same hermeneutical convictions and their application, see Stuhlmacher, *Vom Verstehen des Neuen Testaments*; *How To Do Biblical Theology*; and *Biblische Theologie*.

32. See now the 6th, "student edition" (Stuttgart: Calver Verlag, 1982).

33. Cullmann, *Christ and Time*, 24.

> This has been more correctly and more sharply seen by those who reject Christianity than by many Christians, more sharply even than by many Christian theologians. For it simply is not true that one can give up this entire redemptive history of the New Testament with a perfectly free conscience and yet hold fast to the Christian faith. This attitude, held by many, proceeds from the false presupposition that the redemptive history is only an external framework which the Christian faith can unhesitatingly discard. In reality that which then remains as alleged "kernel" is not at all a particularly characteristic feature of the Christian revelation ... [Contra Bultmann, this redemptive history is not a] "myth" of which the New Testament revelation can be unclothed.[34]

To reject redemptive history as the heart of primitive Christianity is to reject the Christian message itself.[35]

Out of the Closet

For the sake of full disclosure, in aligning myself with the broad approach and convictions of the salvation-history school of thought there are two additional convictions that I bring to my own doing of biblical theology. It must also be said that although these convictions are formative for my own thinking, they are not *necessary* for a recovery of biblical theology itself. Furthermore, these convictions are not unassailable presuppositions; they ultimately stand and fall exegetically. As such, they must take into consideration the evidence brought forth by historical-critical research into the development and textual interrelationships of the biblical writings. And, lastly, these convictions are tied to the existence of the Protestant canon, though not dependent on its eventual ordering of the biblical books, as the final stage of the process of development already initiated within the biblical writings themselves. These convictions, shared by my coeditor, Paul House, were put in the preface to our recent volume on the topic:

> First, we are convinced that the Bible *is* a unity because it is the word of God, who is a unified and coherent being, and that a unified biblical theology should thus span the entire range of the Scriptures because they are all part of the written word of God

34. Ibid., 26–28.
35. Ibid., 29.

. . . . This pursuit of unity does not reject legitimate diversity. Indeed, it affirms that effective literature utilizes tension and diversity to create its unity. Nonetheless, this diversity contributes to the overall unity; it does not negate it.

Second, to do biblical theology is not merely to survey the contents of the Bible. In pursuit of an understanding of God and his ways, a biblical theology that spans the canon seeks not only to unpack the content, but also to establish the conceptual unity of the Scriptures as a whole as they unfold in human events. Thus this type of biblical theology endeavors to reflect synthetically on the history and significance of the relationship between God and his people and God and his world, past, present and future, as delineated in the Scriptures. To achieve this goal, whole-Bible biblical theology does not settle for describing the discrete theological emphases of *individual* writers or sources. Nor does it settle for focusing on reconstructing the religious experiences or historical events *behind the text* that gave rise to the text. Instead, *biblical* theology seeks its content and coherence in the final propositions and basic ordering of the Old and New Testaments read in their entirety, in their final form, and in concert with one another. . . . This sort of biblical theology affirms that God's self-revelation cannot be separated from the historical context in which it was given, and that this context is in concert with the literary record in which it is found.[36]

These convictions led earlier to an unpublished set of "Ten Theses on Biblical Theology," which were formulated together with my former colleague, Richard Schultz, who did his PhD with Childs at Yale:

1. Biblical theology should be biblical, taking the canon in its entirety as its starting point and criterion.

2. Biblical theology should be theological, aiming at making synthetic assertions about the nature, will, and plan of God in creation and redemption, as well as their corresponding implications for the nature, will, and purposes of humanity.

3. Biblical theology should be historical, contextual, and thematic in its methodology, integrating historical development, literary structures, sociocultural factors, and theological concepts within an understanding of the history of redemption.

---

36. Hafemann and House, *Central Themes in Biblical Theology*. For my own contribution to this attempt, see the essay, "The Covenant Relationship," 20–65.

4. Biblical theology should develop its theological categories inductively from the biblical text, not from a predetermined systematic framework.
5. Biblical theology should be exegetically based, taking intertextuality as its starting point, including both the "OT" use of the "OT" and the "NT" use of the "OT" as preserved in the MT and LXX traditions.
6. Biblical theology should be intentionally bi-testamental and unifying, so that neither the OT nor NT are read in isolation from each other nor from the standpoint of a "canon within the canon."
7. Biblical theology should work toward a unity of the canon, going beyond the traditional disciplines of OT and NT theology and beyond providing simply descriptive accounts of the various theological emphases within its individual writings.
8. Biblical theology should strive to incorporate the diversity of the biblical writings within the unity of its theology, without sacrificing either its historical particularity or its overarching history of redemption.
9. Biblical theology should be both descriptive and prescriptive in order to be faithful to its theological task of providing an enduring contribution to the self-understanding of God's people within their contemporary context.
10. Biblical theology should be pursued by means of an intentional dialogue within the body of Christ in order to overcome the lamentable specialization of biblical scholars and be viewed as a profoundly spiritual calling in order to be faithful to the biblical witness.

The Point of Biblical Theology

The point of biblical theology, therefore, is to reaffirm revelation in history within a robust view of the divinely inspired reliability of the biblical text itself, which will require restoring the humility of the theologian before the text and, supremely, before God, whose text it is. This will not be easy in a world bent on disavowing its own finitude. In response, Ernest Becker, in his Pulitzer Prize-winning book, *The Denial of Death*, has unmasked the reality that all of life is the attempt to come to grips with our own death through strategies of heroism, which are made increasingly impossible in the modern world by its rejection of the theological answer.

> From this perspective the problem of heroism and of mental illness would be "who nags whom?" Do men harangue the gods, the armies of other nations, the leaders of their own state, or their spouses? The debt of life has to be paid somehow: one has to be a hero in the best and only way that he can; in our impoverished culture—as Harrington so truly put it—"if only for his skill at the pinball machine."[37]

In a context in which the study of Scripture has been replaced with "biblical studies," all too often our discipline has become merely an arena for our own attempted heroism, in which we venture to show our own superiority by haranguing the biblical text (and each other). As the heirs of F. C. Baur, we seek to vanquish our foes by converting Scripture's diversities into conflicts and then winning the battle by overcoming them, either through taming them into static, coexisting realities, resolving them by our own creative solutions, or simply rejecting them in accordance with our own convictions. But what might happen if we did biblical theology individually and corporately from the standpoint of reason-informed dependence, in our case on the biblical text, since the posture of "faith" is the only abiding acknowledgement and answer to our creatureliness?

On January 22, 1999, I was honored to be a part of a small group of young scholars who met with Dr. Carl F. H. Henry (1913–2003) on the occasion of his eighty-sixth birthday at the Inaugural Summit Conference of the Carl F. H. Henry Institute for Evangelical Engagement. At the end of the day's deliberations regarding the current state of theology, the group asked Dr. Henry, whom *Time* magazine called in 1977 "the leading theologian of American evangelicalism," what he thought was the great need in the church today. After a long pause and some time scribbling on a pad of paper, he answered that it is "the articulation of an enduring Christian life and worldview with revelatory excitement that transcends technological science and heralds an unrevisable truth claim that replies to critics who decry reason." The purpose of biblical theology, if history and theology, faith and reason, "law and gospel" can be wed again, is to answer this need, and in so doing to find doxology at the end of theology. For the final goal of a biblically driven and integrated theology is not knowledge *per se*, but praise.

---

37. Becker, *Denial of Death*, 217, quoting Harrington, *Immortalist*, 93.

Bibliography

Barr, James. *The Concept of Biblical Theology: An Old Testament Perspective.* Minneapolis: Fortress, 1999.
Beale, G. K. *A New Testament Biblical Theology: The Unfolding of the Old Testament in the New.* Grand Rapids: Baker, 2011.
Becker, Ernest. *The Denial of Death.* New York: Free Press, 1973.
Chadwick, Henry. *Lessing's Theological Writings.* Stanford: Stanford University Press, 1956.
Childs, Brevard S. *Biblical Theology in Crisis.* Philadelphia: Westminster, 1970.
———. *Biblical Theology of the Old and New Testaments: Theological Reflection on the Christian Bible.* Minneapolis: Fortress, 1992.
Cullmann, Oscar. *Christ and Time: The Primitive Christian Conception of Time and History.* Rev. ed. Philadelphia: Westminster, 1964.
Graf Reventlow, Henning. *Problems of Biblical Theology in the Twentieth Century.* Minneapolis: Fortress, 1986.
Hafemann, Scott J., and Paul House, eds. *Central Themes in Biblical Theology: Mapping Unity in Diversity.* Grand Rapids: Baker, 2007.
Harrington, Alan. *The Immortalist.* New York: Random House, 1969.
Legaspi, Michael C. *The Death of Scripture and the Rise of Biblical Studies.* OSHT. Oxford: Oxford University Press, 2010.
Mead, James K. *Biblical Theology: Issues, Methods, and Themes.* Louisville, KY: WJK, 2007.
Scobie, Charles H. H. *The Ways of Our God: An Approach to Biblical Theology.* Grand Rapids: Eerdmans, 2003.
Smart, James D. *The Past, Present, and Future of Biblical Theology.* Philadelphia: Westminster, 1979.
Spiekermann, Hermann, and Reinhard Feldmeier. *Der lebendige Gott: Eine Einführung in die biblische Gotteslehre.* Tübingen: Mohr Siebeck, 2011. English translation: *God of the Living: A Biblical Theology.* Translated by Mark E. Biddle. Waco, TX: Baylor University Press, 2011.
Stuhlmacher, Peter. *Biblische Theologie des Neuen Testaments.* 2 vols. Göttingen: Vandenhoeck & Ruprecht, 2005–2012.
———. *How To Do Biblical Theology.* PTMS 38. Allison Park, PA: Pickwick, 1995.
———. *Vom Verstehen des Neuen Testaments: Eine Hermeneutik.* 2nd ed. GNT 6. Göttingen: Vandenhoeck & Ruprecht, 1986.
Yarbrough, Robert W. *The Salvation Historical Fallacy?: Reassessing the History of New Testament Theology.* Leiden: Deo, 2004.

Church Lectionaries as Biblical Theology

Frederik Poulsen

MANY PROBLEMS WITHIN THE field of biblical theology remain unsolved. For Christian interpreters, an enduring issue concerns the relationship between the Old and New Testaments. Despite the numerous moves which have been made to express this relationship—e.g., one God behind all scriptures, a unified salvific history, or certain interpretive schemes such as law-gospel—none of them has been made absolute. The relationship remains a complex one.

Central to the church lectionary—i.e., the book of biblical lessons to be read throughout the Christian church year[1]—is the juxtaposition of smaller sections from both testaments. Rather than approaching the relationship between the testaments on a general level, the lectionary invites reflection on the relationship between discrete passages and on separate theological themes. In other words, the relationship between the testaments must be determined from passage to passage, from Sunday to Sunday.

This article explores the church lectionary as biblical theology. First, I will begin with two thought-provoking observations made by Brevard Childs. Then, I will consider the significance of worship and liturgy for reading and hearing the biblical texts. Finally, I will offer an example from First Sunday of Easter to test the potentials of this approach.

---

1. For a short introduction to the history and development of church lectionaries, see Aland and Baldovin, "Lectionary;" Bower, *Handbook*, 15–33.

Two Observations in Brevard Childs's Biblical Theology

My idea of exploring the church lectionaries as biblical theology partly stems from two observations or claims made by Brevard Childs in his major *Biblical Theology of the Old and New Testaments* from 1992.[2] The first one concerns the problem of determining the relationship between the two testaments; the second one concerns the significance of the liturgical context for reading and hearing the Bible.

First, concerning the relationship of the two testaments, it seems to be a persistent problem for Christian interpreters how to relate the two parts of the Bible. Several scholarly surveys have sketched a manifold of different models for understanding this relationship. David Baker, for instance, presents four modern "solutions."[3] These are: the New Testament as the essential Bible, the two testaments as equally Christian Scripture, the Old Testament as the essential Bible, and the two testaments as one salvation history. Manfred Oeming ends his *Das Alte Testament als Teil des christlichen Kanons?* with a valuable assessment of the strengths and weaknesses of the offered models.[4] Finally, Edward Klink and Darian Lockett have recently examined five current ways of doing biblical theology, including their views on the Old Testament's relation to the New.[5] It seems fair to conclude that no consensus has been reached regarding the relationship of the testaments on a general level.

Central to Childs's view is the observation that in the formation of the Christian Bible the testaments were *juxtaposed* rather than brought into alignment. He states:

> The church not only joined its new writings to the Jewish scriptures, but laid claim on the Old Testament as a witness to Jesus Christ. A variety of different theological moves were made by which to articulate the theological relationship of the two dispensations: the one purpose of God, the one redemptive history (or story), the one people of God, prophecy and fulfillment, law and gospel, shadow and substance, etc. No one theological interpretation of the relationship became absolute for Christian theology, but the simple *juxtaposition* of the two testaments as

---

2. Childs, *Biblical Theology*. For an introduction to Brevard Childs and his approach to biblical theology, see Poulsen, *God, His Servant, and the Nations*, 11–74.
3. Baker, *Two Testaments*.
4. Oeming, *Das Alte Testament*, 247–59.
5. Klink and Lockett, *Understanding Biblical Theology*.

the two parts of the one Bible continued to allow for a rich theological diversity.⁶

In other words, in the early church, the relationship of the two parts of the Bible was never theologically spelled out in a detailed formulation. No single model was made absolute. The relationship of the two testaments remained, and still remains, a complex one.

Second, it remains debated what the proper context is for doing biblical theology. Is biblical theology purely a descriptive and historical enterprise under the ownership of the academy? Or is it a constructive and theological enterprise as the property of the church? Or does biblical theology as a "bridge discipline" mediate between these worlds?

Despite his Protestant persuasion, Childs recognizes the Catholic emphasis on tradition and the church's worship as the proper context for hearing the biblical message. He states: "The Roman Catholic insistence upon the decisive role of tradition in shaping the Christian Bible correctly recognized the role of the church's actual use of its scripture both in proclamation and liturgy. The church's practice of worship provided the context in which the biblical message was received, treasured, and transmitted."⁷ In a word, we need to recognize the significance of liturgy and the worshipping community for grasping the true sense of what the Bible attempts to communicate.

It seems to me that Childs's two statements come together in the church's weekly service: we encounter the juxtaposition of passages from both the Old and New Testaments and we encounter them within the context of the worshipping community.

Hermeneutical Implications

Drawing upon Childs, we will now look at the Sunday worship within which the passages from the Bible are read and heard.⁸ My thesis is that the service's liturgy and lectionary offer a valuable key for understanding the biblical texts. The Christian worship not only constitutes a larger interpretive context for receiving the Bible's message, but small significant markers in its liturgy shape the approach. In what follows, I will refer to

---

6. Childs, *Biblical Theology*, 74; my emphasis.

7. Ibid., 66–67.

8. Parts of the following section have formerly been presented in Danish; see Poulsen, "Gudstjenestens Davidsnøgle."

the Danish order of worship with three biblical readings: the Old Testament lesson, the Epistle, and the Gospel.[9] I will make four hermeneutical remarks:

First, in the context of worship, the Bible is approached not as a religio-historical source for examining some people's long-gone religion, but as the vehicle of the living God whose voice continues to speak directly to its modern audience. According to the words of the introductory prayer sounding every Sunday, we have come into the house of God to hear what he *will speak* to us. The words of the Bible are not dead documents, they are alive—they speak! The service offers the context for the community of faith and its encounter with its Scripture. It is here—in the midst of the people of God—that the biblical texts are properly heard and interpreted; not removed from this context.

Second, the readings from both the Old and New Testaments remind us that our Bible consists of two parts, and that the Old Testament has equal authority compared to the New. Along with the Epistle and the Gospel, the Old Testament lesson provides the textual basis for the worship. Central to the church lectionaries is the *juxtaposition* of smaller sections from both testaments. Although there certainly is a movement from the Old Testament to the Epistle to the crowning moment in the reading of the Gospel, it has not been spelled out how one should interpret the relation between the separate passages.

Nevertheless, as Christopher Seitz very precisely puts it, "every pairing—or tripling—of readings indirectly makes a statement about the relationship between the testaments, which is in turn a statement about biblical theology."[10] A closer glance at the proposals which led to the present Danish lectionary from 1992 reveals that the selection of the specific passages has been guided by many different conditions.[11] Some Old Testament passages have been selected to communicate the theme of creation, the law, and our own situation before God, i.e., under his claim, the consciousness of sin, and the hope for grace. Other Old Testament passages have been selected to communicate the messianic prophecies or to present the historical background for the readings from the New Testament. This manifold of relations confirms Childs's claim that the relationship of the testaments never has been fixed into a final formula.

---

9. See *Hymns in English*, 83–99.

10. Seitz, *Word Without End*, 301.

11. For short reviews of the problems in the church's liturgical use of the Old Testament, see Allen and Williamson, *Preaching*, xv–xix; Zenger, "Herausforderung."

Rather than seeking the relationship of the testaments on a general level, the juxtaposition of readings in the lectionary invites reflection on discrete themes and motifs. As was stated, the relationship of the Bible's two testaments must be determined from Sunday to Sunday.

Due to the logic of the lectionary, however, there is an imminent risk that the preacher and congregation are led to believe that "there is some sort of obvious independent integrity to individual passages read as such, detached from original literary contexts or supplied with new contexts due to the juxtaposition of one discrete reading with several other readings."[12] As Seitz states, "the final effect of the present lectionary implies that individual passages have no inherent relatedness to the literary contexts out of which they have been taken."[13]

Third, in the liturgy, the readings from the Bible appear in close connection with the Apostles' Creed. This implies that the biblical texts sound within an overall frame or "narrative" expressed by means of a rule of faith. As far as I have understood, this is exactly what the church fathers and Irenaeus in particular understood by the concept of canon. For them (as for Childs), canon is not merely a list of books, but rather the framework of reading and interpreting the Bible.[14] The function of the Apostles' Creed in the liturgy is to present this framework or overall plot.[15] The movement from creation over redemption to renewal of life sketches this overall framework within which the biblical witnesses to the triune God and his history with us shall be heard.

Fourth, regarding the role of prayer, the church service does not only contain prayers to God, but its own foundation rests upon a prayer: that God may be present and make himself known to us. In the Danish order of worship, this central motif is articulated by the introductory prayer. As was mentioned, this prayer expresses the longing to hear what God will speak to us. However, the real powerful and profound statement is the one that follows: "Lord, through your Holy Spirit, and for the sake of Jesus Christ, *open my heart*, that I may learn (...)" This statement summarizes the old insight that encounter with and understanding of God is only possible because of God's own initiative. Through his Spirit, God shall *open my heart* so that I can learn and believe. In a word, the

---

12. Seitz, *Word Without End*, 302.
13. Ibid., 302.
14. See Poulsen, *God, His Servant, and the Nations*, 12-14, 36-39.
15. See Jenson, "Hermeneutics," 96-98.

introductory prayer states that we have come to church in order to receive help to open our hearts.

The confession of our failing ability to grasp and comprehend God's word calls for humbleness. Not by our own efforts can we reach God. This is also true for the understanding of Scripture. The hymn preceding the sermon is often a prayer to receive the divine spirit of truth and clarity. As Childs states, "the true expositor of the Christian scriptures is the one who awaits in anticipation toward becoming the interpreted rather than the interpreter. The very divine reality which the interpreter strives to grasp, is the very One who grasps the interpreter. The Christian doctrine of the role of the Holy Spirit is not a hermeneutical principle, but that divine reality itself who makes understanding of God possible."[16]

When the Bible is read in the midst of the community in prayer and in anticipation of the illuminating spirit—when God makes our hearts burning within us—we may hope to hear God's voice through Scripture.

Test Case: First Sunday of Easter

In order to test the potentials of this approach, we will now turn to First Sunday after Easter. In Denmark there are two cycles and the texts that I have chosen as my test case—Psalm 30 and John 20:19–31—occur in the first cycle.[17] As was noted, there are three lessons: the first is from the Old Testament, the second is from the New Testament Epistles, Acts, or Revelation, and the third is from the Gospels. Unlike for instance the Revised Common Lectionary, the Psalms or a portion of them are not used as a response after the first lesson, but appear as readings in their own right. In fact roughly a fourth of all readings from the Old Testament is taken from this biblical book.

In many church lectionaries, it seems to be a common principle that the liturgical year with its familiar and distinct seasons—e.g., Christmas, Easter, and Pentecost—offers an important key to understand the selections from the Bible. Especially in the period between Advent and Pentecost, the themes of the Gospel readings are closely related to the "narrative" of the liturgical year. The other lessons (Old Testament and

---

16. Childs, *Biblical Theology*, 86–87.

17. See *Den Danske Alterbog*. The first cycle roughly follows the old lectionary of the Western church dating from the early medieval era. The second cycle was created in 1885 by picking readings from the New Testament with a similar theme as that of the first cycle. Readings from the Old Testament were added in 1992.

sometimes Epistle) then take their cue from the Gospel readings. This is the case here. The Gospel reading is from John 20:19-31 about Jesus's sending of his disciples and his encounter with Thomas, the latter of which takes place exactly one week after Easter Sunday. The Old Testament reading that has been paired with John has been taken from Psalm 30.[18] The psalm consists of a prayer of thanksgiving for deliverance. God has answered the cry for help and the psalmist offers praise and proclamation in gratitude. Interestingly, one would hardly pair these discrete passages outside the context of the lectionary. First Sunday after Easter thus offers a promising test case for further considerations.

In the following reflections, however, I will leave out the second lesson (1 John 5:1-5 or Acts 2:22-28) and only look at the Old Testament reading and the Gospel.[19] My focus is how to relate Psalm 30 to John 20.[20] I will sketch seven possible entries into reflection on the relationships between these two passages that may be addressed in the sermon. The seven entries relate to each other and should thus not be seen in total isolation.

The first entry which could be labeled "the story of Christ" emerges from the traditional interpretation of the Psalms according to which Christ is the speaker.[21] Psalm 30, thus, reflects his passion and resurrection as recorded in the Easter narrative and furthermore presupposed in the Gospel reading from John. Motifs of relevance to this interpretation are found primarily in verses 1-3 in which the psalmist extols and acknowledges God's deliverance: "you have drawn me up," "you did not let my foes rejoice over me," "you healed me," and "you brought up my soul from Sheol." Furthermore, the experience of the cross may find a parallel

18. As a means of comparison, the Revised Common Lectionary employs Ps 30 as a response on three distinctive Sundays: Sixth Sunday after Epiphany B (along with 2 Kgs 5:1-14; 1 Cor 9:24-27; Mark 1:40-45), Third Sunday of Easter C (along with Acts 9:1-6; Rev 5:11-14; John 21:1-19), and Seventh Sunday after Pentecost C (along with 2 Kgs 5:1-14; Gal 6:7-16; Luke 10:1-11).

19. From a canonical point of view, two readings rather than three accords with the twofold character of the Christian Bible; cf. Seitz, *Word Without End,* 308, who argues in favor of only two lessons each Sunday: "The actual dialectical relationship between Old and New Testaments would remain intact, with the consequence that the fullest possible range of ways of relating the Old and New in witness to Christ might be safeguarded."

20. Cf. the Danish lectionary commentary devoted to interpret the texts from the Old Testament and their relation to the other readings on the single Sundays, see Jeppesen, *Det Gamle Testamente,* 174-79. For similar lectionary commentaries in English, see Allen and Williamson, *Preaching;* Van Harn, *Lectionary Commentary.*

21. See Blaising and Hardin, *Psalms 1-50,* 221-27.

in the motifs of anger-favor and night-morning in verse 5: "For his anger is but for a moment; his favor is for a lifetime. Weeping may linger for the night, but joy comes with the morning." Christ's story of passion and resurrection relates figuratively to the movement from death to life that is testified to in the psalm.

The second entry could be labeled "the story of the disciples." In John 20:19–23, the disciples hide behind locked doors because of their "fear of the Jews"—their *foes* to use the language of the psalm. Moreover, their hiding place represents the dark grave or pit from which they need to be set free (cf. Ps 30:3, 9). The disciples become *witnesses* to the resurrected Christ. And they are sent to spread this witness so that "through believing people may have life in the name of Christ." The disciples must do what the faithful ones are called to do in verses 4 and 9 of Psalm 30, that is, sing praises to God, give thanks to his holy name, and tell about his faithfulness.

The third entry emerges from the narrative of Thomas's doubt in John 20:24–29. It concerns the issue of belief insofar as this theme offers a subtle relation between Psalm 30 and the Gospel reading. Verses 6–7 in the psalm render the words of the psalmist's confession: previously, he was arrogant in a self-confident belief in his own power: "I said in my prosperity, 'I shall never be moved.'" He had *too much* faith, so to speak, and was *shaken* by his illness and experience of God's absence.[22] In the Gospel reading from John, Thomas has *too little* faith as he has doubts about the message of Christ's resurrection. Unless he sees the mark of the nails, he will not believe. Thomas is likewise *shaken* by the overwhelming revelation of Christ and responds to it in faith: "My Lord and my God!"[23] Thomas's confession mirrors that of psalmist, as his prayer is framed by the statement "O Lord my God" (Ps 30:2, 12). Between these extremes, that is, too much and too little faith, one ought to believe solely in the presence and life-giving power of God.

The fourth entry deals with the typology between the temple and the church. Unfortunately, the heading of Psalm 30 is omitted in the church reading. The heading which presumably was added by later editors states that the psalm is "a song at the dedication (*hanukkah*) of the temple." According to rabbinic tradition, the psalm was used in the festival of Hanukka, celebrating the restored temple after its desecration in 165 BCE

---

22. For this interpretation, see e.g. Hossfeld and Zenger, *Psalmen*, 189–90; Mays, *Psalms*, 141–42.

23. Neyrey, *John*, 330–31.

(1 Macc 4). Some scholars, however, propose that the psalm was used earlier in connection with the dedication of the second temple as Ezra and Nehemiah inform us (Ezra 6; Neh 12) or in connection with David's palace (1 Chron 21–22).[24] The heading thus suggests that the psalm can be read as a reflection of the foundation or reopening of a temple. It is a kind of "housewarming"-psalm.

In the reading from John, we also encounter the foundation of a temple, namely the church and its liturgy.[25] In the first day of the week, that is, Sunday, and precisely a week later, Jesus appears in the midst of his assembled disciples, greeting them with "peace be with you." The disciples receive the Holy Spirit and the ministry of the church to forgive sins or not forgive sins—what Matthew refers to as "the keys of the kingdom of heaven" (Matt 16:19). Jesus even *breathes* on them, as God did in the creation of Adam (Gen 2:7). The experience of divine and salvific presence indicates "the beginning of the new creation."[26] In the psalm and in John, the temple or church is founded on the encounter with God's deliverance which provokes joy, praise, and proclamation.

In line with this, the fifth entry concerns the individual vis-a-vis the collective. Common to these passages is the idea that the story of an individual becomes the object of praise of a collective. In the psalm, the experience of the psalmist is made known to his audience—"the faithful ones" in verse 4—and they shall give praise to God. In John, the resurrection of Christ is revealed for the disciples who shall share it with a worldwide audience. A variant of this theme is reflected in the traditional use of the Psalms which takes the first person style to speak of corporate or national experience. The later adding of the heading to Psalm 30 may even serve as a pattern example of a communal interpretation of an original individual psalm of thanksgiving.[27]

The sixth entry takes seriously that the readings occur within the context of the liturgical year. Within this context, Psalm 30 and John 20 present an afterthought to the dramatic events of the preceding Sunday,

---

24. See Eaton, *Psalms*, 142; Hossfeld and Zenger, *Psalmen*, 187; Mays, *Psalms*, 140.

25. The narrative in John 20:19-29 may reflect early Christian worship: it takes place on Sundays (cf. Acts 20:7; 1 Cor 16:2); the disciples are gathered (cf. 1 Cor 11:17; 14:26); Christ is present; the narrative contains typical liturgical elements such as the peace greeting, the gift of the Holy Spirit, and the sending to mission. Cf. also Barrett, *St John*, 573: "indeed the whole passage (. . .) may be liturgical in origin."

26. Barrett, *St John*, 570.

27. Childs, *Old Testament as Scripture*, 519.

that is, Easter Sunday. The language of the psalm expresses the feelings that the community has after having experienced the overwhelming power of the Resurrection story. In the words of verses 11–12, we are in a state where mourning has been turned into dancing: "the glad worship is filled with poetry, music, and dancing."[28] The sackcloth has been taken off and we are clothed with joy. In short, we are in a state of never-ending praise.

The final entry emerges from the encounter with Christ that both passages witness about.[29] In the case of the psalm, we could see ourselves in the place of the psalmist. We are those who are affected by illness—an illness to death. We are those who live in the world of sin, death, and devil. Yet God breaks into our life by means of his word. This moment of revelation is indicated by the decisive movement from illness to healing, from death to life, from God's anger, silence, and absence to his life-giving presence. Christ represents that very moment in which divine anger is turned to sovereign pleasure. Paired with John 20, the psalm invites reflection on the concepts of hiddenness and revelation, God's anger and mercy, and the idea of Christ as the visible image of God's grace.[30]

To conclude: an important implication of doing biblical theology within the context of the church lectionaries is that the church service and its liturgy explicitly offer a framework for approaching the biblical texts. The Bible is read in order to hear what God will speak. The biblical readings occur in close connection with the Apostles' Creed which sketches the overall narrative within which the biblical witnesses should be understood. Moreover, the reading of the Bible emerges from the prayer that God will make us able to understand him and his will. Another important implication has to do with the logic of the lectionary. Rather than approaching the relationship of the two testaments on a general level, the lectionary invites reflection on the relationship between discrete passages and on separate theological themes. As my test case has shown, the lectionary demands reflection on the relation between passages that one hardly would pair outside this context. The reflection on

---

28. Eaton, *Psalms*, 143.

29. Cf. Mays, *Psalms*, 141: "Death and resurrection are not yet in view in the New Testament sense, but the language of the psalm only awaits the Christ event for reinterpretation."

30. Cf. Hans-Joachim Kraus's interpretation of Ps 30:4–5 in which, drawing upon Calvin, he speaks about God's anger and hiddenness as the *opus alienum Dei* and God's life-giving mercy as the *opus proprium Dei*; see Kraus, *Psalmen*, 242.

Psalm 30 and John 20 has demonstrated that the Bible's two parts relate to each other in a manifold of subtle ways.

Bibliography

Aland, Barbara, and John F. Baldovin. "Lectionary." *RPP*. Brill Online, 2015. http://referenceworks.brillonline.com/browse/religion-past-and-present.

Allen, Ronald J., and Clark M. Williamson. *Preaching the Old Testament: A Lectionary Commentary*. Louisville, KY: WJK, 2007.

Baker, David L. *The Two Testaments, One Bible: The Theological Relationship Between the Old and New Testaments*. 3rd ed. Downers Grove, IL: InterVarsity, 2010.

Barrett, C. K. *The Gospel According to St John*. 2nd ed. London: SPCK, 1982.

Blaising, Craig A., and Carmen S. Hardin, eds. *Psalms 1–50*. Ancient Christian Commentary on Scripture, Old Testament VII. Downers Grove, IL: InterVarsity, 2008.

Bower, Peter C., ed. *Handbook for the Common Lectionary*. Philadelphia: Geneva, 1987.

Childs, Brevard S. *Biblical Theology of the Old and New Testaments: Theological Reflection on the Christian Bible*. Minneapolis: Fortress, 1993.

———. *Introduction to the Old Testament as Scripture*. Philadelphia: Fortress, 1979.

Den Danske Alterbog. Copenhagen: Vajsenhus' Forlag, 2010.

Eaton, John. *The Psalms: A Historical and Spiritual Commentary with an Introduction and New Translation*. London: Continuum, 2005.

Hossfeld, Frank-Lothar, and Erich Zenger. *Die Psalmen I: Psalm 1–50*. Würzburg: Echter Verlag, 1993.

Hymns in English: A Selection of Hymns from the Danish Hymnbook. Copenhagen: Vajsenhus' Forlag, 2009.

Jenson, Robert W. "Hermeneutics and the Life of the Church." In *Reclaiming the Bible for the Church*, edited by Carl E. Braaten and Robert W. Jenson, 89–105. Edinburgh: T. & T. Clark, 1995.

Jeppesen, Knud. *Det Gamle Testamente på gudstjenestens betingelser I*. Copenhagen: Anis, 2004.

Klink, Edward W., and Darian R. Lockett. *Understanding Biblical Theology: A Comparison of Theory and Practice*. Grand Rapids: Zondervan, 2012.

Kraus, Hans-Joachim. *Psalmen*. Biblischer Kommentar Altes Testament XV/1. Neukirchen-Vluyn: Neukirchener Verlag, 1972.

Mays, James Luther. *Psalms*. Interpretation. Louisville, KY: John Knox, 1994.

Neyrey, Jerome H. *The Gospel of John*. New Cambridge Bible Commentary. Cambridge: Cambridge University Press, 2007.

Oeming, Manfred. *Das Alte Testament als Teil des christlichen Kanons? Studien zu gesamtbiblischen Theologien des Gegenwart*. Zürich: Pano Verlag, 2001.

Poulsen, Frederik. *God, His Servant, and the Nations in Isaiah 42:1–9: Biblical Theological Reflections after Brevard S. Childs and Hans Hübner*. Forschungen zum Alten Testament II/73. Tübingen: Mohr Siebeck, 2014.

———. "Gudstjenestens Davidsnøgle: Et synspunkt på Det Gamle Testamente i gudstjenesten." *Fønix* 34 (2014) 231–45.

Seitz, Christopher. *Word Without End: The Old Testament as Abiding Theological Witness*. Waco, TX: Baylor University Press, 2004.

Van Harn, Roger E., ed. *The Lectionary Commentary: Theological Exegesis for Sunday's Texts. The First Readings: The Old Testament and Acts*. Grand Rapids: Eerdmans, 2005.

Zenger, Erich. "Das Erste Testament als Herausforderung christlicher Liturgie." In *Leseordnung: Altes und Neues Testament in der Liturgie*, edited by Georg Steins, 11–28. Stuttgart: Verlag Katholisches Bibelwerk, 1997.

Sources for Theology Proper

Heiko Wenzel

THE LAST FEW DECADES have seen significant shifts in scholarship on the Hebrew Bible/Old Testament with ramifications for various religious and theological questions. For example, the diversity of approaches has increased, and so have the available (literary and material) sources of the Ancient Near East along with scholarly discussion of those sources. Unfortunately, the variety of approaches has not always facilitated fruitful dialogue between these approaches. This contribution engages some crucial questions related to theology proper with a particular focus on its sources and on methodological questions. In particular, it seeks to describe a framework that may facilitate a fruitful dialogue between various perspectives and approaches crucial questions related to theology proper from different perspectives. To some degree, my paper addresses some important topics that Rainer Albertz raised in his valuable contribution on "Religionsgeschichte Israels statt Theology des Alten Testaments! Plädoyer für eine forschungsgeschichtliche Umorientierung":

- The bewildering variety of Old Testament theological approaches that have not reached a consensus on *the task, the structure, and the method* of Old Testament theology, as well as the fact that, most often, these approaches hardly interact with each other.[1]
- The problematic notion of an Old Testament theology *in contrast* to Old Testament *theologies*.[2]

---

1. Albertz, "Religionsgeschichte," 6.
2. Ibid., 7–8.

- The presumably inherent tendency to systematize the material, to focus on the history of ideas and concepts and to bear New Testament theology in mind when approaching an Old Testament theology.[3]

In light of these problems, Albertz advocates the primacy of a historical approach and the supremacy of a history of Israel.

Sources for Theology Proper

Historical research on the history of Israel and related to the Hebrew Bible has discussed the questions of primary and secondary (and tertiary and so on) sources. For example, Johannes Renz introduces a functional typology (genuine and subjective primary sources, reflective sources in various forms). These categories seek to account for the degree of subjectivity and temporal distance.[4] In contrast, Christoph Uehlinger only accepts "temporal closeness (zeitliche Nähe)" and "the possibility of dating the material (Datierbarkeit)" as criteria for primary sources.[5] Secondary (tertiary and quaternary sources) receive their information indirectly (without access to archives and combine secondary and tertiary sources for the presentation of a particular interpretation).[6] In light of this distinction the Hebrew Bible is—at best—a secondary source for historical research for the most part.

However, this typology may not apply in the same way when it concerns theological questions. According to Bernd Janowski, the Hebrew Bible is a primary source when it comes to a theology of the Old Testament.[7] He argues for a careful correlation of archaeological, epigraphical, and iconographical data with the Biblical text. Acknowledging the hypothetical character of these reconstructions and the "fragile combination of evidence," Janowski distinguishes the history of Israelite religion from a theology of the Old Testament. The former focuses on the historical context of Old Testament traditions as well as the underlying religious, cultural, and contemporary circumstances. The latter addresses Old Tes-

---

3. Ibid., 11–14.
4. Renz, "Beitrag der althebräischen Epigraphik," 126–31.
5. Uehlinger, "Bildquellen," 34–36.
6. He emphasizes that these categories do not necessarily reflect the degree of reliability because primary sources may already be biased (ibid., 35–36).
7. Janowski, "Theologie des Alten Testaments," 104 n.83.

tament traditions in their literary and redaction-historical context along with their theological concerns.[8] When it comes to particular theological topics, this approach may present the history of a theological idea or concept like the presence of God or the tradition of Zion. It also addresses theological ideas in a particular tradition-historical context such as the priestly tradition. Martin Leuenberger's *God on the Move* exemplifies a similar approach for theology proper.[9] In particular, his conclusion summarizes his integration of biblical texts and extra-biblical evidence: the dynamic God on the move—turning to Israel, humankind, and the world, *and* changing over time and in history—thereby remains the same. These stimulating and valuable contributions seek to integrate theological and historical concerns by identifying, tracing, and building on the history of Israelite literature (Literaturgeschichte). These approaches identify two fundamental sources for theological questions: the biblical texts and extra-biblical evidence. In the following I engage these approaches by identifying crucial questions, by reflecting on reasons for the complex discussion, and by advocating a literary approach that is informed by Mikhail Bakhtin's ideas on literature.

Crucial Questions

A brief survey of the lively discussion on the topic also demonstrates the multifaceted variety of perspectives, concerns and questions, for example the relationship between

- Old Testament Theology *and* a History of Israelite Religion
- Old Testament Theology *and* a Theology of the Hebrew Bible
- Old Testament Theology *and* Biblical Theology
- Old Testament Theology *and* Systematic Theology
- (Theological) Unity *and* Diversity in the Hebrew Bible
- Synchronic *and* Diachronic Approaches
- Descriptive *and* Normative Approaches
- Approaches with *and* without a center ("Mitte") of the Hebrew Bible
- Israelite Religion *and* Ancient Near Eastern religions

---

8. Ibid., 111. These two perspectives may be supplemented and contrasted with theologies of the ANE (ibid., 112).

9. Leuenberger, *Gott in Bewegung*.

This list is hardly exhaustive but illustrates the complexity of the discussion. This complexity derives from a variety of reasons, for example, the complexity of the scholarly field. It should not come as a surprise that many major books on Old Testament theology are written by senior scholars towards the end of their career. In a sense, it is almost arrogant to approach this topic at my age. I ask the reader for forgiveness as I simply want to get started on some aspects of this important discussion and seek to benefit from your scholarly interactions. The sheer mass of scholarly material requires a time-consuming learning process. Perhaps it is hardly possible to write an Old Testament theology and simultaneously interact with other approaches and cover the complexity of the field of research on a scholarly level. Albertz supports his plea for a history of Israelite religion instead of a discipline of Old Testament theology by reminding us of the limitation of our (human) power/capability to do the work.[10] Perhaps this reality requires scholarly settings and attitudes that focus *more* on how my scholarly research can benefit from the research and insights of others and *less* on how I can convince others of my position or approach.

The complexity of the discussion also derives from the very nature of the texts (as well as from the world inside and outside the Hebrew Bible. The Hebrew Bible is dominated by narratives that cover a time frame of several hundred years. So the idea of a story[11] is prevalent, not a system of doctrines or a collection of divine instructions. A story is always selective and exercises (some) control over its parts. I would even argue that, above all, a story seeks to engage the reader; only secondarily does it function to pass on information or present a system of ideas. Therefore, I agree with Albertz to a significant degree when he suggests that the Hebrew Bible eludes a "theoretical and systematizing approach,"[12] because it not only covers a variety of historical periods, but also documents significant changes and exhibits the dynamic of a people on several levels. Any scholarly attempt to approach this material (much less mastering it) must account for this complex reality. In addition, any scholarly attempt to cover and summarize this material is therefore in the process

---

10. Cf. Albertz, "Religionsgeschichte Israels," 24.

11. *This idea of a story* is neither identical with salvation history ("Heilsgeschichte") nor with the reconstruction of a history of Israelite religion. Rather, it is consists of various literary connections (guidelines for reading = *Leseanweisungen*) and describes the whole (which is more than the collection of its parts) that emerges from it.

12. Cf. Albertz, "Religionsgeschichte Israels," 11.

of construction. It seems to me that the variety of approaches is tied to this very nature of the Hebrew Bible.

Many scholars account for the complex historical reality of the Hebrew Bible by emphasizing the variety of traditions, their historical nature, and their historical dynamic. So the adjective "historical" or the plea for a sufficient (historical) depth (or the critique when it is lacking) become almost technical terms for the only appropriate way of accounting for this complexity. However, this is hardly the case. Meir Sternberg's description of Biblical texts points to an alternative that may fruitfully supplement the discussion: "Biblical narrative emerges as a complex, because multifunctional, discourse. Functionally speaking, it is regulated by a set of three principles: ideological, historiographic, and aesthetic. How they cooperate is a tricky question."[13] The aesthetic principle requires a careful appreciation of the literary form of the material that we encounter in the Hebrew Bible and—in my opinion—it must be offered a seat at the table when we discuss the ideological/theological aspects and implications. In particular, paying close attention to the aesthetic/literary aspects of the texts matches one important goal of narratives or stories: to engage the reader. To put it differently with regard to the inquiry of this contribution, the literary architecture of passages or books in the Hebrew Bible display important theological concerns and convictions, i.e., "a purposeful reflection of various perspectives."[14] An attempt at writing an Old Testament theology must account for these dynamics and bring it to the table of our scholarly discussion. Therefore, a dialogue between historical and literary approaches seems indispensable to me when seeking to trace theological ideas, concepts, dynamics, and their developments.

A Dialogue between Historical and Literary Approaches

In a sense, I extend Albertz's discourse model for the history of Israelite religion.

> Ich möchte darum vorschlagen, in Anlehnung an H. G. Kippenberg ein Diskursmodell in die Religionsgeschichte Israels

---

13. *Poetics of Biblical Narrative*, 41.
14. "Sie sollte dabei aber nicht übersehen, daß die Letztgestalt des Alten Testaments nicht von ungefähr gekommen ist, sondern sich weither als ein gezieltes Zusammen-Denken bezeichnen (läßt), das in theologischer Hinsicht vor allem durch das Wissen um das wirkungsmächtige Wort Gottes geprägt wurde." Janowski, "Theologie des Alten Testaments," 123, quoting Sæbø, "Vom Zusammendenken zum Kanon," 124.

einzuführen, weil es mir am ehesten geeignet erscheint, den der alttestamentlichen Tradition inhärenten dialogischen Charakter historisch aufzuschließen. Aufgabe ist es dann, mit Hilfe historischer Rekonstruktion den in den alttestamentlichen Texten »gefrorenen« Dialog in ein lebendiges Streitgespräch verschiedener israelitischer Menschen und Gruppen zurückzuübersetzen.[15]

Albertz's model seeks to disclose the inherently dialogical character of Old Testament tradition(s) with a historical method that identifies various perspectives by historical analysis and construction. I suggest that this perspective may be supplemented by a literary approach that is informed by the literary theory of Mikhail Bakhtin. To put it differently, Albertz's historical and analytical approach identifies and constructs the sources for his synthesis of a history of Israelite religion. Extending this perspective, I mean to start from the theological syntheses of texts from the Hebrew Bible as they are given to us in the texts themselves and engage the various voices from that angle.

Bakhtin reads literature as unified, coherent pieces of art. Coherence does not entail a simplifying schematization that reduces the complexity of texts at the expense of significant details in the literature. Rather it describes Bakhtin's active engagement with incompatible parts of texts in order to trace how an author (for biblical texts we may say a redactor/s) intentionally organizes different perspectives. This engagement builds on Bakhtin's conviction that parts of a text may not be isolated from the whole: "A work's author is present only in the whole of the work, not in one separate aspect of this whole, and least of all in content that is severed from the whole."[16] In light of this perspective, unity and complexity or coherence and tensions are not incompatible. Rather, they may not only reflect multi-faceted aspects of reality, their coexistence and interaction,[17] but they display Bakhtinian ideas of unfinalizability, openness or human surplus. Complexity and tensions do not circumvent but facilitate dialogue and understanding between the voices.

In contrast to other appropriations of Bakhtin and his ideas, my approach is informed by Bakhtin's reading of literature. It should guide the application of his ideas rather than promoting ideas in the literature

15. Albertz, "Religionsgeschichte Israels," 23.
16. Bakhtin, "Methodology," 160. See also the discussion of some historians on parts and the whole of history, Acham and Schulze, *Teil und Ganzes*.
17. Bakhtin, "Methodology," 27–30.

read by him. One must, therefore, distinguish Bakhtin's way of reading Dostoevsky and Rabelais from their way of authoring their own works. Bakhtin's own advice for reading scholarly books offered to students can be a guideline:

> The "active engagement in [the] subject matter" of a scholarly book is "the most important precondition for the productive reading" of it. "The greater and more insistent are our demands towards the book, the more will it speak to us. It does not care for indifferent readers and does not respond to them. The true, engaged work on a book is not a passive appropriation but a living and passionate dialogue with it."[18]

Bakhtin distinguishes two tasks and stages in the dialogue with a work:

> The first task is to understand the work as the author himself understood it, without exceeding the limits of his understanding. This is a very difficult problem and usually requires introducing an immense amount of material. The second task is to take advantage of one's own position of temporal and cultural outsideness. Inclusion in our (other's for the author) context. The first stage is understanding (there are two tasks here); the second stage is scholarly study (scientific description, generalization, historical localization).[19]

The idea of "outsideness" demands proximity and distance. Bakhtin is not concerned about fully entering the text and he does not want to treat texts merely as objects of scholarly studies. His emphasis on dialogue responds to the impossibility of fully entering the text and seeks to facilitate dialogue instead of hindering it. Such an approach neither focuses solely on the author nor on the reader when reading the text. Bakhtin affirms both foci, but challenges their respective monological claims to adequately engage a text. The otherness of the text is not a problem to be overcome but an invaluable opportunity to engage it.[20]

---

18. Mihailovic, *Corporeal Words*, 97.

19. Bakhtin, "From Notes," in *Speech Genres*, 144–45.

20. Having investigated outsideness and "creative understanding," Emerson and Morson note that "[u]nlike alternative forms of interpretation, then, creative understanding demands a double and dialogic activity. In contrast to relativism and modernization, it presumes that the text is truly *other* and contains semantic depths otherwise unavailable; in contrast to enclosure within the epoch, it demands what Bakhtin calls the interpreter's own 'outsideness,' which includes the resources of his

Bakhtin's concern for dialogue may stimulate some reflections when opposite hermeneutical presuppositions and approaches in Biblical studies talk past each other or do not engage each other.

This dialogue within the texts as pieces of literature and between various texts or books is not an end in of itself. It is only the first step in understanding a piece of literature. "Taking advantage of one's own position" requires an engagement with constructions and evidence related to the historical, sociological and religious world of the texts. Thus a dialogue with historical approaches must follow.

Ramifications for Theological Research

By identifying the ongoing dialogue the reader accounts for different and perhaps contradicting perspectives by tracing their coexistence and their interaction. This approach acknowledges the very nature of language and builds on the dialogical orientation of the word or statement. This orientation captures the idea that every word is a response[21] and anticipates a response.[22] Response is crucial for Bakhtin; he argues that "primacy belongs to the response, as the activating principle: it creates the ground for understanding, it prepares the ground for an active and engaged understanding."[23] *Bakhtin's ideas of unfinalizability and openness emphasize that people (and I would add, a "story") always have the potential of developing differently.*

> There is neither a first nor a last word and there are no limits to the dialogic context. . . . Nothing is absolutely dead: every meaning will have its homecoming festival. The problem of great time.[24]

These aspects may also describe the framework for a fruitful dialogue between Jewish and Christian perspectives and engagement with

---

or her own culture's experience" (*Mikhail Bakhtin*, 289; cf. ibid., 429). The common assumption of a bifurcation of politics and religion, social and individual, and church and carnival thus needs to be revisited for the Russian context (Mihailovic, *Corporeal Words*, 132, 135, 147–58).

21. Bakhtin, "Discourse in the Novel," 279; Bakhtin, "Problem of Speech Genres," in *Speech Genres*, 92, 94.

22. Ibid., 75, 145; Bakhtin, "Discourse in the Novel," 280.

23. Ibid., 282.

24. Bakhtin, "Methodology," in *Speech Genres*, 170.

the Hebrew Bible. The idea of openness towards the future (and the development of the "story") is important to the Hebrew Bible as a whole and—in light of the dialogical orientation of the word—also to its parts.

In addition to the benefits related to the story in the Hebrew Bible and its human protagonists, a literary approach informed by Bakhtin seems to be most appropriate for questions of theology proper in the Hebrew Bible. On a hermeneutical and foundational level, important aspects for it describe the framework for the investigation and hold them in tension: unity and diversity, definiteness and definitiveness, continuity and discontinuity, and most of all, openness towards the future. The collection in the Hebrew Bible claims unity (not uniformity) in light of or despite various theological perspectives, disparate historical developments and distinguishable emphases and topics, in particular when it comes to theology proper.

Moreover, the simple fact that the Hebrew Bible is more complex than any given center or framework can describe does not justify that we abandon the possibility of a center or a unifying framework for the Hebrew Bible. The very fact of the Hebrew Bible in its canonical form requires at least a unifying framework, if not a center (cf. Zimmerli's "Glauben an die Selbigkeit Gottes"). The limited collection of books and traditions bears witness to the conviction that there is something that holds them together in distinction from other books and traditions. So it seems to me that it is not a question whether there is a unifying framework; rather, the degree of complexity or ambiguity with regard to this unifying framework should be at the center of our discussion.

Two Illustrations

I would like to illustrate some implications of these ideas with two examples. First, it is widely acknowledged that Zech 1:1-6 function as an introduction to the first chapters of the book, but it is hardly discussed how this observation impacts the reading and the reception of these chapters or whether it might even have ramifications for discussing the transition from Zechariah 8 to Zechariah 9-14. In particular, discussions how and why Zechariah 9-14 is attached to Zechariah 1-8 are rare and, most often, short. Regardless of the results of such discussions, this attachment affects not only the reading of the book of Zechariah but also the Book of the Twelve. The reality is complex; not only the historical but also the literary reality. Whoever added these chapters expects us to engage (or respond to it, speaking with Bakhtin) this surprising and unexpected unit,[25] because it may also exhibit some of their theological reflections and concerns.[26]

Take Job 1:6-12 as a second example. On a literary level, I would describe these verses as a guideline for reading. The information presented in these verses is of no relevance to the development of the story. None of the protagonists show any familiarity with these ideas. But accounting for these verses impact the interpretation of several passages in Job (e.g., chapter 28 or Job 41:1ff) and/or the story as a whole regardless of how the historical process of production is perceived. The importance of this guideline for reading may be illustrated briefly with one example. Satan challenges God by suggesting that Job may not be that pious after all (Job 1:9). He suggests that Job simply follows a utilitarian *do ut des* (Job 1:10):

הֲלֹא־אַתְּ שַׂכְתָּ בַעֲדוֹ וּבְעַד־בֵּיתוֹ וּבְעַד כָּל־אֲשֶׁר־לוֹ מִסָּבִיב מַעֲשֵׂה יָדָיו בֵּרַכְתָּ וּמִקְנֵהוּ פָּרַץ בָּאָרֶץ:

Have you not surrounded him and his family and all that he has with your protection? You have blessed the work of his hands, and his livestock are spread over the land (*NAB*).

The expression captures שׂוּךְ בַּעַד divine action in this context. In Job 3:23 a very similar expression סכך בַּעַד describes the despair of those bitter in soul (Job 3:20) who do not want to be alive but hope to die (Job 3:21):

לְגֶבֶר אֲשֶׁר־דַּרְכּוֹ נִסְתָּרָה וַיָּסֶךְ אֱלוֹהַּ בַּעֲדוֹ:

Men whose path is hidden from them,
and whom God has hemmed in (*NAB*)!

In both cases the expression does not describe divine action in a very positive way. In both cases the line is part of a lamentation or an accusation and it challenges God himself. Nevertheless, they represent completely opposite perspectives. The reader is thereby invited to reflect on Job's and his friends' statements from the perspective of Job 1-2 in general and of Job 1:6-12 in particular: what is the appropriate way of

---

25. I avoid the term "unity" intentionally because it suggests to many the notion of uniformity.

26. See the respective discussion in Wenzel, *Reading Zechariah*.

conceiving and describing divine action in this case? How should the divine itself be understood in light of this action (or non-action for this matter)? These observations shed an interesting light on the ambivalent presentation of divine presence in the book of Job. But this discussion must await further research.

In particular, the second example not only demonstrates the value of Bakhtin's literary approach, it also illustrates how important these foundational reflections are for the discussion of theology proper and its sources.

Points of Departure

In light of these examples, a literary approach informed by Bakhtin emphasizes two (hermeneutical) aspects for articulating a theology of the Hebrew Bible that supplement and interact with other approaches (historical or literary-historical). First, guidelines for reading the various books of the Hebrew Bible exhibit an indispensable and valuable source for theological reflection of these literary units themselves. This precious resource repeatedly elucidates how various and conflicting perspectives have been positioned to dialogue with each other. I suggest that any attempt at reflecting on theological perspectives in the Hebrew Bible must account for this positioning. Second, intertextual relationships within the Hebrew Bible indicate theological concerns to correlate various topics and positions.[27] Through these relationships the Hebrew Bible creates connections that significantly inform theological reflections.

In addition to these hermeneutical aspects, two ideas may stimulate and guide further discussions on theology proper related to the Hebrew Bible. Divine presence and divine absence[28] in Israel has been a fruit-

---

27. As noted, this is *a* point of departure that seeks to highlight important aspects of our discussion. These aspects have not always received the attention I think they deserve. They are not meant to replace other points of departure. In particular, intertextual relationships (in a broader sense because of the difference in culture, language, and the frequent, hermeneutical difficulty of identifying them) to the literature of the ANE is of significant importance.

28. I am grateful for having had the opportunity to present a draft of this paper at the relevant SBL session in Vienna in 2014. Many questions and comments have been very helpful and stimulating. In particular, I was cautioned about the use of the term "divine absence." Some scholars would prefer to speak about divine hiddenness. This comment illustrates well the importance of terminology as well as the significance of theological and hermeneutical presuppositions. My reference to the term "divine

ful venue for discussion. Spieckermann rightly notes that these topics may be "so comprehensive and at the same time so essential to religious perception in the Old Testament and in the Ancient Near East that it may provide the framework for various analyses/or models."[29] They may function as two focal points of a theological ellipse that circumscribe the field of theology proper in the Hebrew Bible. Therefore, in the course of future research, Samuel Terrien's work *The Elusive Presence* deserves detailed discussion on a methodological and thematic level. His impressive survey demonstrates that the idea of divine presence is woven into many books and collections of the Hebrew Bible. The frequency and the variety of this topic make it a valuable focus for reflection. In particular, divine encounters frequently mark crucial points in the development of narratives like Genesis 3 or Genesis 12 or Exodus 19-20.

In light of the ideas of divine presence and absence in the Hebrew Bible in general and Terrien's treatment of epiphanies and theophanies in particular, the relationship between two topics specifically requires hermeneutical and theological reflection: the frequent emphasis on the fact that divine initiative is crucial to these encounters between the human and the divine realm and the idea of an inapproachable God. These topics are frequently combined with openness or an almost defining aspect of surprise with regard to how and when the divine presence manifests itself. If a certain degree of surprise is so important, scholarly research on this topic may have to expect the unexpected when undertaking this task. Statements about divine closeness and distance may surprise, but need not necessarily be amended by adding an "only" like many translation do in the case of Jer 23:23:

הַאֱלֹהֵי מִקָּרֹב אָנִי נְאֻם־יְהוָה וְלֹא אֱלֹהֵי מֵרָחֹק׃

Am I a God near at hand only, says the LORD,
and not a God far off (NAB)?

But all this must await future research.

---

absence" merely reflects its usage in the literature and, for the moment, only serves a heuristic purpose. A detailed interaction with Samuel Terrien's work as well as crucial passages in the Hebrew Bible and an examination of the use of the term "divine absence" in scholarly literature might lead to the conclusion that this term is inappropriate. However, this must await future research.

29. Cf. "so umfassend und zugleich zentral für die religiöse Wahrnehmung des Alten Testaments und im Alten Orient ist, dass sich in seinem Schatten mannigfaltige Darlegungen bergen können"; Spieckermann, "Der nahe und der ferne Gott," 115 n.2.

Bibliography

Acham, Karl, and Winfried Schulze, eds. *Teil und Ganzes. Zum Verhältnis von Einzel- und Gesamtanalyse in Geschichts- und Sozialwissenschaften*. München: dtv, 1990.

Albertz, Rainer. "Religionsgeschichte statt Theologie des Alten Testaments! Plädoyer für eine forschungsgeschichtliche Umorientierung." In *Religionsgeschichte Israels oder Theologie des Alten Testaments?*, edited by Ingo Baldermann, et al., 3-24. Jahrbuch für Biblische Theologie 10. Neukirchen-Vluyn: Neukirchener Verlag, 1995.

Bakhtin, Mikhail M. "Discourse in the Novel." In *The Dialogic Imagination*, edited by Michael Holquist, translated by Caryl Emerson and Michael Holquist, 259-422. UTPSS 1. Austin, TX: University of Texas Press, 1981.

———. *Speech Genres and Other Late Essays*. Translated by Vern W. McGee. Edited by Caryl Emerson and Michael Holquist. UTPSS 8. Austin, TX: University of Texas Press, 1986.

Emerson, Caryl and Gray Saul Morson. *Mikhail Bakhtin. Creation of a Prosaics*. Stanford: Stanford University Press, 1990.

Janowski, Bernd. "Theologie des Alten Testaments. Zwischenbilanz und Zukunftsperspektiven." In *Theologie und Exegese des Alten Testaments/der Hebräischen Bibel*, edited by Bernd Janowski, 87-124. SBS 200. Stuttgart: Katholisches Bibelwerk, 2005.

Leuenberger, Martin. *Gott in Bewegung. Religions und theologiegeschichtliche Beiträge zu Gottesvorstellungen im alten Israel*. FAT 76. Tübingen: Mohr Siebeck, 2011.

Mihailovic, Alexandar. *Corporeal Words. Mikhail Bakhtin's Theology of Discourse*. SRLT. Evanston: Northwestern University, 1997.

Renz, Johannes. "Der Beitrag der althebräischen Epigraphik zur Exegese des Alten Testaments und zur Profan- und Religionsgeschichte Palästinas." In *Steine—Bilder—Texte*, edited by Christof Hardmeier, 123-158. Leipzig: EVA, 2001.

Uehlinger, Christoph. "Bildquellen und 'Geschichte Israels'—Grundsätzliche Überlegungen und Fallbeispiele." In *Steine—Bilder—Texte*, edited by Christof Hardmeier, 25-77. Leipzig: EVA, 2001.

Sæbø, Magne. "Vom Zusammendenken zum Kanon. Aspekte der traditionsgeschichtlichen Endstadien des Alten Testaments." In *Zum Problem des biblischen Kanons*, edited by Ingo Baldermann, et al., 115-33. Jahrbuch für Biblische Theologie 3. Neukirchen-Vluyn: Neukirchener Verlag, 1988.

Hermann Spieckermann, "Der nahe und der ferne Gott. Ein Spannungsfeld alttestamentlicher Theologie." In *Gottes Nähe im Alten Testament*, edited by Gönke Eberhardt und Kathrin Liess, 115-34. SBS 202, Stuttgart: Katholisches Bibelwerk, 2004.

Sternberg, Meir. *The Poetics of Biblical Narrative. Ideological Literature and the Drama of Reading*. Bloomington: Indiana University Press, 1985.

Wenzel, Heiko. *Reading Zechariah with Zechariah 1:1-6 as the Introduction to the Entire Book*. CBET 59. Leuven: Peeters, 2011.

Historical Paul and "Systematic Theology"

To Start a Discussion

N. T. Wright

Introduction

Once upon a time, those who worked in faculties of Theology or "Divinity" made a working assumption about the relationship between exegesis and systematic theology. I don't know if this working assumption ever actually worked, but then, as Bernard Williams said in his last book, pragmatism is undoubtedly true, the problem is it doesn't work. So perhaps we should call it a non-working assumption. Anyway, it went like this: the biblical exegetes do their work, constantly refining what we know about what the Bible says; they then pass this work down the hall to the Systematic Theologians, who arrange it into the larger constructs which can then be used for wider discourse, including teaching in church, apologetics, and so on. Underneath this assumption is, of course, the frequently stated character of Christian theology, namely that it is in some sense or other grounded in the Bible, so that for theology to get too far away from the Bible would be to deny its own supposed presupposition.

As I say, however, the problem with this is that it doesn't work. I have taught in theology faculties on and off for nearly forty years, and the closest I have come to seeing this model in action was once when I met Henry Chadwick on the corner of Broad Street in Oxford and he spoke warmly to me about my then supervisor, George Caird, as someone from whom I ought to learn a great deal. He was right; but I'm not sure that Caird's work ever had visible impact on Chadwick, and I'm quite sure it didn't on John Macquarrie, the Lady Margaret Professor of the time. Nor did systematicians like Maurice Wiles expect to get help from the exegetes, unless the exegetes were people like Dennis Nineham who were, rather obviously, themselves reading the New Testament in the light of some radical theological proposals. If anything, Caird sometimes pointed me in the other direction, saying that if one was ever puzzled by something in New Testament Christology, one should re-read Donald Baillie to check one's bearings.

The situation has, in fact, frequently been much worse than this. In a famous conversation between Paul Tillich and C. H. Dodd at Union Seminary in New York, Tillich basically said that there was no point twiddling his thumbs waiting for some nugget of useful exegesis to emerge from the lexical and text-critical work going on down the hall. This negative comment has frequently been reciprocated, as biblical scholars see theologians who not only claim to be "biblical" but write books about the authority of scripture making more or less no use of the Bible itself in their deliberations. In some quarters, biblical scholars explicitly reject "theological" proposals, as though they were bound to corrupt the pure historical study of the text. If there is supposed to be a marriage of biblical studies and theology, then as Paul says about marriage in Ephesians 5—but in a different sense—it is a great mystery.

Underneath this uneasy situation there lies the question of history. It isn't just that systematic theology claims to be biblical; it is that all Christian thinking focuses, in some sense, on Jesus; and, traditionally, this Jesus is fully human as well as fully divine. In other words, he is firmly situated and rooted in real human history. Unless we are to embrace some sort of Docetism, then not only does it matter that he was "crucified under Pontius Pilate"; it matters that he was a first-century Palestinian Jew living in the Greek-speaking Middle East under the rule of the early Roman empire. People sometimes ask—they sometimes ask *me*—if it would make any difference had Jesus lived in tenth-century China, or twentieth-century Africa; but the very question betrays a complete misunderstanding of what Christian theology is all about. "When the time had fully come," wrote Paul in Galatians 4, "God sent forth his son." The Jewish context, and all the rich blend of history, suffering, prophecy, aspiration, and expectation that it contained, is a non-negotiable element of the meaning of Jesus.

Perhaps I should say that I believe it is a non-negotiable element; because part of the burden of my song today is that for many theologians it has in fact been neglected almost completely. There are two types of this neglect. First, there are those who have quite properly spent their time studying Augustine or Aquinas, Luther or Calvin, Schleiermacher or Tillich or the great Barth himself—but who seem to have little or no idea of what made first-century Jews tick and hence what meaning should be given to that collection of first-century Jewish texts we call the New Testament. That is dangerous enough; but there has recently emerged a second type, which, flying under the false colors of a first-century technical term, "apocalyptic," have claimed that it is actually a *virtue* of Christian theology to see it in a de-historicized form, to sustain the pious fiction that when the theologian reads the New Testament the historical wall between them becomes porous and disappears altogether so that the text speaks directly, "immediately" in the technical sense of that word, into the interpreter's mind and world. Such a move, of course, renders careful linguistic, textual, and historical study of the original texts in their setting irrelevant and even counter-productive: a convenient fiction for those who want to indulge pious fancy without hard work. One sometimes meets a popular version of this—one such was reported to me just last night—according to which the supposed perspicuity of Scripture means that it will speak as God's word to every generation and that any attempt to situate it historically is therefore both unnecessary and distracting.

I hope I do not have to argue against these extraordinary suggestions. But I have the sense nevertheless that a great deal of Christian theology has taken a not dissimilar position in practice, and my task here, beginning from my own historical (and of course theological) study of Paul, is to propose not only that there are many things in such a study which can refresh the particular topics of systematic theology but also that when we really study Paul for all he's worth we discover that he himself addresses the larger structural question as well. Fresh study of Paul thus not only enables us to glimpse new angles on Christology, soteriology, eschatology, and so on—though of course it does that, and I shall include those centrally in this presentation—but also to see more clearly what theology itself might be. And, since Paul is himself an exegetical theologian one might say that he models for us something of what it means to wrestle with ancient texts and contemporary meanings . . . though, importantly, he himself would say that the texts with which he was wrestling, the scriptures of ancient Israel, stood in a different relation to his work than his own writings should do to ours. More of that, perhaps, anon.

So, to put down a marker from the start: Christian systematic theology cannot do *without* Paul, but it often hasn't known what to do *with* him. It has often reduced him to a few passages on justification, or a couple of examples of early Christology, and for the rest has regarded him as a polemical figure whose sharp and angular words do not fit easily into the delicately shaped boxes of our proposed constructions. Theology has not even glimpsed, I think, the central point I have argued in my recent book (*Paul and the Faithfulness of God*), that Paul actually *invents* the discipline we now, with long hindsight, call "Christian theology"; that he does so for a very particular purpose; that he gives it a particular shape and character; and that he, like the Jesus whom he loved and served, can only be properly understood when we locate him within the turbulent and multi-layered world of his day.

Putting Paul in His Place

That task of location has, supposedly, been the aim of much biblical study. However, even in the hallowed halls of the historical critics things have often been very different. A hundred years ago a genuine effort was being made, by people like Adolf Deissmann, to locate Paul within that complex world; but this was largely abandoned in the long years of existential and neo-Kantian interpretation led by Rudolf Bultmann. Instead, exegetes have arranged their Pauline work around a string of essentially theological debates, which swirl around one another confusingly and routinely twist the texts to fit. These debates grow out of, and flow into, one another, though, again confusingly, they do not map on to one another. Was Paul basically writing about anthropology or cosmology (Bultmann vs. Käsemann)? Was the center of his thought justification or salvation history (Käsemann vs Stendahl, echoing older debates between the followers of F. C. Baur and those who were arguing for some form of *Heilsgeschichte*, ending notably with Cullmann)?

Or, taking a different tack, was Paul really an *apocalyptic* theologian, or a proponent of salvation-history (Martyn)? Or is the real opposition "apocalyptic" against "justification" itself (Campbell)? And so on. In particular, of course, we have had thirty-five years of trench warfare between something which I originally labelled the "new perspective," but which is now both quite old and certainly highly pluriform—"not-so-new perspectives," in other words—and something which inevitably gets called the "old perspective." And the heat aroused by this debate is certainly not caused by rival hypotheses of historical exegesis. Everyone knows that there are big theological issues at stake, though since the exegetes are not trained to address them and the theologians don't want to know about the historical basis for the argument this remains a dialogue of the deaf. As Bertrand Russell said of a long-standing argument he had had with one of his former wives: She still thinks she is right, and I still think I am right. Once again: the mystery of the non-marriage of theology and exegesis.

At the heart of my argument, both in the book and here, is the belief that the so-called historical-critical school of exegesis, as it has spent its energies prolifically over the last century, has by and large led us into a quagmire of false antitheses: *not because it was historical and critical but because it was not nearly historical or critical enough.* Here is the irony of the school that runs from Baur to Bultmann to Käsemann and on to Martyn and others today: they have used enough "history" to fill their pages with learned footnotes, but part of their "critical" stance has been precisely and explicitly to stand over against the text, helping Paul to say more clearly what they thought he was really trying to say, peeling away not only layers of later glosses but also the parts where Paul, unaccountably to this school, persisted in thinking and writing more like a first-century Jew and less like a good existentialist Lutheran. This method, dignified with the name *Sachkritik*, "material criticism," has bedeviled some of the main work of the last hundred years.

While we acknowledge and even applaud the intention to enable the biblical text to speak into very specific and dangerous situations, such as Germany between the wars, the elevation of that unique and peculiar moment, with all its cultural and philosophical currents, into a hermeneutical grid for interpreting the New Testament, was itself a triumph of an essentially anti-Jewish, anti-historical, and I believe, anti-Pauline impetus. Even when it celebrates its great triumphs, such as Käsemann's commentary on Romans, it always needed, but alas did not always have, a slave in the back of the chariot to whisper in the great man's ear, "Remember, you too are historically situated."

In particular, and this brings us closer to my central concern, so much mainstream Pauline study of the last century has proceeded on the assumption that since Paul taught justification by faith rather than works his religio-historical situation must be non-Jewish. He picks up early Jewish formulae, say Bultmann and Käsemann, in order to twist them into a new shape relevant for his Gentile audience. He abandons the idea of Davidic messiahship in order to present Jesus as the *kyrios*, a word familiar to the pagans both in cult and in imperial rhetoric. And so on. Thus the study of Paul, in these highly influential movements at least, has partaken of what I perceive actually to be the problem afflicting so much systematic theology to the present day: the assumption that the Jewish setting of the original texts can and even must be set well aside in order to allow a non-Jewish discourse to proceed unchecked.

To this, for the moment, I merely say one thing: that at least in Paul's mind the idea of worldwide mission was itself a profoundly *Jewish* idea, based precisely on biblical messianism: "his dominion shall be from the one sea to the other, and from the river to the ends of the earth." When Paul launches Romans by speaking of the Davidic messiah as the heart of the gospel, and ends his theological exposition by speaking of the Root of Jesse who rises to rule the nations, these are not accidental throwaway remarks. They provide the telling framework for the whole thing. Paul believed that the God of Israel, the creator of the world, had been faithful to his promises, both *to* Israel and *through* Israel to all humanity, both *to* humanity and *through* humanity to all creation. This "faithfulness of God," one possible translation of Paul's biblically allusive phrase *dikaiosynē theou*, lies at the heart of his theology, both explicitly in Romans and implicitly throughout the rest of his letters. And it is this motif, I suggest, much misunderstood in both exegesis and theology, which gives us the clue to his fundamental contribution to Christian theology— and by "fundamental contribution" I don't just mean "the main thing Paul had to say," but "the thing Paul said which ought to be foundational for all systematic theology worthy of the name." Paul, the apostle to the pagans, was a theologian who taught about the one true God over against the world's idols; and this true God was both the creator and the God of Israel. These matter, not just as points to be acknowledged before moving on to other more interesting topics, but as strands to be visible all the way through.

Paul in History: Worldview and Mindset

For the last twenty years and more I have used one particular tool of historical analysis, and I perhaps need to say a word about it here since my main argument first focuses on it and then hinges on it. This tool is the analysis of what I and some others call "worldviews." Three things to note. First, a worldview in this sense (as opposed to the sense used by some post-Schaeffer American writers) is not what you look *at*; it is what you look *through*. It is the normally unstated and unexamined set of background phenomena—not only ideas but activities and physical objects—which form the unseen lens through which people perceive their world. Second, I use "worldview" to indicate the lenses shared by a community, and I use "mindset" to indicate the particular personal variation on that worldview belonging to a person within it. Third, this corresponds quite closely to what social scientists such as Clifford Geertz have written about, though the terminology sometimes differs. The word "worldview" may appear to privilege the metaphor of sight, which can be unfortunate, but I and others use it in a technical sense where this should not be a problem.

I have devoted considerable space, both in *Paul and the Faithfulness of God* and in earlier works, to trying to understand the worldview of second-temple Judaism. This obviously involves sharp focus on what for many in theology and the church is a dangerous area, the long dark years between (if you like) Malachi and Matthew. Some have criticized me for thus allowing non-canonical materials—Josephus, Qumran, the Pseudepigrapha—to influence my reading of the biblical text. To this I reply that if you want to understand how ideas and phrases are used in the first century it helps to look at the first century, not the fourth century BC or the fourth century AD (still less the sixteenth century AD!); and that in fact until fairly recently most clergy had on their shelves not only Whiston's *Josephus* but also Edersheim's *Life and Times of Jesus the Messiah*, and they plundered these works cheerfully when preaching on the New Testament. To suggest that the pure canonical text ought to be self-explanatory without such aids is to commit again a form of Docetism, and to invite the rejoinder that if you don't want to use first-century non-biblical materials you're going to have difficulty simply translating Paul, never mind understanding him. A theology that supposes it can be "biblical" without also being firmly "historical" is like someone trying to dance on one leg only.

At the heart of worldview-analysis stands the *symbol*. This is usually something concrete, either an object or a particular style of behavior or life. For second-temple Jews, it was the Temple and the Torah, with Torah playing out in circumcision, the food laws, the Sabbath and so on: these were the *symbols* which marked out the Jews from their pagan neighbors.

For first-century Romans, it was the Empire. I recently went with some students to the Augustus exhibition in Rome, and the symbols are very clear, on statues and coins and decorative artwork found from Spain to Syria, from Gaul to Galilee. Symbols form the concrete expression of the worldview: they are the things which say, in a thousand small but telling ways, "this is who we are." And my argument in chapter 6 of this book is that the central symbol of Paul's newly shaped worldview was *the church itself*: the church as the *united* and *holy* community. The church didn't have the normal Jewish symbols—though we should note that Paul clearly wants his ex-pagan converts to embrace certain aspects of Jewish life, such as the rejection of idolatry and sexual immorality. But the church certainly didn't take on the symbols of the pagan world. The church itself—a community living with an astonishing social mix, and living an astonishing lifestyle of holiness and care for the poor—was the sign, the symbol, the thing you could see on the street that said something new was happening. Paul's churches didn't mint coins, but they believed they could see the face of Jesus in one another, as the Spirit transformed them. They didn't keep the Jewish food-laws, but they practiced a new sort of Passover meal whose radical egalitarianism was a major challenge to the social and cultural structures of the day. And so on.

Along with the symbol goes the *narrative*. Here is I think a key element against which many theologians, and some exegetes, push back hard (why?). Ever since Hans Frei's work we have been alerted to the importance of narrative in the Bible and to its suppression in the modern period. Many still regard narrative theology, or exegesis, as a fad which they can do without. But narrative, properly understood, goes precisely with the ancient Jewish, and early Christian, emphasis on *the goodness of creation*: the one God has made this world of time and change; and on *the call of Israel*, and the story of God's people from Abraham through Moses and David and the prophets and the exile . . . and the strange puzzle about whether exile has really ended, and whether Yhwh has really returned to his temple. Once again, to try to avoid all this, in the interests of an abstract timeless theology, is I think a large step away from the Bible, away from Paul, away from Israel, away from Jesus himself. It is like trying to understand the tenth game of the fifth set of a Wimbledon final without any reference to the previous games and sets. To say that this reduces everything to the horizontal dimension rather than the vertical, as people often do, is to miss the point altogether. In the Bible, the divine rescue operation following Eden and Babel is the call of Abraham. To flatten that out is to risk both Docetism and Marcionism. Many there are who go that route.

From Worldview to Theology

All this leads to the central point I want to make: in Paul we not only see the first flowering of Christian theological reflection on topics which have remained central from that day to this—Christology, soteriology, eschatology, and so on. We see also, and at a deeper level, *the reason why such theological reflection was necessary in the first place, and the reason why it remains necessary in the church ever afterwards*. My central case is that *Paul believed theology to be the necessary task of the church if it was to be the church*. Without the symbols of Judaism, and without taking on the symbols of paganism, you might think it was asking for the moon to expect people to form united, holy communities, living as a kind of radically renewed Israel within the pagan world. If you know anything about human nature and sociology it looks like a ridiculous experiment. For Paul, the thing that would hold it all together was the constant, radical fresh exploration of the central themes of ancient Judaism: God himself, God's people, God's future for the world. Monotheism, election, eschatology.

But the point was not simply that these topics needed to be worked out—as though a couple of generations might do the hard work, write the books, and leave all subsequent generations to put their feet up and look the answers up when they needed them. No: this theological task is, for Paul, the ongoing task to which the whole community, and every member of it, must be devoted. Here is the genius of Paul's vision: as he says in Colossians, to warn everyone and teach everyone in all wisdom, in order to present everyone mature in the Messiah. Or, in 1 Corinthians: be babies when it comes to evil, but in your thinking be grown-ups. Or, in Romans: do not be conformed to this world, but be *transformed by the renewing of your minds*. For Paul, theology was the task of the whole church, each one contributing their particular gifts. It was constantly rooted and grounded in worship and prayer, and we can see that going on in Paul's letters themselves, as some of his greatest theological formulations look very much like prayers and hymns. Each community, then, and each generation, has to engage in the same exercise, the same discipline, the same activity; because this activity, this theologizing, is what will enable the central symbol to stand firm. It's hard enough trying to get a Christian community to be both united and holy. Trying to do so without prayerful, scriptural theology is simply impossible. If you don't believe me, look around the western world today.

Within this, the choice of central topics is, I think, vital. It is notorious that Pauline theologians have had trouble fitting together all the various things he says, not only on the Law—always controversial—but on many other things like Christology. (Did he believe that Jesus was fully divine? Was Messiahship important for him? And so on.) I believe, and the thought experiment at the heart of this book reflects this, that our problem has been not least that we have approached Paul with the categories of much later questioning. Commentaries from a hundred years ago often assume that Paul was basically supplying material for later debates, so that for instance Rom 1:3–4 was a statement of Jesus' humanity followed by a statement of his divinity. I think Paul would have been very puzzled: he certainly assumed Jesus was fully human, he certainly believed he was fully divine, but (as I've said elsewhere) these beliefs, like two sharp signs on the musical stave for the Hallelujah Chorus, tell you what key the music is to be played in, not the particular tune that you are going to hear. More recently, the great majority of Pauline scholars have assumed that the best way to organize his theology is through the topics bequeathed to us by sixteenth-century soteriology, which was itself a reaction to fourteenth- and fifteenth-century soteriology, with a massive focus on something called "justification," a topic which was allowed to swell out of all biblical proportions to cover the whole of soteriology, and a corresponding downplaying of ecclesiology and/or ethics.

We have then approached these questions through the lens, not of first-century thinking, but of the various philosophies of Kant, Hegel and more recently Heidegger and others. We have thus often spent our energies giving nineteenth-century answers to fifteenth-century questions, with occasional reference to the fourth century as well. My central proposal is that systematic theology would do well to try to give twenty-first century answers to first century questions; and that the first century questions might themselves give us some clues as to how to do that.

I have therefore proposed, in line with various Jewish scholars, that the central theological topics ought to be monotheism, election, and eschatology—one God, one people of God, one future for God's world; and that one of Paul's greatest achievements was to rework each of those topics, quite thoroughly, around Jesus himself and around the Spirit. This, of course, needs working out in exegetical detail, and the book supplies plenty of that. But let me tell you how what I think I now see in Paul challenges (what I take to be) the normal proposals of systematic theology.

This is my main point to you, from a position of great ignorance about modern systematics but also of great puzzlement whenever I do look over people's shoulders and see what's going on. *From at least the fourth century onwards, Christian theology has constantly been trying to make theological bricks without the biblical straw.* Here, at a very broadbrush level, is what I have seen going on. People used to say things like, "Of course, the first Christians were monotheists, so they couldn't think of Jesus as fully divine; it was only when they moved out of the Jewish world into the Gentile world that this became possible." Or they used to say, "The Trinity was a philosophical construct of the fourth century which of course the New Testament never for a moment envisaged." They would often say, "Well, perhaps the early Christians did move in a binitarian direction; but it was only with the Cappadocian Fathers that the Spirit was recognized as fully divine." And so on.

This line of thought has been assiduously propagated by two quite different strands of thought. First, there have been the Roman Catholic and Orthodox theologians whose vision of theology, and indeed of revelation itself, of God's Word itself, was that the Bible was only ever part of it, only ever the start of a longer process. With a strong view of Spirit-led tradition, they were very happy to affirm that the apostolic writings themselves were only as it were a preliminary exploration, which needed to be filled out with the more mature reflections of Irenaeus or Athanasius or whoever. Thus it was clearly in the interests of those who believed in the equal importance of Scripture and tradition, if not the primacy of the latter over the former, to insist that you don't find the key theological *topoi* clearly stated in Scripture, but only in the later Fathers and indeed their successors.

Second, however, the same point has been made *ad nauseam* by a very different school: the liberal theologians of the last two centuries who accepted the historical analysis just offered but read it the other way round. There you are, they said: the New Testament knows nothing of Trinity, Incarnation, and so on—so we can discount all that Patristic stuff as so much Hellenistically inspired philosophical speculation. I have met this in liberal Anglican theology; I have also met it in various Jewish writers, notably Geza Vermes. This was what lay behind that nine day's wonder, *The Myth of God Incarnate*, in the 1970s.

All this has left conservative protestants looking extremely vulnerable. They want to resist not only that liberalism but also the many evils they see flowing from it. But, in their tradition (oh, irony), they don't want to put any weight on tradition, only on Scripture! What can they do? This is what has driven many in recent years to lay aside their former suspicions of ecclesial tradition and to place a new emphasis on creeds and councils and the "great tradition," and to join their Catholic friends in looking down their noses on the mere exegetes who try to call them back to the scriptures which used to hold pride of place. No, they say: look what happens when you say *"sola scriptura"*: you have the chaos and confusion of modern north American Protestantism. To which I reply: that's because they are not doing *sola scriptura* properly. They, like their radical counterparts in Germany and elsewhere, have operated a radical canon within the canon. And when you put the canon back together again, and put Paul back together again, you will find a new angle of vision on all your key topics, and a new frame of reference within which they can be stated robustly and creatively.

The result of all this is, I believe, that we need to tell the story of the Bible and theology very differently. Let's begin with monotheism. Ancient Jewish monotheism was never, until the later Rabbis, an inner analysis of the being of the One God. It was always a polemical doctrine, against paganism on the one hand and dualism on the other. Paul reaffirmed this in countless ways. But, as a result of what he believed about Jesus, he believed that the One God had now been made known as the God who sent the Son and the God who sent the Spirit of the Son. Galatians 4:1–11 says it all: you either have something remarkably like the trinity, or you have paganism. Many other passages—extraordinarily ignored or downplayed by both liberal exegetes and conservative theologians!—point in the same direction. Of course, Paul doesn't use the language of substance and nature. But that is precisely my point. I believe that the later philosophical language represents a noble attempt, like that of the Rabbi when asked to summarize the Torah standing on one leg, to say what has to be said but without the benefit of the framework in which it actually makes the best sense. Yes, if you are addressing conversation partners whose universe of discourse is neo-Platonism or late stoicism or whatever, no doubt you will want to try to say things in their language. But the tragedy then, which has never I think been resolved, is that the church forgot, perhaps deliberately (?), the Jewish narrative within which what they wanted to say made much better sense still.

What is this Jewish narrative? I have argued in various places that the key story is the double story of exile and return. On the one hand, second-temple Jews were still looking for the fulfilment of the 490 years spoken of in Daniel 9. The true exile—the political and spiritual exile, much deeper than the geographical one—was not yet over. On the other hand, the same Jews were still looking for the return of the divine glory, the Shekinah, the radiant Presence of Israel's God, to the temple. The great promises of Isaiah 40 and 52, of Ezekiel 43, of Malachi 3, had not yet been fulfilled. There may have been a sense, based on faith and memory, that when they rebuilt the temple God had somehow resumed his residence; but there is no second-temple scene corresponding to Exodus 40, 1 Kings 8, or Isaiah 6. One writer after another in the New Testament exploits exactly this gap to say, very clearly: these promises are fulfilled in Jesus and the Spirit.

The word became flesh, *kai eskenosn en hemin, kai etheasametha ten doxan autou*. Paul belongs exactly here. He tells and retells, in particular, the story of the Exodus, which is not only the story of rescue from Egypt, of the giving of Torah, and the wilderness journey to the inheritance—all of which play vital roles in his exposition. He tells, in particular, that element of the Exodus narrative which we often forget: that this constitutes a fresh revelation of who Israel's God is, and that the climax of the narrative, bringing in a sense a closure to the two-volume work Genesis and Exodus, is this God coming to dwell, as an act of sheer grace despite Israel's sin, in the tabernacle beside the camp. The glory of Yhwh dwells with the people, and leads them through the desert to the promised land, constituting them as the new-Eden people, even though that will bring tragedy as well as promise. My case here, then, fully consonant with fourth-century Trinitarian theology but I believe setting it on much firmer foundations than people had realized it possessed, is that so far from the early Christians telling stories about Jesus and then gradually realizing they had to say something about God, they rather found themselves telling the story of how this God had visited and redeemed his people, had accomplished the new exodus, had constructed the new tabernacle—and found themselves compelled to tell this story by talking about Jesus as the place where the living God had come to dwell with his people, and about the Spirit who, like the pillar of cloud and fire, led them through the desert to their inheritance.

They weren't telling Jesus-stories and embellishing them with God-language. *They were telling God-stories*, indeed, the ancient Jewish

God-story, *and claiming it had all come true in Jesus and the Spirit.* If I am even half right here then the last two hundred years of attempts to put exegesis and theology together have been missing the point. The Fathers did a great job of expressing all this in fresh language, but by ignoring the ancient Jewish and biblical roots they gave huge hostages to fortune. Chalcedon itself looks like a confidence trick. It didn't need to. The tools were at hand, but the narratives had been forgotten, and the scriptures reduced to collections of *topoi*, or allegorized into the teaching of virtue and spirituality. Virtue and spirituality are very important, but the scriptures are more than collections of *topoi*. Systematic theology needed them in the fourth century, and it needs them today. Better late than never.

When it comes to soteriology, the central Jewish category is election itself: Israel, chosen for the sake of the world. This does not "instrumentalize" Israel, as some have wrongly charged—or, if it does, it does no more than what in the Bible God always seems to do, making humans in his own image so that they can run his world for him, calling specific people for specific tasks. This is not a form of abuse, as is sometimes ridiculously suggested, but a great ennoblement and honor. Abraham's seed will bring blessing to the world. Israel will be the light to the nations. The Messiah will rule from sea to sea. The new covenant which will result from the Servant's work will bring renewal to the whole creation: myrtle instead of briar, cypress instead of thorn. The great narratives of scripture, particularly those which speak of exile in terms of punishment for sin and hence of return from exile in terms of atonement and rescue, provide the rich resource from which the whole New Testament, and particularly Paul himself, launch their particular expositions of how the one God has rescued the world through the death and resurrection of Jesus and the gift of the Spirit. In Paul's hands—perhaps I should say in his heart, because he regularly speaks of this with a sense of grateful love—the ancient Jewish themes come rushing together into fresh configuration. The cross and resurrection stand at the heart of this, of course, though Paul never says the same thing twice about either of them, but allows them to act as the lens through which one argument and line of thought after another is brought into specific focus. One of the most frustrating things for me, after thirty-five years of new and not-so-new perspectives, is to see systematic theologians still going round and round in circles discussing justification with minimal reference to the story of Israel and, often enough, with minimal reference to the Holy Spirit. Yes, there are notable exceptions. But this speaks to me of an attempt to address sixteenth-century issues without first-century help—merely using Paul's text as a source for phrases and ideas, and treating Romans in the usual low-grade way, as a text about how to get saved in which Abraham plays only a small back-up part and the whole story of Israel becomes a detached treatise on a different topic. This sort of theology, if I may be so bold, is like sex without marriage: an attempt, so to speak, to get the climax without the covenant. And from this all sorts of ills have arisen, as you might expect. Let me just mention two.

I know that in some rules of contemporary rhetoric any mention of the Third Reich automatically causes points to be deducted—it's basically morality by cliché—but in this case it's very relevant. Generations that had used forms of *Sachkritik* to help Paul shuffle off his Jewish coil; generations that had been told that Judaism was "the wrong sort of religion"; generations that had read not only Luther's wonderful expositions of the love of God but also his terrible denunciations of "the Jews"—these traditions paved the way, only too obviously, for many in the church to find themselves ill-equipped to stand against the blasphemous nonsense of 1930s anti-semitism. Equally, generations that had read Paul from a Reformed standpoint but had systematically screened out the fact that every time he talks about justification he was also talking about Jew and Gentile coming together in a single family where ethnic differences were irrelevant—such generations had prepared the way for another great twentieth-century blasphemy, the heresy of Apartheid, and indeed its transatlantic counterparts which in a measure continue to this day. Of course, in all these situations there were many other factors involved. And of course the greatest wickednesses of the last few centuries have been perpetrated by avowed atheists. But my point remains: a curtailed and truncated reading of Paul's soteriology, one which for generations had refused to allow him to say what he was actually saying in Romans and Galatians in particular, was crucial in preparing the way for supposedly Christian viewpoints in which ethnic divisions, and ethnic hatreds, were allowed to become normative, rather than being ruled out before they could begin.

All this applies as well to theories of atonement and justification. Here there is a particular problem which arises from the privileging of Romans—something of which I am sometimes accused. If you treat Romans as a systematic exposition of soteriology, rather than as a Christologically grounded exposition of the faithfulness of God—in which of course soteriology plays a central role—you will be tempted at once to treat, say, Rom 3:21–26 as a more or less complete statement both of atonement and of justification. It isn't. It summarizes what Paul says at much greater length on these topics elsewhere, in Romans and other letters, in order to set out the *main* argument, which is about the *dikaiosyne theou*, the faithfulness of God, revealed through the faithful death of the Messiah for the benefit of all the faithful.

That is why the treatment of Abraham in Romans 4 is a decisive part of the same argument: Paul is there explicitly expounding Genesis 15, the chapter where God made the covenant with Abraham, in order to demonstrate that in the Messiah these promises are fulfilled. Let this small example serve metonymically for the larger point I want to make. Again and again, theology has approached exegesis not with the desire of hearing what the text is actually saying, but with the hope that it will speak to the particular questions we bring to it. Answer: it will, but only if you pause long enough to let it first reframe the question and then answer it in the reframed terms. That pause is, I think, part of what it means to believe in the authority of Scripture. And I regret that, like the pause between the two halves of a chanted psalm-verse, it is all too often omitted in the hurry to get on with the job.

The same could be said on the third topic, eschatology. Many in the last few centuries have written about eschatology, but it's often been hard to get the focus exactly right, not least because most western theologians have still been thinking in terms of the mediaeval question of heaven, hell, and perhaps Purgatory (or perhaps not). The biblical idea of God's kingdom coming on earth as in heaven has been quietly sidelined. For Paul, however, it was clear: the Messiah was already reigning, in fulfilment of the Psalms and Isaiah, and the last enemy to be destroyed, like the enemy king being killed at the end of a triumphal procession, would be death itself. It is a matter of astonishment to me that some systematic theologians who are otherwise apparently orthodox in their views can suppose the bodily resurrection, including Jesus' empty tomb, to be an optional extra. That speaks of a theology that has forgotten what Paul was all about. But it's more than this. The inaugurated eschatology of the New Testament, the "now and not yet" for which Paul is rightly famous, can only be understood in second-temple Jewish terms—which means that rich blend of what has misleadingly been called "apocalyptic" and what has misleadingly been called "salvation history." The end has come forward into the beginning, which is both a total and unexpected shock and, in retrospect, the fulfilment of all that had been promised. And Paul's teaching on the *parousia*, the second coming, owes a great deal to his Christologizing of the ancient biblical "day of the Lord," just as his ethics, also to be understood eschatologically, owe a great deal to his rethinking, around the Spirit, of the Jewish vision of a fully human life.

When we put all this together, as I've tried to do in the final part of the book, we find a rich engagement, already there in Paul, with the political, religious, and philosophical worlds of his day, as well as with his own Jewish context. From all this I want to highlight, in conclusion, one of the philosophical points which comes out very strongly. It has to do with epistemology, always a vital topic in theology as well. For Paul, it is part of his inaugurated eschatology that the full and final revelation not only of God's purposes but also of his personal identity had been revealed in Jesus, and particularly in his death and resurrection. "He is the image of the invisible God," he writes in Colossians; in other words, as in John 1:18, Jesus is the starting-point for the knowledge of God.

It isn't that we know who God is, ahead of time, and somehow fit Jesus into that. It is that Jesus requires that we take all our earlier ideas of who God is and allow them to be remade around him. That is why the gospel is "foolishness to the Greeks," as well as scandalous to the Jews, and it is on the horns of that dilemma, I believe, that so much systematic theology has found itself impaled. Rather than articulate the scandal, we have avoided the deeply Jewish meanings which a true historical exegesis would reveal; then, leaving behind the foolish Jewish message of the gospel, we have translated it into something a bit less foolish. Paul would insist, for reasons anchored in the cross and resurrection themselves, that this is not the way. The *method* of his theology is itself rooted in the *message*. The old world is crucified to Paul, and he to the world, and this must work out epistemologically as well as morally and spiritually. Likewise, with the resurrection the new creation has been born, a new world coming into existence within the ongoing old one; and the appeal of Rom 12:2, not to be conformed to the present age but to be transformed by the renewal of the mind, is therefore essentially an appeal for a resurrection-based epistemology. We are to see everything, beginning with God himself, in the light of the renewed-Jewish eschatology, through which we understand how election has been and is being fulfilled, through which the faithfulness of the one God comes at last into full view. I know that many theologians would insist on all this as well. I hope I have provided a more solid foundation, should that be necessary, for this understanding of a theological epistemology.

All this is focused, finally and fully, in the rich life of prayer where, once again, Paul takes essentially Jewish forms and reworks them through Messiah and Spirit. I have spoken elsewhere of the way in which Romans 9–11 is book-ended with a classic short lament and a classic short doxology. I have argued in detail that in 1 Cor 8:6 Paul takes the central Jewish prayer, the Shema, and discovers Jesus at the heart of it. I end with Ephesians 1, which is a great reworked Jewish *Berachah*, a blessing of the one God of creation and covenant, of exodus and tabernacle. As all great systematic theologians have always known, Christian theology is never more truly itself than when it is prayer, and vice versa: "Let us bless God, the father of our Lord Jesus, the king, who has blessed us in the king with every spirit-inspired blessing in the heavenly realm . . . he chose us in him, he foreordained us for himself, to the praise of the glory of his grace . . . we have deliverance, the forgiveness of our sins; his plan was to sum up the whole cosmos in the Messiah, everything in heaven and on earth. In him we have been made heirs, and have been marked out with the spirit of promise, the guarantee of our inheritance; and, once more, all this is to the praise of his glory."

Every topic in Christian theology is rooted in this prayer. There is no need to move away from it and seek another foundation. From this standpoint, as Paul says in 2 Corinthians, he is able to take every thought captive to obey the Messiah. That is, of course, harder than it sounds. All too often the captives have taken over the camp. My underlying aim in *Paul and the Faithfulness of God*, and this paper, is to reclaim Paul's perspective: to let Paul teach us not only *what* to believe but *how* to believe, not only the basic content of systematic theology but its ongoing method. Only if we recover this perspective, I believe, will theology be able to serve the purpose for which Paul believed it existed: to enable the church to live as the united and holy community, so that the powers of the world would be confronted with the symbol which declares, more deeply than words and books, the fact that that Jesus is Lord and they are not.

III. FUTURE: CONSTRUCTIVE WAYS FORWARD FOR BIBLICAL THEOLOGY

The Wisdom in Rupture

Brueggemann's Notion of Countertestimony for Postmodern Biblical Theology

Carey Walsh

WALTER BRUEGGEMANN'S NOTION OF biblical countertestimony includes texts that portray divine hiddenness, ambiguity, the unreliability of God, and distressful, negative experiences of Israel's God. In discussing this concept, Brueggemann gives credit to ancient Israel for its remarkable theological candor, its willingness to confront God, to entertain *God's* failure in the covenantal relationship, as well as its own disappointments and doubts about this relationship. Such testimony is indeed counter to the affirmative, compelling depictions of God elsewhere in biblical tradition. The relationship of Israel to its God, so constitutive of its identity, was nevertheless critically examined from all angles. A chief benefit to biblical theology of countertestimony, then, is its realism; it speaks to a dynamic, living relationship that allows for the expression of difficulties. Another benefit of attention to Israel's countertestimony is that it enables Brueggemann to incorporate Wisdom literature into his biblical theology, which has for too long been neglected, being regarded as, he notes, the "embarrassing stepchild" of Old Testament theology for most of the twentieth century.[1] Indeed, Wisdom has more often been considered the lesser material of the Old Testament, characterized as a worldly, practical philosophy with none of ancient Israel's trademark features such as covenant, providence, Sinai, patriarchal promises, creedal formulae, etc.

---

1. Brueggemann, *Theology*, 334. Gerhard von Rad, he notes, is an important exception. His two-volume *Old Testament Theology* addressed Wisdom literature in the fourth section of the first volume and in his last major work, *Wisdom in Israel*.

This essay explores the textual testimony of negativity about God most evident in the theodicy of Job and asks: What is gained *theologically* from reading negativity? Can a negative portrayal of God perform a theologically constructive service? I agree with Brueggemann that there is a theological function to disputatious texts, not only in the dialogues of the debating friends where we might well expect it, but also in the book as a whole. My thesis is that the Book of Job addresses a bitter ambivalence toward God, along with the suffering of the righteous and problem of evil. Job is an abrasive text that scours reader complacency and expectations of God. In effect, it smashes any conceptual idols of who God *ought* to be, whether this be the retributionist God of the Deuteronomist, or the God pleased by Wisdom's advice for following the correct path down the road to a good life and avoiding promiscuous Dame Folly. Reader expectations about who God is supposed to be would also include, I suggest, a concept more pronounced in Christian theology, namely, omnipotence, so that Job offers a powerful prophylactic against omnipotence and the other Omnis of renown (e.g., omniscience, omnipresence, omnibenevolence), which can become dangers when they constrain the divine to predictability by insisting that God fulfill our human categories.

The conceptual abstraction of omnipotence, "all powerful," vouchsafes a divine all-ness that has to "be there" and so acts as a theological assurance of security in matters of faith. It illustrates Derrida's claim that Western philosophy has privileged the category of essence.[2] Other relational aspects of God are relegated to background so that pure, expansive power can be asserted. The nature and quality of that power and its effect on God's people and the surroundings is secondary to power alone. Any such abstractions, of all-power (omnipotence), all-presence (omniscience), and all-goodness (omnibenevolence), however, strain the human ability to know and encounter God. Abstractions about the essence of God reify the divine life force, its living freedom. The theological conundrum is and always has been that God cannot be captured by human articulation, no matter how precise. Negativity in texts, then, can serve a vital function by protecting divine freedom to exist and flourish beyond the conceptual categories enlisted by biblical writers and theologians alike. This emphasis on uncertainty in knowledge, and the limits and even deconstructive quality of language finds a receptive audience in postmodern theological discourse. Hence, Brueggemann rightly sees

---

2. Caputo, *Prayers and Tears*, 15.

a great deal of benefit for postmodern endeavors in biblical theology to reading the texts that are contained in Israel's countertestimony. The theodicy in Job presents a negative space for God, since so much of the book is given over to dialogue of the friends about God, while God makes no appearance until the end. The negative space or absence of God in the book reveals the heady theological ruptures in understanding the divine, that while frightening, also pose a unique opportunity for a fragile opening into a God beyond concepts, even beyond the covenant.

Divine power is in dispute in Job. There are two appearances of God in the book (chapters 1–2 and 38–41), but dialogues about God's absence fill the rest of its pages. Scholarly consensus views the prose prologue (1–2) and epilogue (42:7–17) as originally independent traditions that were attached to the poetic dialogues comprising the rest of the book. However, literary analysis of these two originally independent traditions does nothing to diffuse the theological bomb their juxtaposition triggers: God, by being present with the Satan in concocting sufferings for Job to endure, *is* a knowing, fully complicit accessory to Job's torture.[3] In fact, God voices only a single limitation for the Satan: "The Lord said to Satan, 'Very well, he is in your power; only spare his life.'" (2:6). Restraint against the murder of an innocent man is hardly a showcase for divine mercy. The two celestial beings wager over whether catastrophic suffering would alter Job's faith. Further, it is God, *not* Satan, who mentions Job as exemplary in faith and in avoiding evil (1:8). Since exemplary faith has actually attracted catastrophe in this instance, the story would seem to counsel readers to aim safely lower for a spiritual mediocrity, beneath God's radar for praise. What began as an idle hypothetical between God and Satan quickly turns deadly. Job is an ambiguous testimony of a potent God, since divine absence persists for the majority of the book, and, the God who does appear in the prologue and whirlwind theophany is a handful of negativity. My contention is that the God evident in Job acts as an inner biblical critique—a proto-postmodern one—against omnipotence.

The well-known theophany of Job occurs near the book's end.[4] God clearly appears to Job, is interventionist about it, and is utterly commanding in presence. From the whirlwind, God booms a soliloquy on all he has created. Experientially, Job is finally and unmistakably before God for which he has long been petitioning. Yet, even in this potent, almost men-

---

3. It is not until later, with 2 Enoch and the New Testament that the figure of Satan represents the embodiment of evil. See Pagels, *The Origin of Satan*.

4. The Lord appears from the whirlwind, 38:1—41:6. Cf. Jer 23:19 and 30:29.

acing, display of divine presence, the theophany itself is all words. God is the subject of talk, first between Job and his friends for most of the book, then by God himself in the whirlwind speech. This is no dialogue here, and Job has petitioned precisely for a dialogue, his day in court with God, a day to present his case. Instead, it is a flurry of rhetorical questions, asked and answered by God. Job, for his part, speaks or is permitted to speak only twice (40:4–5; 42:2–6). Indeed, there is so much talk, so many words, that it is as if God is *not* there, narcissistically too full of his own presence to notice the presence of an Other, Job.[5] God does all of the talking and none of it is about his faithful servant Job, the grieving, exhausted man standing before him. This meeting of two becomes only a divine monologue, which erases the presence of the other, by muting him utterly. This sort of narcissistic absenting is further confirmed when God's idea of restoration is to give Job a second batch of children to replace the ones destroyed in the celestial bet, *as if* this makes up for it. The largesse of such gift giving does not address or even acknowledge Job's grief. Divine omnipotence is clear, clearly on display, but wholly unimpressive.

The whirlwind theophany has negative elements about the divine in that it delimits the holy to power alone. The dialogues throughout the book have revolved around God's potency and the aptness of when it is deployed. The painful silence of God for thirty-six chapters follows with a four chapter long torrent of talk by him. This divine talking spree would certainly answer the silence that has pained especially Job. The whirlwind speech acts as a kind of conceptual idol. It is, in Jean-Luc Marion's sense,[6] an idol because it is fixed presumably by the gaze of what humans—the friends of Job and all subsequent Bible readers—want of their God, a mighty, all-powerful, *deus-ex-machina*, deity booming out of the sky with certain authority. Marion criticizes conceptual abstractions in theology because they limit God and are really only a mirror of our own wishes projected. If we examine the whirlwind speech in Marion's terms, then, we can critique our need to create a conceptual idol of omnipotence. For, we and Job's friends want *essentially*, not YHWH, "who is who he is" (Exod 3:14), some ineffable, dynamic life source or existence itself, but a Greek god, a Zeus controlling the fates, to explain the fate of their pitiable friend. In the whirlwind account, we get one, a

---

5. This inability to see the Other is a glaring weakness of the deity, in its refusal to have "renounced all claims to domination or sovereignty." Levinas, *Difficult Freedom*, 8.

6. Marion, *God Without Being*, 7–18.

God not only in control of the fate of humankind but one so thoroughly omnipotent that he both manages the constellations of the heavens, the weather patterns of the earth, and even micromanages each sneeze of the Leviathan,[7] the flight of the raven, and the crude mothering instincts of the ostrich (38:41; 39:14; 41:25).[8] This God of Job, then, is frozen by the *human* need for divine, 'bring-it-on' omnipotence. If this whirlwind speech is conceptually descriptive of who God really is, there is no actual room for relationship with others. A narcissist is too preoccupied with himself to notice others, and such an omnipotent display is otherwise uncharacteristic of the God of the Bible, who has predicated his entire creation on interaction. Feuerbach was correct to note that so much of theology *is* projection on a blank screen of what humans want God to be, need him to be.[9] The negative image (like negative theology) is biblical prophylactic against this temptation.

The dialogues throughout the Book of Job have critiqued the notion of retributive justice, namely, that God reliably punishes the wicked and rewards the righteous. This notion has a long history, particularly in the Deuteronomistic traditions and the early Wisdom traditions of Proverbs. But, in the epilogue of Job, a shift occurs, for the God portrayed in the final chapter reverts right back to it, rewarding Job and punishing his friends, as if the new brood of children could possibly make up for Job's trauma. But this time, after a book-length critique of it, the portrait of the familiar, a retributionist God itself looks diminished. Its use in the epilogue savagely dismantles the doctrine of retribution precisely by demonstrating how bizarre its theology is in relation to innocent suffering. The prologue and epilogue function as a satire that reduces God to puppeteer, experimenting on his people and then grandly rewarding them punitive damages at the end. Job's ten children are still dead, even as he receives a second set in the epilogue (Job 42:13). The silence of Mrs. Job (she is nameless) in response to God's "reward" speaks volumes.

---

7. The Leviathan is envisioned here to be some sort of large, water beast, perhaps a crocodile, with allusions to the chaos monster in Ugaritic mythology. At the very least, it manifests the alien Other, Newsom, *Book of Job*, 248–50; Smith, *Early History of God*, 85–86.

8. Newsom suggests that the ostrich symbolizes not only an absence of wisdom, but also an "anarchic joy," which may have drawn the attention of a dominating God. *Book of Job*, 247.

9. Feuerbach, *Essence of Christianity*, 20.

The wisdom of Job, then, is radically deconstructive. It offers in parable a critique of a retributionist, omnipotent God. It exposes the limiting idol of God as all-controlling creator, hovering over creatures to manage each and every last detail, *except* the broken heart of his faithful servant, Job. The doctrine of retribution must be retired if Israel—or any of us—is to move forward in faith. God is no sniper, picking off the innocent for no other reason than that he can, thinking all the while that they make for such easy targets they almost deserve what they get. Job, we recall, was singled out for his laudable faith in God.

One revelation offered in the book of Job is the severe ambivalence we have toward God and how that finds an outlet in our theological imaging of him. The prologue elicits ambivalence about God. Indeed, it forces the issue. This stark notion of God's complicity with evil remains in the text as is. It reveals not so much a doctrine of God-as-he-is-in-himself but, more tellingly, the hidden human fear that this is how it all really works behind the scene. The prologue exposes a truth all right, namely, that humans are often caught up short by uncomprehending pain, with their assumptions about God as caring, aloof, attacking, vacillating wildly.

The whirlwind speech may be the climactic scene of the book of Job, depicting as it does the long longed-for presence of God. But as brute cipher for providential control over everything, it is functionally an idol. An idol debases God, biblical discourse is throughout fiercely insistent on this. Here though, in the book of Job, biblical discourse about idolatry gives way to an enacted occasion—a parable—of it.[10] Readers have long been unsatisfied and disturbed by the God of the whirlwind speech. Perhaps they are meant to be. The theophany is not theologically descriptive but rather provocative; not of what God *is*, but of who he cannot *merely* be. The biblical image evokes protest.[11] It directly challenges the theological tendency to limit God to any one element, be it divine power, mercy, gender, etc. The exposé of God's power in Job serves, by its very overreach (e.g., ostrich nurturance), as a biblical critique of omnipotence for the divine.

In fact, Mrs. Job may have been the only working theologian in that household when she said, "Curse God and die" (2:9). The Death of God movement begins, then, not in the mid-twentieth century but back even

---

10. McFague, *Speaking in Parables*, 66–91.

11. For discussion of the multiplicity of voices and the dialogic character of texts over and above their descriptive elements, see Newsome, *Book of Job*, 21–31; Green, *Makhail Bakhtin and Biblical Scholarship*.

further with Mrs. Job.[12] Curse *this kind* of God, she would seem to be saying: the one who takes bets with the Satan; the one who singles out the righteous for experimentation; the one who is bracingly omnipotent, *way* above their own pitiful sorrows, yet also curiously impotent. For, this all-powerful God had been vulnerable to the Satan's questions in the first place, much as Eve had once been to the serpent's. Moreover, this divine speech about divine power thrums on for far too long. Job had conceded the issue at 40:4–5, but God continues for the rest of the chapter and the next for a total of sixty-one verses. This theophany dedicated to divine power, in effect, protests too much. If God is no better than an insecure mortal, subject to the dares of others far less powerful, or defensive to the point of overkill, or if God is merely divinized abstraction, namely, Omnipotence Unquestioned, then perhaps theology should heed Mrs. Job's counsel and "curse him and die."

A God, then, *reduced* to omnipotence is not a God worth knowing. He is an idol only of power, of what humans need him to be, namely, a security system against uncertainty. The whirlwind theophany in Job transgresses into the idolatrous because it restores the God of interventionist and retributive power, which the book otherwise takes such great pains to debunk. While God's display of omnipotence in the whirlwind theophany indeed may soothe our anxiety about "who's in charge here, anyway?" it leaves a distasteful ambivalence about encountering this hectoring Captain of Fate, who commands that we ready for battle by girding up our loins (38:3; 40:7). Gone is the marriage metaphor in Israel's relationship with its God, gone is the "slow to anger and abounding in steadfast love" deity (Exod 34:6–7; Num 14:18–19; Ps 86:15 103:8; 145:8; Jonah 4:2; Joel 2:13; Neh 9:17). Ironically, the friends of Job might have appreciated this encounter more than Job himself could, since they have been advancing God's undisputed sovereignty and right to retribution. In the epilogue, the friends are chastised by God and accept it in silence: "the LORD said to Eliphaz the Temanite: 'My wrath is kindled against you and against your two friends; for you have not spoken of me what is right, as my servant Job has'" (42:7). Perhaps, they even welcome it, for divine wrath confirms the basis of their theology even as it is directed at them. The whirlwind God is an idol, almost a bully of one, where power is vouchsafed, but at the expense of other signal divine characteristics,

---

12. Altizer, *Radical Theology*; Rubenstein, *After Auschwitz*.

for example, loving-kindness, love, covenantal awareness of the other, steadfastness, relational encounter, mercy, etc.

Divine love still exists in this whirlwind portrait but it is remote, evident in how God daily takes care of all the species he has made, and how he has the sun and stars come to the skies. It is indeed full-time work for this creator to keep the diversity of the cosmos going: the whirlwind speech is essentially a curriculum vitae of the creator's efforts. Hence, while the divine encounter champions a creation theology, the price is steep, namely, a God isolated by divine power. It has the effect of reminding Job that his problems, as *one* member of *one* of these species, in the vast expanse of the universe God maintains, are quite small in comparison. The whirlwind theophany for Job is, at best, then, an exercise of divine "tough love."

Job perhaps catches up with his wife's perspicacity at the end when he says, "I disown what I have said, and repent in dust and ashes" (42:6). His response to the whirlwind speech is ambiguous, as ours might be. It can be humble contrition or the sheer brokenness of wanting to be left alone. "Dust and ashes" signals the self-mortifying humility that accompanies grief,[13] while "disowning one's words" is biblically impossible (as surely the deity would know); it is the reason why there are strict biblical laws governing vows (e.g., Num 30:6–7; Ps 76:11; Matt 5:37). Words, once spoken are "out there" they have reality, and cannot be taken back (e.g., Jephthah's vow, Judg 11:30–31). Interpreters have long wondered if Job's contrition is genuine or rather a mocking dismissal of this brutish God, an idol of power, "By hearsay I had heard of you, but now my eye has seen you" (42:5). If genuine, then Job is cowed and appropriately reverent. But if mocking, then his words overplay deference, with sarcasm really the covert dismissal of such totalizing power.[14] Brueggemann understands in Job's reply nothing more than a general "existential trust" in the effect of this text, and of life in general. That uncertainty is a constitutive facet of relating to the divine. There is a divine presence and power in Job, but it is not on human terms. Nor is it for biblical interpreters to erect theological conceptualizations of divine essence. Instead, countertestimony emphasizes a suffusing, dynamic divine presence who will not be domesticated.

---

13. As "sackcloth and ashes" do elsewhere in the Bible: Jer 6:26; Jon 3:6; Dan 9:3; Neh 9:1; Esth 4:1–3; Matt 11:21.

14. In situations where the powerless are so completely outmatched by the powerful, they nevertheless find covert means of resistance through sycophantic playacting and mockery. Scott, *Domination and the Arts of Resistance*.

The purpose of attending to the negativity of God in such cases is not to proffer an abject theology, nor is it an exercise in rebellious pleasure. It is instead to see negativity as corrective of human distortions, then and now, about God. Biblical theology is interested in what the texts mean, not only what they meant in Israel's time and so the clashing of testimonies has an instructive effect beyond that of Israel. Brueggemann is insistent that there is always uncertainty with interpretation, i.e., that textual meaning can never be locked down by methods. A living God cannot fully yield to the interpreter's methods because God's very life force is beyond both language and the interpreters' full cognition. Brevard Childs nicely articulates the paradoxical twist of biblical interpretation: "The very divine reality which the interpreter strives to grasp, is the very One who grasps the interpreter."[15] With Job's ambiguous response, then, the interpreter is fully grasped by a omnipotence's discomfiting edges, and forced to revisit its theological aptness. Where postmodern thinkers would run with the indeterminacy of Job's reply to his divine encounter, Brueggemann sees a theological purpose even in texts that reveal negative notions of God. The cognitive uncertainty of Job and of the biblical author after all is a creaturely humility that allows divine freedom to flourish beyond biblical theophanies. And such humility before vastness is no defeat. It allows divine presence to be free even from biblical imaging.

Bibliography

Altizer, Thomas J. J. *Radical Theology & the Death of God*. Indianapolis, IN: Bobbs-Merrill, 1966.
Brueggemann, Walter. *Theology of the Old Testament: Testimony, Dispute, Advocacy*. Minneapolis: Fortress, 1997.
Caputo, John D. *The Prayers and Tears of Jacques Derrida: Religion without Religion*. Bloomington, IN: Indiana University Press, 1997.
Childs, Brevard. *Biblical Theology of the Old and New Testaments*. Minneapolis: Fortress, 1992.
Feuerbach, Ludwig. *The Essence of Christianity*. Translated by George Eliot. Lawrence, KS: Digireads, 2012.
Green, Barbara. *Makhail Bakhtin and Biblical Scholarship: An Introduction*. Atlanta: Society of Biblical Literature, 2000.
Levinas, Emmanuel. *Difficult Freedom: Essays on Judaism*. Translated by Seán Hand. Baltimore, MD: Johns Hopkins University Press, 1997.

---

15. Childs, *Biblical Theology*, 86–87.

Marion, Jean-Luc. *God Without Being*. Translated by Thomas A. Carlson. Chicago: University of Chicago Press, 1991.
McFague, Sallie. *Speaking in Parables: A Study in Metaphor and Theology*. Minneapolis: Fortress, 2000.
Newsom, Carol A. *The Book of Job: A Contest of Moral Imaginations*. New York: Oxford University Press, 2003.
Pagels, Elaine. *The Origin of Satan: How Christians Demonized Jews, Pagans, and Heretics*. New York: Vintage, 1996.
Rubenstein, Richard L. *After Auschwitz: History, Theology, and Contemporary Judaism*, 2nd ed. Baltimore, MD: Johns Hopkins University Press, 1992.
Scott, James C. *Domination and the Arts of Resistance: Hidden Transcripts*. New Haven, CT: Yale University Press, 1992.
Smith, Mark S. *The Early History of God: Yahweh and the Other Deities in Ancient Israel*, 2nd ed. Grand Rapids: Eerdmans, 2002.

The New Testament as the Covenantal-Liturgical Consummation of the Biblical Story?

A Critical Evaluation of Scott Hahn's Biblical Theology of the New Testament

Janghoon Park

Introduction

AN INFLUENTIAL CATHOLIC BIBLICAL theologian well known for his conversion from the Protestant faith, Scott Hahn deserves our attention for his fresh way of understanding the concept of covenant and liturgy as two organizing principles of the biblical canon.[1] Unlike the existing biblical-theological understandings of covenant,[2] Hahn's biblical theology is characterized by God's three-stage developmental covenant-making with Israel, aimed at achieving "the restoration of the filial relationship with all humanity."[3] Interwoven with this unique developmental view of the biblical covenant is Hahn's notion of liturgical trajectory and teleology, namely that the liturgical dimension is central in understanding the unity of the biblical canon in both its content and context. My goal in this paper is

---

1. The comprehensive information regarding Scott Hahn's ministry and theology, along with a list of Hahn's published works, can be found in http://www.salvationhistory.com.

2. For a survey of the studies on the concept of covenant, see Hahn, *Kinship by Covenant*, 1–22, and "Covenant in the Old and New Testaments," 263–92. For various biblical-theological models built around the theme of covenant and some critical appraisals of those models, see Niehaus, "Theologically Constructed Covenants," 259–73.

3. Hahn, *Kinship by Covenant*, 336.

to show that this covenant-oriented, liturgy-focused, biblical-theological framework proposed by Hahn fails to find support from relevant biblical texts. Towards this end, I will first investigate the covenantal dimension of Hahn's view, and then critically assess the liturgical aspect of his biblical theology.

A Description and a Critical Assessment of the Covenantal Dimension in Hahn's Biblical Theology of the New Testament

A Description of Hahn's Three-Stage Developmental View of the Biblical Covenants

Hahn constructs his own three-stage developmental view of God's covenant-making, from the current historical critical research on the ANE covenant types.[4] For Hahn, covenant is a way of establishing a familial bond, especially a father-son relationship, between two parties. This is a serious relationship that involves obligations and promises and is ratified by an oath-taking ceremony, a way of appealing to the deity as witness and invoking his curse in the event of breaking the covenant stipulations.[5] Covenants can be classified into three types depending on how obligations are distributed: in a "kinship-type" covenant, both parties share obligations; in a "treaty-type" covenant, the superior party imposes obligations on the inferior one; in a "grant" type covenant, the superior party obligates himself to bestow a grant on the inferior party in return for the latter's meritorious service.[6]

On the basis of this understanding of the nature and types of the ANE covenant, Hahn constructs a threefold developmental view of the historical outworking of the biblical covenant. In his view, God's covenant relationship with his people consists in a father-son relational dynamic, in which God progressively reconfigures the relationship by moving from a kinship-type covenant, to a treaty-type covenant, and then finally to a grant-type covenant.[7] In other words, God starts with a kinship-type covenant—which involves mutual obligations—and when the other party

---

4. Ibid., 22–33, 332–38.
5. Ibid., 3–9.
6. Ibid., 29.
7. Ibid., 332–35.

fails to fulfill the covenant obligations, he moves into a disciplinary mode by making a treaty type covenant—which imposes obligations only upon the inferior party. But when the inferior party provides an exceptional obedience to the covenant stipulations, God renews the relationship by making a grant type covenant, in which he takes an oath to bestow blessings in response to the inferior party's extraordinary obedience.

For Hahn, this three-stage relational adjustment occurs first in the life of Abraham, and then in the history of Israel. God initially makes a kinship-type covenant with Abraham in Gen 15, but when Abraham engages in "illicit sexual relations" in Gen 16, God reconfigures the covenant relationship into a more severe, treaty-type covenant in Gen 17 where he imposes the obligation of circumcision upon Abraham and his descendants.[8] But when Abraham shows an extraordinary fidelity to God by offering his son Isaac in Gen 22, God responds by making a grant-type covenant with Abraham and thereby takes an oath to grant all of the promises unconditionally—i.e., not only the promises made in this third covenant but also all of the promises made in the previous two covenants.[9]

The same three-stage covenant making is also observed in relation to Israel. God begins with a kinship-type covenant at Sinai, but when Israel commits idolatry God alters the covenant relationship into a stricter, more disciplinary configuration: he implements penalties of relational distance by introducing the mediation of the Levitical system (in response to the first generation's Golden Calf incident), and by making the Deuteronomic covenant in a treaty-type configuration (in response to the second generation's Baal worship at Beth-peor in Num 25).[10] These alterations reflect God's disciplinary attitudes and forebode Israel's ultimate failure to remain faithful to the covenant.[11] God then reconfigures the covenant relationship under grant type covenants, first in response to Phinehas' exceptional zeal for God at Beth-peor (i.e., the Levitical covenant which unconditionally guarantees the perpetual priesthood of Phinehas' descendants in Num 25:6–13),[12] and then in regards to David's holy desire to find a place for God's dwelling (i.e., the Davidic covenant

8. Ibid., 117.
9. Ibid., 120–23.
10. Ibid., 68–83.
11. Ibid., 66–67, 77–78.
12. Ibid., 155–60.

which unconditionally ensures the everlasting royal priestly reign of the son of David in 2 Sam 7).[13]

These three grant-type covenants (i.e., the Abrahamic, Levitical, and Davidic covenants) resulting from God's three-stage relational adjustment converge and find fulfillment in the consummate covenant relationship made possible by the new covenant, which is itself another grant-type covenant established on the basis of Christ's exceptional obedience to God.[14] In Hahn's view, the New Testament writings assume this transhistorical tripartite relational trajectory and affirm its consummation in the new covenant. They do so by highlighting the ways in which the new covenant fulfills one or more previous covenants involved in the three-stage development of the covenant relationship in the Old Testament.[15]

A Critique of Hahn's Three-Stage Developmental View

Does this three-stage developmental view of the biblical covenant adequately reflect the perspectives of the New Testament authors? Many criticisms can be made, but we have room here for only one, namely that Hahn's developmental paradigm misleadingly represents the Deuteronomic covenant as a failed covenant arrangement with nothing positive to contribute to God's fulfillment of his redemptive purposes through the new covenant. In Hahn's scheme, the Deuteronomic covenant is essentially God's way of administering fatherly discipline to Israel for their idolatry; it serves the "remedial" or "pedagogical" purpose of rehabilitating the sinful Israel and restoring them as God's obedient son.[16] However, as revealed in the history of Israel, this supposed remedial purpose of the Deuteronomic covenant is thwarted by Israel's persistent breach of the covenant stipulations. Hahn himself indeed recognizes the ultimate ineffectiveness of this alleged disciplinary measure attributed to God, especially since God's redemptive purposes in his developmental scheme are advanced *only* by the grant type covenants made with a few extraordinary individuals on the basis of their exceptional covenant faithfulness.[17] In Hahn's scheme, therefore, the Deuteronomic covenant ultimately repre-

13. Ibid., 176–213.
14. Ibid., 271–72.
15. Ibid., 237, 276–77, 325–27.
16. Ibid., 90.
17. Ibid., 265–67.

sents God's failure, functioning only to reveal the severity of Israel's unfaithfulness and divulge the naivety and incompetence in God's dealing with Israel.

Hahn's assignment of this exclusively negative role to the Deuteronomic covenant, however, fails to do justice to the New Testament writers' recognition of at least two ways in which the Deuteronomic covenant contributes to God's fulfillment of the covenant promises. First, contrary to Hahn's understanding of God aborting the interim Deuteronomic covenant arrangement and resorting to the grant type covenants, Paul, particularly in Rom 5–8, shows that God's giving of "the law" (i.e., the Deuteronomic covenant) is not an unsuccessful interim measure that merely highlights the necessity of a better solution. Rather, the law is part of God's single overarching redemptive plan, in which it serves the secret purpose of paving the ground for Christ's task of dealing with sin once for all. It is important here to consider N. T. Wright's observation of the way in which Paul's thought progresses from Rom 5:20 through 7:13 and 8:3. In Rom 5:20, Paul says that "the law came in that the transgression might increase."[18] In Rom 7:13, he elaborates on 5:20 by stating that sin produced death through the law "*in order that* sin might be shown to be sin" and "*in order that* through the commandment sin might be utterly sinful." This sin-increasing and sin-highlighting role of the law is meant to serve the purpose revealed in Rom 8:3: "God condemns sin in the flesh [of Christ]." In other words, Paul's point emerging from these verses is that the law functions to highlight the essence of sin and thereby captures *sin as a whole*, so that God may be able to "condemn sin in the flesh" of Christ *once for all* (cf. Rom 6:10).[19] This shows that at least in Romans, the law is not merely a former disciplinary measure now superseded by a more mature relational dynamic. Rather, it is God's designed confederate in his Christ-centered redemptive strategy of capturing the totality of sin in Christ and dealing with it once for all.[20]

Hahn further downplays the significance of the Deuteronomic covenant when he argues that it is not the Deuteronomic covenant but the Abrahamic covenant that provides the mechanism by which the sin of the world can be transferred to Christ and be dealt with by his death.

18. The English Bible version quoted in this essay is *NASB*.

19. This reading is persuasively presented by Wright, "Romans," 551.

20. Paul does talk about a pedagogical role of the law in Gal 3:23–25, as pointed out by Hahn (*Kinship by Covenant*, 265–67). However, Hahn's heavy attention to Galatians (a whole chapter devoted to Gal 3–4) should have been balanced by taking Romans into consideration.

It is difficult to deny that the New Testament writers, especially when communicating the atoning significance of the death of Christ, draw on the sacrificial images from the Levitical system (e.g., Rom 3:25; 8:3; Heb 9:1—10:25, esp. 9:25 and 10:12) and refer to the Deuteronomic covenant (e.g., Rom 8:1-4; Gal 3:13; Heb 9:15-22).[21] In Hahn's developmental scheme, however, the Levitical sacrificial system and the Deuteronomic covenant are merely the bygone interim covenants overridden by the permanent arrangements of the grant-type covenants. For this reason, Hahn appeals to the Abrahamic covenant—i.e., the grant type covenant made in Gen 22 at the end of the three-stage covenantal adjustment in Abraham's life—as the place where the principle of Christ's vicarious, atoning death is revealed. More specifically, Hahn's focus is on the principle of oath-making in the Abrahamic covenant of Gen 22 as the very mechanism by which Christ's death becomes vicarious and acquires atoning significance.

Hahn reasons as follows. When making a grant-type covenant, the superior party's oath-making is necessary, as it functions to guarantee unconditionally the fulfillment of the promised blessings in response to an exceptional obedience provided by the inferior party.[22] This oath-making is performed through a self-maledictory ritual, a ritualistic demonstration of what will happen to the oath-maker in the event that he fails to keep the sworn promise.[23] Applying these principles to his reading of Gen 22, Hahn identifies Abraham as the inferior covenant party who shows an exceptional fidelity (i.e., his offering of Isaac) and views God as the superior covenant party who guarantees the fulfillment of the promises with a self-maledictory ritual. Hahn then makes a problematic exegetical move: he claims that Abraham's offering of Isaac, the very act that demonstrates Abraham's fidelity, should be understood *also* as God's self-maledictory ritual.[24] That is, Abraham's attempted murder of Isaac should be seen as Abraham and Isaac acting together in God's stead to demonstrate ritually what will happen to God if he fails to fulfill the sworn promises. Abraham's offering of Isaac then, is on the one hand, a meritorious act offered to God (the act that merits God's reward), and on the other hand, a ritual act performed on behalf of God (the

---

21. See e.g., Finlan, *Paul's Cultic Atonement Metaphors.*
22. Hahn, *Kinship by Covenant*, 93.
23. Ibid., 50-59.
24. Ibid., 126-27.

act that guarantees a reward for the demonstrated merit)—both at the same time! This collapse of distinction between Abraham's meritorious service and God's self-maledictory ritual implies a *virtual identification* between Abraham-Isaac and God. In Hahn's own words, "God identifies himself so closely with Abraham and his seed that he has to share in whatever curses their sins provoke, if that is necessary to fulfill his oath."[25] For Hahn, it is precisely this identification made here between God and Abraham-Isaac (and also their descendants) that serves as the curse transferring mechanism in Gal 3:13.[26] For "by swearing a covenant oath [through his self-curse enacted by Abraham-Isaac] God subjected himself to the curse that rightly belonged to Israel and Gentiles" and had Christ bear this curse vicariously.[27]

This way of prioritizing the Abrahamic covenant of Gen 22 and deriving the mechanism of Christ's atonement from it is unconvincing for at least two reasons. First, there is no reason for viewing Abraham's offering of Isaac as God's self-maledictory ritual. According to the current covenant research on which Hahn heavily relies, oath-making in a grant-type covenant can be performed in so many different ways that self-malediction can be expressed *implicitly* without involving an explicit self-maledictory ritual.[28] Oath swearers, for example, can simply make "a solemn confession of the deity's existence" or show mere "acknowledgement of God as a witness."[29] In Genesis 22 then, God's invocation of himself by saying "I swear by myself" (Gen 22:16) is sufficient to function as a covenant ratifying oath. There is no need, therefore, to identify Abraham's offering of Isaac as God's self-maledictory ritual.[30]

---

25. Ibid., 127.

26. At this point, Hahn also draws on the Aqedah tradition by positing a typological relationship between Isaac's potentially atoning near death and Jesus' atoning death (ibid., 256). However, the Aqedah tradition's prioritization of Isaac's obedience (i.e., his obedient consent to be bound) rather than that of Abraham's, and its speculative description of Isaac's atoning death (e.g., voluntarily shedding blood and reduced to ashes) are congruent neither with the emphases of the text of Gen 22 nor with Hahn's covenantal reading of Gen 22. For more details regarding this point, see Davies and Chilton, "Aqedah," 515; Daly, "Soteriological Significance," 45; Vermes, "New Light," 143.

27. Hahn, *Kinship by Covenant*, 256.

28. Hugenberger, *Marriage as a Covenant*, 210.

29. Ibid., 201.

30. In fact, Hahn himself does not identify self-maledictory ritual as a necessary feature of the grant-type covenant applicable to Gen 22 (*Kinship by Covenant*, 93,

Second, even granting that Abraham's offer of Isaac is God's self-maledictory ritual, this enacted event will materialize only if God breaks the covenant. In other words, if we consider the definition of self-maledictory ritual, the enacted curse will be actualized *only if God fails* to keep the promise. Until such failure occurs on God's part, the ritually enacted curse is never actualized. Exactly the opposite is true, however, in the case of Christ. Christ's vicarious bearing of the curse is the proof, not of God's covenant breach, but of God's covenantal faithfulness! The curse borne by Christ, therefore, was not generated by God's breaking of the covenant, nor was it transferred to Christ by the identification between God and Abraham-Isaac. The mechanism of covenant-making Hahn ascribes to the Abrahamic covenant in Gen 22 simply does not work. A key to understanding the origin of the curse and its transfer to Christ is the Deuteronomic covenant. It was because of Israel's breach of the Deuteronomic covenant that the curse was incurred by Israel. And it is by embodying Israel under the Deuteronomic curse that Christ had the curse transferred onto himself and bore it vicariously, with the result that the Abrahamic promises were fulfilled (Gal 3:13; 4:4–5).[31] Hahn wrongly identifies the Abrahamic covenant, rather than the Deuteronomic covenant, as providing the mechanism by which the curse is incurred by Israel and transferred to Christ.

In summary, Hahn's failure to recognize the contributions of the Deuteronomic covenant to God's redemptive history, and his concomitant prioritization of the Abrahamic covenant in Gen 22, show that his three-stage developmental scheme of God's covenant-making fails to capture adequately the New Testament understandings of the nature and function of the Deuteronomic covenant.

101–2).

31. Debate continues regarding the nature, manner, and scope of Christ's connection with humanity that accounts for the atoning efficacy of Christ's death.

A Description and a Critical Evaluation of the Liturgical Dimension in Hahn's Biblical Theology of the New Testament

A Description of the Liturgical Dimension of Hahn's Biblical Theology of the New Testament

Perhaps in an attempt to complement his covenantal scheme, Hahn emphasizes the liturgical dimension of his covenantal framework in his later work.[32] In Hahn's covenantal framework, God's people are primarily a covenant people within the liturgical settings. That is, they enter into a covenant relationship with God through covenant rituals, and they define and celebrate their identity and life according to the covenant document—all within the liturgical settings.[33] For Hahn, it is also within this liturgical context that both the Old Testament and the New Testament are canonized, interpreted, and appropriated, serving the purpose of establishing, maintaining, and renewing God's covenant relationship with his people. This liturgical context of Israel's existence as a covenant people exerted profoundly shaping influences on the composition and final form of the biblical canon.[34] Hahn argues that this can be seen in the "liturgical trajectory" and "liturgical teleology" found in the overall story emerging from the canonical text.[35]

By "liturgical trajectory" and "liturgical teleology," Hahn means that the biblical meta-narrative is unfolded in such a way that God's liturgical intentions for humanity and the world—namely, God's design of the world as a cosmic temple and his intention to make Adam and his descendants priest-kings who worship God—are sustained after Adam' fall. More specifically, these original liturgical intensions are re-expressed in Israel, and are ultimately fulfilled through Christ's restorative ministry.[36] This pattern is first detected when God's choice of Abraham and his deliverance of Israel from Egypt are seen as the divine process of establishing Israel as a kingdom of priests who serve God and rule the world with God's presence among them in the tabernacle.[37] Hahn notes

---

32. Hahn, "Canon, Cult, and Covenant," 207–33.
33. Ibid., 209.
34. Ibid., 210.
35. Ibid., 208.
36. Ibid., 220–24.
37. Ibid., 215–17.

that this liturgy-oriented vision of God's kingdom is further sustained in the centrality of the temple in David's priestly kingdom. Despite Israel's Adam-like fall, namely exile, this liturgical vision of God's kingdom is realized finally through Christ's accomplishment of the new exodus deliverance, which establishes the new priestly kingdom under the rule of Jesus the Davidic Messiah.[38] Hahn describes the consummation of this new priestly kingdom as follows: "in the new heaven and new earth, the new Jerusalem of Revelation, the children of the new Adam worship as priests and rule as kings, and the entire universe is revealed to have become a vast divine temple."[39]

For Hahn, this "liturgical trajectory" and "liturgical teleology" of the biblical canon are closely related to the liturgical context in which the canonical text is understood and used. Just as Israel finds her identity as the Adamic priestly king from the canonical text and applies this truth to herself through liturgical practices—such as the Passover, Sabbath, and the festivals and other various liturgical regulations—so also the new covenant community enters into the new covenant and is brought into contact with the covenant God through the sacramental liturgy.[40]

To summarize: the liturgical context and content of the New Testament writings mean that the New Testament, together with the Old Testament, reveal God's ultimate liturgical purposes for humanity and the world. They also mean that the New Testament writings, by virtue of being the canonical text of the new covenant community, are meant to actualize these liturgical purposes for the covenant community precisely in the liturgical settings. In Hahn's own words, "when proclaimed in the church's liturgy, Scripture is intended to 'actualize' what is proclaimed— to bring the believer into living contact with the wonders of God, the mighty saving works of God in the Old and New Testament."[41]

A Critique of Hahn's Understanding of the Liturgical Dimension

Does this view of the liturgical dimension of the biblical canon adequately capture the perspectives of the New Testament books? My critique will focus on one point of Hahn's view, namely that the New Testament

38. Ibid., 218–19.
39. Ibid., 225.
40. Ibid., 220–23.
41. Ibid., 228.

writers point to the liturgy as the means by which the new covenant people realize God's liturgical purposes for humanity and the world. To quote Hahn, when "proclaimed sacramentally and accompanied by the ritual washing of water, the Word brings the Spirit upon people, making them sons and daughters of God through a real sharing in his life, death, and resurrection."[42] This implies that there is something special about the liturgy itself that makes the proclamation of Scripture Spirit-empowered and thus effective in bringing people into a covenant relationship with God. And this special capacity of the liturgy, Hahn seems to believe, can be construed from his demonstration of the liturgical context and content of Scripture.

It is my argument that neither the liturgical context nor the liturgical content of the canon warrants Hahn's ascription of salvific effectiveness to the liturgical practices. Two points are in order. First, the liturgical context—i.e., that the covenant community interprets and appropriates both the Old and New Testament in its liturgical settings—may mean that the liturgy forms the context for the use of the canonical text, but it affirms little about the necessity and the effectiveness of the liturgy itself. In fact, the New Testament writers are pessimistic about the effectiveness of the liturgy in both the Old Testament and the New Testament canon. In the Old Testament, Israel was the covenant people on whom God's liturgical intentions were realized and maintained through their liturgical practices. But the New Testament writers, after coming to the united realization that the whole of humanity, including Israel, is incorrigibly sinful and hard-hearted, are disillusioned about the effectiveness of the liturgy in ensuring that Israel remains God's true people. This point is poignantly emphasized in Romans 9–11, where Paul deplores the fact that Israel, despite her zealous adherence to the law and diligent participation in the liturgical practices commanded in the law (Rom 9:30–33), is ultimately revealed as disqualified from the covenant. With regards to the new covenant community also, the New Testament writers do not emphasize the liturgical practices as if they are the means by which the new covenant reality materializes. Rather, their focus is on the Spirit and the Spirit-generated faith as the efficacious means by which people are brought into the new covenant relationship with God (e.g., Acts 2; 2 Cor 3; Rom 8; Gal 5). Hahn might argue that he also recognizes this point, claiming, as he does, that the power of the liturgy lies in its ability to cause or facilitate

---

42. Ibid.

the coming of the Spirit when Scripture is proclaimed in the liturgical setting.[43] But this ability, too, is not supported by the New Testament. Numerous instances of Paul's evangelistic preaching performed in non-liturgical settings—which gave rise to Gentile churches (e.g., Acts 13–14; 16–20)—undermine the claim that the work of the Spirit is dependent on or bound with the liturgical setting.

Nor does the liturgical content of Scripture—which Hahn explains in terms of the liturgical trajectory and teleology—generate Scriptural support for the special importance that Hahn confers on the liturgy itself. Hahn is right when he observes that the liturgical concept and imagery are used in such a way that "the meaning of the earlier texts is discerned in the later texts ... [and] later texts can only be understood in relation to ones that came earlier."[44] It is also true that the liturgical imagery is consistently used in the canonical description of Adam and the Garden of Eden, Israel and the Temple, and the church and the New Jerusalem. But the whole point of this canonical emphasis on the liturgical dimension is, not that the liturgy itself is essential—as seen in the history of Israel—but that the liturgy is merely a pointer to the liturgical reality. In other words, worship is no longer confined to particular formalized events; it is the ultimate ontological and existential orientation of humanity and the world. The liturgy itself is only a signpost to this larger and deeper reality. When the reality comes, signposts are no longer essential. This is Paul's point when he affirms that the glory of God Moses encountered in the Tent of Meeting is now available through the Spirit (not through the liturgy) to anyone who turns to Christ in faith (2 Cor 3:16–18). Similarly, when the book of Revelation describes the coming of the New Jerusalem, there is no temple in the city because "its temple is the Lord God the Almighty and the Lamb" (Rev 21:22). Rather than confined to particular events or particular settings, the glory of God will be the shining light by which "the nations will walk" (Rev 21:24). In the end, all reality will be God-focused and worship-oriented. This is the liturgical reality towards which the liturgical trajectory and teleology progress. Hahn is not justified in placing undue weight on the liturgy itself when fuller emphasis on the liturgical reality itself would be salutary.

---

43. Ibid., 228–29.
44. Ibid., 227.

Conclusion

Hahn's three-stage developmental view of God's trans-historical covenant-making and Hahn's emphasis on the liturgical context and content of the biblical canon represent a fresh attempt to capture the complexity of the biblical-theological patterns that undergird the New Testament books. Hahn's suggested framework, however, would have been more convincing if it had not downplayed the contributions made by the Deuteronomic covenant to God's overall redemptive strategy and if it had not overemphasized the significance of liturgy itself.

Bibliography

Daly, Robert J. "Soteriological Significance of the Sacrifice of Isaac." *CBQ* 39 (1977) 45–75.

Davies, P. R., and B. D. Chilton. "The Aqedah : A Revised Tradition History." *CBQ* 40 (1978) 514–46.

Finlan, Stephen. *The Background and Content of Paul's Cultic Atonement Metaphors.* Academia Biblica 19. Atlanta: Society of Biblical Literature, 2004.

Hahn, Scott. "Canon, Cult and Covenant: The Promise of Liturgical Hermeneutics" In *Canon and Biblical Interpretation*, edited by Scott Hahn et al., 207–35. Scripture and Hermeneutics Series 7. Grand Rapids: Zondervan, 2006.

———. "Covenant in the Old and New Testaments: Some Current Research (1994–2004)." *CBR* 3 (2005) 263–92.

———. *Kinship by Covenant: A Canonical Approach to the Fulfillment of God's Saving Promises.* London: Yale University Press, 2009.

Hugenberger, G. *Marriage as a Covenant: A Study of Biblical Law and Ethics Governing Marriage Developed, from the Perspective of Malachi.* Vetus Testamentum Supplemental Series 52. Leiden: Brill, 1994.

Niehaus, Jeffrey. "An Argument Against Theologically Constructed Covenants." *JETS* 50 (2007) 259–73.

Vermes, G. "New Light on the Sacrifice of Isaac from 4Q225." *JJS* 47 (1996) 140–46.

Wright, N. T. "The Letter to the Romans: Introduction, Commentary, and Reflections." In *The New Interpreter's Bible, vol 10: Acts to First Corinthians*, edited by Leander E. Keck, 395–770. Nashville: Abingdon, 2002.

The Place of God in the Bible

Between Jewish and Christian Theology

Zvi Shimon

THE TERM THEOLOGY, TAKEN literally and in its originally confined meaning, relates to the study of God. Its meaning has expanded in modern use to a wider definition encompassing the nature of religious truths or the descriptive study of matters of ultimate concern.[1] In the field of biblical theology, the term has come to be used by most theologians in reference to the study of the central ideas of the Bible, and not exclusively to the study of the deity. A survey of biblical theologies reveals the more expansive definition to be the more prevalent. Delineation of the purview of theological inquiry include "those ideas and thoughts, and concepts of the Old Testament which are or can be important";[2] "to construct *a complete picture of the OT realm of belief*";[3] "the intellectual and cultural world-image that lies behind the individual texts ... the general world-picture that may have been assumed."[4] These definitions are not confined to the understanding of God alone, but are geared to a more encompassing understanding of the biblical world view.[5]

---

* The writing of this paper was financially supported by the Bet Shalom Foundation, Kyoto, Japan.

1. See *Webster's Dictionary*, s.v. "theology," def. 1C(2). See also *Oxford Reference Dictionary*, s.v. "theology," def. 2.
2. Koehler, Foreword to *Old Testament Theology*.
3. Eichrodt, *Theology of the Old Testament*, 1.25.
4. Barr, *Concept*, 248.
5. Not all theologians adopt the wider definition of the term theology. For a confined approach to the purview of biblical theology limited to the study of the divine, see, for example, Westermann, *Elements*, 9; Brueggemann, *Theology*, 117.

God as the Focus of the Bible

Although most modern biblical theologians have adopted the wider definition of the term theology, examination of their work reveals an approach conforming to the confined definition. The central idea of the Bible has been defined almost unanimously in relation to God.[6] Proposed foci of the Bible include: divine salvation, divine redemption, knowledge of God, holiness of God, divine covenant, divine promise, or the divine plan.[7]

The two classical and prototypical theological works—the theologies of Eichrodt and von Rad—are cases in point. Eichrodt's *Theology of the Old Testament* includes three parts: God and the People, God and the World, and God and Man. As is evident from the titles, the common denominator of the sections is God. The central concept underlying Eichrodt's theology is covenant.[8] Covenant, by nature, exists between different parties, and hence the term invites a balanced treatment of the two sides of the covenant—God and the people of Israel; however, examination of the content of Eichrodt's work reveals a propensity towards focusing on

---

6. Two noteworthy, albeit partial, exceptions are von Rad, *Theology* 1, 48–56, and Brueggemann, *In Man*, 22, 30, 33. They relate to a biblical focus on humanity but confine its literary scope and attribute it to a theological revolution which takes place in the United Monarchy period. Von Rad identifies this change in focus of biblical historical writing particularly in the Succession Narrative and Brueggemann focuses on the wisdom traditions in the Hebrew Bible, especially on the book of Proverbs. It is instructive to note that Brueggemann considers his proposal to be "radical from the perspective of our usual Bible interpretation with its commitment to a theology of sin and salvation." (Foreword to *In Man We Trust*).

7. For lists of proposed foci and references see Preuss, *Theology* 1, 21; Levenson, *Hebrew Bible*, 54; Barr, *Concept*, 338. This close to consensual scholarly position persists to the present. Georg Fischer, SJ, in a paper presented at the International Society of Biblical Literature meeting in Amsterdam, July 2012, surveyed the recent developments in biblical theological research. He described the pluralism in method and content characteristic of recent research and summarized that, for all the diversity in the field, one point is accepted by all theologians: God is the center of the Bible.

8. The term covenant is present in the title of all of the first eleven chapters of Eichrodt's theology, excluding the opening chapter. For a critique of the view that covenant is the central focus of the Bible, see Levenson, *Hebrew Bible*, 36; Preuss, *Theology*, 8–9. It is noteworthy that throughout most of biblical narrative sins are not described as breaches of the covenant but rather as perpetration of evil. Even though the book of Genesis mentions the covenants between God and Noah and between God and Abraham, it does not describe sins as infringements of the covenant. See Gen 18:20; 19:13; 37:21; 38:7,10; 39:9. This is also the case regarding sins recounted in other biblical narratives: see, for instance, Judg 20:3; II Sam 12:9; I Kings 21:20.

God.⁹ Eichrodt's final work—*Man in the Old Testament*—raises expectations for a counterbalance to the emphasis on God in his previous works; however, despite the title, "man" holds no substantial advantage in this work. The study focuses on humanity primarily in light of its relationship with God and stresses the place that this relationship holds in the biblical conception of humanity. Most theologies that follow the Eichrodt model in searching for the central message of the Bible suggest different nuances but do not stray from the premise that God stands at the heart of the Bible.¹⁰

Gerhard von Rad proposed a different model for the study of biblical theology. He correctly perceived that the Bible does not focus directly on the nature of God and therefore shifted the focus to God's *actions* throughout history. According to von Rad, it is not the concept of God which stands at the heart of the Bible but his workings.¹¹ He believed that theological study should focus on the different traditions surrounding divine intervention in history and their depiction throughout the biblical account. In line with this approach, von Rad's theology is not organized, like Eichrodt's, according to theological concepts, but rather according to the order of the books of the Bible. Even though von Rad forged a new direction in biblical theological research, he did not deviate significantly from the traditional focus on God at the expense of humanity. Von Rad and scholars following his approach view the biblical narrative as material from which to glean knowledge about the ancient Israelite understanding of the divine.¹² Von Rad did not change the content of theological research, just the method and nature of the discussion—from a systematic abstract analysis to a study focused on the actions of God throughout history as recounted in the biblical account.¹³

Von Rad acknowledged that the Bible does not focus solely on God and he therefore believed that theological study should not be confined

---

9. The focus on God is evident from the section and chapter headings throughout the two volumes of his work.

10. Zimmerli, *Theology in Outline*, 14–21, for instance, sees God's name–Yahweh–as the focus of the Bible. Snaith, *Distinctive Ideas*, 9, suggests knowledge of God. Analysis of Snaith's chapter-headings is particularly instructive. The majority of the headings include God: Holiness of God, Righteousness of God, Salvation of God, Covenant-Love of God, Election-Love of God, and Spirit of God. For additional bibliography see Preuss, *Theology*, 1.21.

11. See von Rad, *Theology*, 1.105–6, 111–12, 115, and, 2.v–vii.

12. See, for instance, Wright, *God Who Acts*, 38; Westermann, *Elements*, 9–10.

13. Von Rad, *Theology*, 1.106; Westermann, *Elements*, 9–10.

to the study of the nature of the divine. However, he believed that all other topics treated by the Bible should to be viewed as secondary to the study of the deity.

> It will certainly not be possible for us to confine our theological work to testifying to the divine historical acts. Other things as well took place for Israel in the orbit of these acts of God. Men emerged whose function within this activity was to clarify it; offices came into being and cultic usages became necessary, because they were meant to make life in proximity to this revealed God possible for Israel. The various officials often stood up wonderfully to the test, and they often failed. Israel told the story of all of this, and of much besides, and then she thought the whole thing through again. . . . In particular Israel became revealed to herself in the sphere of this divine activity: she recognized herself, both her refusals and the completely new possibilities which opened up for her in the history, whenever she laid herself open to the working of her God. . . . This too must be dealt with in a Theology of the Old Testament. But its starting point and its centre is Jahweh's action in revelation.[14]

Accordingly, biblical historiography serves as the central source for the study of God. God is revealed through his actions in history and hence it is through the historiographic account that knowledge of God can be accrued. In Ludwig Köhler's categorical formulation: "All history has its source in God and takes place for God."[15]

Is such a position supported by biblical historiography? Is the primary goal of biblical historiography to teach of the essence of God? Part of the answer to this question depends upon the evaluation of God's role in biblical historiography. James Barr relates to this very point:

> But the divine guidance or control of all history seems to be poorly indicated in the narrative. Often it seems more as if history is conducted by humans, and God sometimes reacts. He "raises up" adversaries in response to bad behavior. . . . In the light of his commands and his promises, history happens to a large extent against his will.[16]

---

14. Von Rad, *Theology*, 1.114–15.

15. Köhler, *Old Testament Theology*, 93. See also Wright, *God Who Acts*, 38; Albrektson, *History and the Gods*, 11.

16. Barr, *Concept*, 358–59. See, similarly, Alter, *Biblical Narrative*, 12. See also Zimran, "Divine Will."

The view that God is the centerpiece of the Bible is not confined to theological study; a similar approach underlines certain literary studies of the Bible, as well. A very instructive example is Amelia Devin Freedman's *God as an Absent Character in Biblical Hebrew Narrative*. In her introduction she states:

> There is a startling contradiction here. While there can be no questions that the HB as a whole is centered on God and God's relations with Israel, God appears in most biblical stories only indirectly. The question raised by this paradox is as follows: What methods can modern readers use to understand the character of God, who is both the single most important character in HB narrative and absent from the majority of it?[17]

The "startling contradiction" with which the book grapples exists if one assumes, like Freedman, that the Bible is centered on God. However, why assume so if, as Freedman concedes, the biblical text does not support such an assumption?

The Disappearing God

One would think that the centrality of God's role in the Bible, in general, and in biblical historiography, in particular, would be a rather simple quantitative question: how often is God mentioned in the Bible and how do his numbers match up in comparison to other biblical characters? However, such an approach is misleading. God is certainly the most often-mentioned character in the Bible—no character even approaches the number of appearances of God in the Bible. However, this in no way makes him the central character of the Bible. God's immortal nature gives him a slight advantage over all other characters. Evaluating the role of God is not a quantitative question so much as it is qualitative. It is not the final tally of mentions of God that determines centrality. The decisive factor is the number of narratives in which God is the *central* character. In this category, I would argue that God does not get first place.

Even if one focuses on narratives in which God is explicitly present and active, there are very few, in my mind, in which God can be construed as the central and dominant character. The narrative that has the most impressive stretch of divine intervention is the Exodus Narrative: miracle follows miracle climaxing with the splitting of the Red Sea. God

17. Freedman, *God*, 3.

is clearly a central character of the Exodus Narrative and is determining the course of events. Is the Exodus Narrative representative of biblical narrative? The Bible itself answers this question by presenting the Exodus as an exception:

> For ask now concerning the days that are past, which were before you, since the day that God created man on the earth, and ask from one end of heaven to the other, whether any great thing like this has happened, or anything like it has been heard. Did any people ever hear the voice of God speaking out of the midst of the fire, as you have heard, and live? Or did God ever try to go and take for Himself a nation from the midst of another nation, by trials, by signs, by wonders, by war, by a mighty hand and an outstretched arm, and by great terrors, according to all that the Lord your God did for you in Egypt before your eyes? (Deut 4:32–34)

The Exodus Narrative, like the Sinai Revelation, is depicted as an exception that proves the rule. The uniqueness of these narratives set them apart as standouts for future generations, as examples that display the power of God and his magnificent actions for his people. It is specifically their being an aberration in the realm of divine intervention that gives the Exodus Narrative and the Sinai Revelation their special status in the Bible.

Furthermore, the issue of momentum as the reader progresses through the Bible is also an important consideration. Richard Elliott Friedman points to the gradual diminishing of God's appearances throughout the Bible:

> God disappears in the Bible.... Gradually through the course of the Hebrew Bible ... the deity appears less and less to humans, speaks less and less. Miracles, angels, and all other signs of divine presence become rarer and finally cease.[18]

The decrease in the explicit mention of God within biblical narrative is noticeable within a macro-biblical perspective as well as within specific books of the Bible.[19] Hence, even if one argues that God is the central focus in the earlier parts of the Bible—a claim I would contest, with the

---

18. Friedman, *Hidden Face*, 7.

19. On the changing role of God within the opening chapters of the book of Genesis, see Steinmetz, "Vineyard, Farm and Garden," 193–207; within the whole book of Genesis, see Humphreys, *Character of God*; within the conquest narrative in the book of Joshua, see Assis, *Conquest Narrative*, 158–59, 193–94, 206–7.

exception of the opening story of creation—the lead role of God is certainly not maintained as the reader progresses in the biblical narrative.

Samuel E. Balentine concludes his study titled *The Hidden God* by emphasizing the hiddenness of God as an intricate characteristic of the Hebrew Bible's depiction of the divine:

> God's hiddenness is . . . an integral part of the nature of God which is not to be explained away by theological exposition of human failures or human limitations. God is hidden just as he is present; he is far away just as he is near. Once this fact is given due consideration, then it is possible to understand the Old Testament's witness to the absence of a present God: "Truly thou art a God who hidest thyself, O God of Israel, the Savior." (Isa 45:15)[20]

It is hard-pressed and implausible to claim that the "hidden God" be regarded as the central character of the extended biblical narrative. God's literary absence surely doesn't deny a behind the scenes role for God in the turning of events; however, it does call into question the claim that God is the focus of the Bible.

Protestant Theology

The phenomenon of the gradual disappearance of God in the Hebrew Bible pointed out by Richard Elliott Friedman and the motif of the hidden God discussed by Balentine, call into question the norm in theological research of viewing God as the central character of the Bible. How did it come about that so many studies accept as an axiom that God is the center of the Bible even when the sources themselves do not support this assumption? The answer rests not in the scriptures but rather in the "scribes"—the background of most of the scholars in the field of biblical theology. With few exceptions, theological research is by and large a Christian discipline, and for the most part, although not exclusively, from the Protestant perspective.[21] Many theological studies aim at validating Christian perspectives and assumptions, and are characterized by Christian orientations such as determining the relationship between the

---

20. Balentine, *Hidden God*, 175–76.

21. See Childs, *Old Testament Theology*, 7–8; Levenson, *Hebrew Bible*, 45; Sweeney, "Jewish Biblical Theology," 192.

Hebrew Bible and the New Testament.[22] The Protestant background of many theological scholars leads to a focus on abstract and faith-oriented components at the expense of the more concrete aspects of ancient Israelite thought. Similarly, the historiosophic perspective adopted by most theological research tends to focus upon the acts of salvation of God (salvation history), in accordance with emphasis in Christian thought.[23] Walter Brueggemann, in a noteworthy exhibition of honesty and self-awareness, comments:

> We have done our Scripture studies in terms of man's sin and God's grace, informed primarily by Paul and more particularly his letter to the Romans. . . . In our tradition, perhaps in contrast to Catholicism, we have been concerned to witness to the Lordship of God over history and have been zealous to claim for him the decisive role in every turn in history. This indeed is the assumption of a salvation-history approach to Scripture. On the other hand, wisdom and the derivative discussions do not celebrate his intervention. They do not credit him with every major turn in history.[24]

This state of affairs is somewhat surprising. The primarily Protestant theological stance that God is the focus of the Bible goes counter to scriptural evidence and seems to undermine the foundational tenet of Protestant doctrine—*sola scriptura*. If the Bible is regarded as the supreme authority in matters of doctrine then the focus of biblical narrative should be determined and supported by Scripture. It would appear that another of the five solas—*sola fide*—has overridden *sola scriptura*. Faith has conquered its textual source and interpreted it in its own image.

Humanity as the Focus of the Bible—A Jewish Theological Perspective

If, as opposed to the dominant position in theological research, God is not the focus of the biblical narrative, then what is? There are those who

---

22. See, for example, Westermann, *Elements*, 217-32. Regarding this tendency in Old Testament Theology, see also Levenson, *Hebrew Bible*, 37-39; Barr, *Concept*, 172-88, 253-65; Knierim, "On Biblical Theology," 118-28.

23. See, for example, Eichrodt, *Theology*, 472-511; von Rad, *Theology*, 1.121-28; Westermann, *Elements*, 35-84; Zimmerli, *Theology in Outline*, 167-240.

24. Brueggemann, *In Man We Trust*, 61-62. See also Levenson, *Hebrew Bible*, 45-46, 51-61; Gerstenberger, *Theologies*, 283-84.

deny *a* central idea underlying the biblical narrative, and emphasize the heterogeneous nature of Scripture.[25] According to this approach, it is impossible to generalize and propose one theological/ideological core underlying so many diverse sources. While I agree with the claim that the Bible does not present a unitary outlook, and different sources and books evince diverse and at times conflicting emphases, this, in my opinion, does not preclude the possibility of pointing to an idea/topic that stands at the center of *many* biblical narratives and can therefore be considered the central, although certainly not the exclusive, focus of the Bible.

An alternative approach to the theological focus of the Bible may be found amongst certain Jewish theologians. There are scholars who have contested the very existence of Jewish biblical theology while others have pointed to the limited interest of Jewish scholars of the past in the field.[26] Although it is true that Jewish scholarship has put far less of a focus on theological studies, it has certainly not ignored the field.[27] Two Jewish theologians of the twentieth century, Leo Adler and Abraham Joshua Heschel, proposed an alternative direction. Adler is unfortunately little known in academic circles. He was born in Germany in 1915, received a PhD in philosophy, and served as Rabbi of Basel. In his opus, *The Biblical View of Man* (German original published in 1965) he rejects the prevailing position in biblical theological research of construing God as the center of the Bible, and proposes humanity as the focus:

> God, of whom Isaiah (55:8) tells us that His thoughts are not our thoughts and His ways are not our ways, is neither fathomable nor knowable. But that which the Bible itself considers to be outside the realm of potential human experience cannot be at the center of biblical interest. It is clearly the human who is the central object of the Bible's religion.[28]

Abraham Joshua Heschel, although also ignored in many theological discussions, is nevertheless recognized by some scholars as a

---

25. See, for example, von Rad, *Theology*, 1.115; Westermann, *Elements*, 9; Levenson, *Hebrew Bible*, 36, 54–56; Gerstenberger, *Theologies*, 1–2, 280–81. Knohl, *Biblical Beliefs*, 4, 143.

26. Tsevat, "A Jewish View," 33–50 esp. 33–34; Goshen-Gottstein, "Tanak Theology," 617–44 esp. 618–22; Levenson, *Hebrew Bible*, 33–61. See additional bibliography cited in Ben Zvi, "Constructing the Past," 31–32.

27. See surveys of Jewish theological research in Greenspahn, "Jewish Theologies," 13–29; Ben Zvi, "Constructing the Past," 31–50; Barr, *Theology*, 286–311.

28. Adler, *Biblical View of Man*, 6.

representative of "Jewish biblical theology."[29] Similarly to Adler, Heschel suggests:

> The Bible is primarily not man's vision of God but God's vision of man. The Bible is not man's theology but God's anthropology, dealing with man and what He asks of him rather than with the nature of God.... It was not the aspiration of Israel to know the Absolute but to ascertain what He asks of man; to commune with His will rather than with His essence.[30]

Heschel who ascribed to the minimalist definition of the term theology as the study of the concept of God, preferred the term *anthropology* over *theology*, for defining the focus of the Bible. Semantics aside, it is clear that the two Jewish thinkers proposed a common center of the Bible: humanity.[31] The almost consensual position in primarily Christian biblical theology of viewing God as the focus of the Bible is ironically rejected on theological grounds. The Jewish theologians reject the possibility of "knowing" God and of comprehending that which is beyond human comprehension and knowledge. However, the suggestion for an alternative focus in the Bible requires further elaboration. The term anthropology relates to a very wide spectrum of interests in the study of humans. What aspect of anthropology is the Bible interested in?

The focus on humanity in biblical narrative is of a very specific nature. Biblical narrative does not delve into elaborate descriptions of material reality in biblical times nor does it give lengthy insights into human psychology or political thought. The focus of the biblical narrative is primarily on human behavior and more specifically, on human wavering and choices in the moral sphere.[32] From Eve's contemplating eating from the forbidden fruit to Esther's hesitation whether to intervene on behalf of her people, from Cain's grappling with divine rejection and ensuing jealousy to King Ahab's wavering between the influences of Jezebel and Elijah, the biblical narrative focuses on human choices of a moral-religious nature with an emphasis on choice between good and evil. History, as it is depicted in most of the Bible, is not "salvation history" but rather a

---

29. See Dentan, *Old Testament Theology*, 81, cited by Levenson, *Hebrew Bible*, 34, and Ben Zvi, "Constructing the Past," 47, who mention Heschel in passing.

30. Heschel, *Man is not Alone*, 129. See also, Heschel, *God in Search of Man*, 412.

31. Jewish theological focus on humanity in the analysis of biblical texts is also evident in the work of Joseph B. Soloveitchik, particularly in *Lonely Man of Faith*.

32. For a development of this idea see, recently, Shimon, *Human Choice*.

history of human choices and their consequences–of sin and retribution, and virtue and reward; hence, the emphasis of Jewish theology not on knowing God, but rather on understanding the divine expectations of humanity—the path one should choose.[33]

This last point brings us back to God. The shift in emphasis in Jewish theology from God to humanity does not dismiss God from the narrative nor remove him from history. God is certainly a central figure in the biblical narrative, but his role is primarily as promulgator of law and morality, and judge of humanity. If human choice between good and evil is the focus of the Bible, then God's narrative role is judge of human actions. Divine judgment of humanity is expressed in many of the biblical narratives in the form of election and rejection of characters. This process of divine election lies at the heart of the book of Genesis, in determining inclusion in the Abrahamic covenant and in the chosen people; it continues throughout biblical historiography in electing the leadership of the people and ultimately in determining the destiny of the nation of Israel.

The substantially different suggestions for central foci of the Bible proposed by Christian and Jewish theologians reflect differing understandings of history, of the role of humans in generating history, and may ultimately reflect different conceptions of humanity. A divine-focused theology will tend to see history as generated by God, and will often view humanity, as is evident in certain understandings of the doctrine of original sin, as inclined to sin and failure. Accordingly, humanity depends upon divine grace, and salvation is only in the hands of God. An anthropocentric-focused theology will tend to see history as determined by human action, and view humanity as capable of bringing spiritual-moral progress and salvation. The biblical focus on human choice is ultimately founded upon the tenet of freedom of choice and upon the consequent responsibility of humanity in determining the course of history.

---

33. See Levenson's interesting comment regarding theological studies ignoring as a candidate for the center of the Bible "humankind's duties, a theme that occupies most of the biblical materials, legal, prophetic and sapiential alike." Levenson, *Hebrew Bible*, 54. See, further, Levenson, *Sinai and Zion*, 42–45.

Bibliography

Adler, Leo. *The Biblical View of Man*. Translated by Daniel R. Schwartz. Jerusalem: Urim, 2007.
Albrektson, Bertil. *History and the Gods: An Essay on the Idea of Historical Events as Divine Manifestations in the Ancient Near East and in Israel*. Coniectanea Biblica Old Testament Series 1. Lund: CWK Gleerup, 1967.
Alter, Robert. *The Art of Biblical Narrative*. New York: Basic, 1981.
Assis, Elie. *From Moses to Joshua and from the Miraculous to the Ordinary: A Literary Analysis of the Conquest Narrative in the Book of Joshua*. Jerusalem: Magnes, 2005.
Barr, James. *The Concept of Biblical Theology: An Old Testament Perspective*. London: SCM, 1999.
Balentine, Samuel E. *The Hidden God: The Hiding of the Face of God in the Old Testament*. Oxford: Oxford University Press, 1983.
Ben Zvi, Ehud. "Constructing the Past: The Recent History of Jewish Biblical Theology." In *Jewish Bible Theology: Perspective and Case Studies*, edited by Isaac Kalimi, 31–50. Winona Lake, IN: Eisenbrauns, 2012.
Brueggemann, Walter. *In Man We Trust: The Neglected Side of Biblical Faith*. Richmond, VA: John Knox, 1972.
Brueggemann, Walter. *Theology of the Old Testament: Testimony, Dispute, Advocacy*. Minneapolis: Fortress, 1997.
Childs, Brevard S. *Old Testament Theology in a Canonical Context*. Philadelphia: Fortress, 1985.
Dentan, Robert C. *Preface to Old Testament Theology*. New York: Seabury, 1963.
Eichrodt, Walther. *Theology of the Old Testament*. Vol. 1. Translated by John A. Baker. London: SCM, 1961.
Fischer SJ, Georg. "Biblical Theology in Transition–An Overview of Recent Works." Paper presented at the annual international meeting for the Society of Biblical Literature, Amsterdam, July 22–26.
Freedman, Amelia Devin. *God as an Absent Character in Biblical Hebrew Narrative: A Literary-Theoretical Study*. Studies in Biblical Literature 82. Frankfurt am Main: Peter Lang, 2005.
Friedman, Richard E. *The Hidden Face of God*. New York: HarperOne, 1996.
Gerstenberger, Erhard S. *Theologies in the Old Testament*. Translated by John Bowden. Minneapolis: Fortress, 2002.
Goshen-Gottstein, Moshe H. "Tanak Theology: The Religion of the Old Testament and the Place of Jewish Biblical Theology." In *Ancient Israelite Religion: Essays in Honor of Frank Moore Cross*, edited by Patrick D. Miller, Jr. et al., 617–44. Philadelphia: Fortress, 1987.
Greenspahn, Frederick E. "Jewish Theologies of Scripture," in *Jewish Bible Theology: Perspective and Case Studies*, edited by Isaac Kalimi, 13–29. Winona Lake, IN: Eisenbrauns, 2012.
Heschel, Abraham J. *God in Search of Man: A Philosophy of Judaism*. New York: Farrar, Straus & Cudahy, 1955.
———. *Man is not Alone: A Philosophy of Religion*. New York: Jewish Publication Society of America, 1951.

Humphreys, W. Lee. *The Character of God in the Book of Genesis: A Narrative Appraisal.* London: Westminster John Knox, 2001.
Knierim, Rolf P. "On Biblical Theology." In *The Quest for Context and Meaning: Studies in Biblical Intertextuality in Honor of James A. Sanders,* edited by Craig A. Evans and Shemaryahu Talmon, 117–28. Biblical Interpretation Series 28. Leiden: Brill 1997; republished in *Reading the Hebrew Bible for a New Millenium: Form, Concept, and Theological Perspective,* vol. 1, edited by Deborah L. Ellens et al., 11–20. Harrisburg, PA: Trinity, 2000.
Knohl, Israel. *Biblical Beliefs.* Jerusalem: Magnes, 2007.
Koehler, Ludwig. Foreword to *Old Testament Theology.* Translated by A. S. Todd. Philadelphia: Westminster, 1957.
Levenson, Jon D. *The Hebrew Bible, the Old Testament, and Historical Criticism: Jews and Christians in Biblical Studies.* Louisville, KY: WJK, 1993.
———. *Sinai and Zion: An Entry into the Jewish Bible.* Minneapolis: Winston, 1985.
Preuss, Horst D. *Old Testament Theology.* Vol. 1. Translated by Leo G. Perdue. Edinburgh: T. & T. Clark, 1995.
von Rad, Gerhard. *Old Testament Theology.* Vol. 1. Translated by D. M. G. Stalker. London: Oliver and Boyd, 1962.
———. *Old Testament Theology.* Vol. 2. Translated by D. M. G. Stalker. London: Oliver and Boyd, 1965.
The Oxford English Reference Dictionary. 2nd ed. Oxford: Oxford University Press, 1996.
Shimon, Zvi. *Human Choice: Biblical Narrative and the Drama of Choice.* Jerusalem: Magnes, 2015.
Snaith, Norman H. *The Distinctive Ideas of the Old Testament.* London: Epworth 1944.
Soloveitchik, Joseph B. *The Lonely Man of Faith.* New York: Doubleday, 2006.
Steinmetz, Devora. "Vineyard, Farm and Garden: The Drunkenness of Noah in the Context of Primeval History." *Journal of Biblical Literature* 113 (1994) 193–207.
Sweeney, Marvin A. "Jewish Biblical Theology." In *The Hebrew Bible: New Insights and Scholarship,* edited by Frederick E. Greenspahn, 191–208. New York: New York University Press, 2008.
Tsevat, Matitiahu. "Theology of the Old Testament: A Jewish View." *Horizons in Biblical Theology* 8 (1986) 33–50.
Webster's Third New International Dictionary of the English Language Unabridged. Springfield, MA: G. & C. Merriam, 1968.
Westermann, Claus. *Elements of Old Testament Theology.* Translated by Douglas W. Stott. Atlanta: John Knox, 1982.
Wright, G. Ernest. *God Who Acts: Biblical Theology as Recital.* Studies in Biblical Theology 8. London: SCM, 1952.
Zimmerli, Walther. *Old Testament Theology in Outline,* Translated by David E. Green. Atlanta: John Knox, 1978.
Zimran, Yisca. "Changes of Divine Will Following Human Request." Master's thesis, Bar-Ilan University, 2008.

Middle Narratives as an Aspect of Biblical Theology

John Goldingay[1]

MEMORY HAS BECOME A topic of interest in biblical studies. As a category for thinking about the past, it has several advantages over the more traditional term "history." One advantage is its being an English equivalent to Hebrew and Greek words that do come in the Bible, as "history" is not. Remembering is a key imperative in the Old Testament, especially in Deuteronomy but also elsewhere. Its significance is taken up by Jesus and by Paul ("Do this in remembrance of me"). Whereas history might seem implicitly to embrace everything, the notion of memory presupposes the selective nature of our relationship with the past, a selectivity based on the significance of the past for the present and the future. Historical study, too, works in light of the significance of the past for our concerns, but we may present it as otherwise. Further, for better and for worse a focus on memory also subverts the inclination to focus on the question whether events happened.

"History" is inclined to refer especially to the past of a community; we may well add an adjective such as "personal" if we use the word to refer to an individual's past. The opposite may apply to "memory." In Western culture we may think of memory as an individual affair, but the Bible assumes that an entity such as Israel has a corporate memory, and modern memory studies especially emphasizes "cultural memory" or "social memory." In biblical studies one can therefore think of the Bible

---

1. An expanded version of this paper appears in Goldingay, *Do We Need the New Testament?*.

as embodying, or at least including, the corporate memory of Israel and/or of the Second Temple community and/or of the early Christian community. It comprises what they wanted to remember or wanted people to remember or wanted to be remembered by.

Narrative is then the way in which an individual or a group organizes its memory, and the Scriptures are dominated by narratives that articulate the past in the form that these cultures wanted to affirm. In particular, what I call "middle narratives" do so. I base the notion of middle narratives on the idea of middle axioms in ethics. One significance that can attach to the idea of middle axioms is that they articulate tenets lying between concrete imperatives on one hand and general principles on the other. The Bible talks both in terms of specific duties such as "build a wall around the roof of your house" and of general obligations such as "love your neighbor." Middle axioms help mediate between these by providing tenets that are less specific than the former but more concrete than the latter.

In parallel, the Bible contains many individual narratives expressing theological insights: stories about Israel, about individual Israelites, about Jesus, and about the infant church. It also implies a grand theological narrative, which the creeds aim to encapsulate. In addition, however, the Bible includes a series of extensive explicit or implicit middle narratives, which form a distinctive way in which it does theology. In this paper I examine the theological implications of some of these middle narratives, consider how they may be seen as part of a grand theological narrative that emerges from the Bible as a whole and is (I suggest) a key aspect to biblical theology, and consider the relationship between the middle narratives and the grand narrative. In the terms of one of the questions underlying the book in which this paper appears, I am putting forward one answer to the question, "What is a 'biblical theology of the New Testament'"? A "biblical theology of the New Testament" is, or at least involves, the drawing up of the grand narrative that extends from the Old Testament into the New.

I should note that the word narrative itself and the idea of a grand narrative are cultural clichés. Following Jean-François Lyotard himself, people who talk about narratives and about a grand narrative sometimes simply have in mind ideas or theories or worldviews. In a more traditional sense, a narrative is an account of a sequence of events. In the Bible, narratives in the narrower sense are prominent, and it is narrative in this sense that I am studying.

My first middle narrative is Genesis to Kings, which is a *grand* theological narrative in its own right. At one level it is one long exercise in memory and in memory formation. I take it as reaching its final form not long after the last event it relates, during the exile; it embodies a way of understanding Israel's history from its beginnings to the time of the community for which it was written. This assumption about its date goes against a trend in Old Testament study that reads this narrative as reflecting the Persian period, but I don't think my reading will be greatly affected if one takes that approach. I do assume that much of the contents has a long history and I am not averse to the idea that the narrative had seen earlier editions, but I am focusing on the work as we have it.

One way to read this middle narrative is to focus on the significance of four key figures, Abraham (who can stand for the ancestors in general), Moses, Joshua, and David. Abraham stands for the way Israel's life is lived in the context of God's promise to its ancestors. Moses stands for the assertion that Yahweh reigns as king in the world and over Israel. Joshua stands for the people's entering into possession of Canaan. David stands for the way Israel's life is lived in the context of God's commitment to him and to Jerusalem. But the story in which these four figures stand out is framed by two further motifs characterized by some ambiguity. The story begins with God's creation of the world and of humanity as a whole. The implication of Genesis is that God's involvement with Israel is designed to fulfill God's intention to bless the world, yet that motif all-but disappears within the main story. The narrative eventually ends with the unraveling of all that has preceded. The people find themselves back in the Babylonia from which Abraham had been summoned. That fate overwhelms them because more often than not they flout the will of their sovereign, expressed through Moses. It results in their losing the land into whose possession Joshua led them. The Davidic monarchy comes to an end. Rudolf Bultmann called the Old Testament the story of the miscarriage of God's plan.[2] This understanding is inappropriate as a summary of the Old Testament as a whole but it is a fair description of Genesis to Kings.

Reading Genesis to Kings would thus be a sobering experience for Judahites during the exile. How could it not be profoundly discouraging? There are two sorts of answers to that question. One might start from Gerhard von Rad's description of the Books of Kings, in particular, as a

---

2. See Bultmann, "Prophecy and Fulfillment," 50–75.

Gerichtsdoxologie, an act of praise at the justice of the judgment of God.[3] Admittedly in light of memory studies I no longer think this description is quite right, because a *Gerichtsdoxologie* would need to be addressed to God, and the Books of Kings are addressed to people, as a statement of how they need to remember their past, but some aspects of their effect are similar. They invite people to face the facts about their story, and in this sense to make their own *Gerichtsdoxologie*. It will involve them standing naked and vulnerable before God (or owning that such is their position). Given their story, all they can do is cast themselves on God's mercy. But one encouragement towards their doing so is God's showing himself as one characterized by faithfulness and mercy through their story; perhaps these qualities have not come to an end (as Lamentations notes). Another sort of encouragement in the story is God's making those promises to Abraham, as 2 Kings 13:23 notes. More prominent is God's making those promises to David, which have inhibited God from casting off his successors (1 Kings 15:4; 2 Kings 8:19; 19:34; 20:6). The closing scene of 2 Kings, relating the release of King Jehoiakin in exile, constitutes a sign that God has not abandoned his promises to David.

This first middle narrative declares, then, that God has a purpose for the world as a whole, that his plans for implementing his purpose have not so far been fulfilled, that likewise he has not been able to fulfill his purpose for Israel to be the means of implementing that purpose, but that all might not be lost.

The Scriptures' second middle narrative is Chronicles-Ezra-Nehemiah. Again, I do not assume that this narrative came into existence in one go, but two things are clear. One is that the overlap between the closing verses of Chronicles and the opening of Ezra invites readers to read these works sequentially. The other is that those closing verses of Chronicles indicate that, like Ezra-Nehemiah, Chronicles belongs at least a few decades after that little note of hope at the end of 2 Kings, which refers to the release of King Jehoiakin in 561. Chronicles knows that Cyrus's conquest of Babylon in 539 was a more significant indication that Yahweh was still at work. The reference to it leads into the account of the restoration of the temple in Ezra; the policies of subsequent Persian kings make possible the further works of restoration by Ezra and Nehemiah.

Chronicles begins its actual recounting of Israel's story with David; the story from Adam through Abraham, Moses, and Joshua to Saul is told

---

3. von Rad, *Old Testament Theology*, 1.357-58; cf. von Rad, *Gesammelte Studien*, 2:245-54.

by means of a list of names occupying the first third of 1 Chronicles. Its account of David's importance then focuses on his significance for the temple, which links with the importance of the temple in the account of the return from exile in Ezra 1–6. One could thus say that the three key figures in this middle narrative are David, Ezra, and Nehemiah, and that its focus lies on Jerusalem: its temple and its worship, Ezra's renewal of its life, and Nehemiah's rebuilding of its walls.

There is again some ambiguity about this middle narrative. Beginning with Adam throws into sharper light its saying nothing about God's purpose for the world as a whole. Yet its treatment of emperors such as Cyrus, Darius, and Artaxerxes gives them a more positive relationship to Israel and to Yahweh's purpose than one finds in references to emperors in Genesis to Kings. At the same time, Chronicles-Ezra-Nehemiah frets over the fact that the community is still under the control of a superpower. While it sees Yahweh as having fulfilled his promise to restore Israel after the exile, it portrays the Second Temple community as struggling in various ways with adversity and with its own failure. And it does not reach any closure. At the end of Nehemiah, the story simply stops.

The third middle narrative I consider is the one expressed in the visions in Daniel. Here the superpowers, which were more prominent in Chronicles-Ezra-Nehemiah than in Genesis to Kings, come into the forefront of the narrative; and in association with that fact, the visions declare that God is going to bring his purpose for the world to its consummation. The sequence of superpowers comprises Babylon, Medo-Persia, and Greece. Daniel may be picking up an older scheme that began with Assyria, the actual first Middle-Eastern superpower; if so, the scheme has been adapted to fit a framework that begins with Daniel himself, living in the Babylonian period. At the other end, the scheme later comes to be adapted to include Rome, and subsequently to cover later superpowers. But within Daniel, the scheme embraces Babylon, Medo-Persia, and Greece, which eventually give way to the implementing of God's reign through his people. This middle narrative, then, offers a perspective o n the entire history of Israel from the exile to the end.

In Daniel 7 the animals that symbolize the empires emerge from the sea, which is likely a negative image; the sea is a symbol of dynamic power that operates independently of God, at best (in the new heavens and the new earth in Revelation 21, there is no more sea). The vision does not go back to creation but begins with the emergence of the superpowers. Their sequence involves neither consistent degeneration nor progress. Babylon is bad, Medo-Persia is less awful, Greece is truly bad. The evaluation corresponds to Judah's experience at the hand of the empires. The last of the visions is noteworthy for its detailed account of the conflicts between the Seleucid and Ptolemaic monarchies and their relationship with Judah, which stands between them. The theological significance of this account is the way it portrays history as going nowhere, a tale "full of sound and fury, signifying nothing." Yes,

> To-morrow, and to-morrow, and to-morrow,
> Creeps in this petty pace from day to day
> To the last syllable of recorded time.

(Only after typing those words did I recall that they were uttered by Macbeth in Dunsinane Castle, twenty miles west of the St. Andrews where the paper was read).

Yet the visions do not portray history as petering out or just jogging along, as might be the implication of our first two narratives. When it has reached its darkest point and when the last superpower in the sequence has reached a height of arrogance and blasphemy in relation to God, and of oppression over God's people, God intervenes, terminates the superpower's rule, and gives over power to the his saints. The visions were vindicated by the defeat and withdrawal of the Seleucid forces from Jerusalem in 164, after which Judah gained control of its own destiny, though it held it only for a century until the next superpower arrived.

The narrative expounded by Daniel's visions complements the one in Genesis to Kings, which offers a perspective on the story from creation to the exile. Indeed, combining these two generates a suggestive Old Testament grand narrative. Its first half indeed takes the story from the world's creation to a plan that reaches miscarriage under the Babylonians. Its second half exponentially increases that gloom in the way it also sets Israel's continuing story against the backcloth of the history of the world as a whole from the Babylonian empire onwards, a history that has no meaning. But it declares that the absence of meaning from history does not indicate that miscarriage has the last word or that things are out of God's control. The goal of history will not be reached by Israel's obedience or by the nations' initiative, but that goal will be reached by God's intervention. It deserves noting that neither the three middle narratives we have considered nor this grand narrative incorporates a messianic figure.

There are other middle narratives one could infer from the Old Testament, notably from Isaiah, from Jeremiah, and from Ezekiel (and they would incorporate a messianic figure). But I now move to some New Testament middle narratives. While these belong to the other side of the gap we assume exists between the Testaments, in my view they are probably as near temporally to Daniel's visions as Daniel's visions are to Chronicles-Ezra-Nehemiah, and these New Testament narratives are nearer to Daniel's visions than Daniel's visions are in relation to Genesis to Kings.

I begin from Mark. Mark arguably has so short a time frame, three years, that it hardly counts as a middle narrative. Most of the Gospel relates incidents from Jesus' ministry; the last third covers the closing week of his life; one final paragraph relates his resurrection. Whether this brief ending is original or something has been lost, readers apparently thought its brevity unsatisfactory, and added alternative endings to take the narrative on into the story of the proclaiming of the gospel. Within Mark's own work, for our purposes more significance attaches to Jesus' declarations in Mark 13 about a coming persecution, a desolating sacrilege, and a coming of the Son of Man. If we take Mark 13 into account, this middle narrative extends forward in a parallel way to Daniel's visions, from which it derives its imagery. Yet its focus lies resolutely on Jesus' story, and its implication for its readers is that they need to focus resolutely on the life and death of Jesus, and on the coming crisis and its resolution.

Matthew's middle narrative also takes Jesus' story forward with a brief account of events following the resurrection, and it also incorporates Jesus' declarations concerning what Matthew calls his coming and the end of the age. It contrasts with Mark in a more striking fashion in the way it takes Jesus' story back from his ministry to his birth, and behind his birth to his ancestry; the account traces Jesus' origins into the past, to Abraham via the exile and David. While Mark referred to the beginning of Jesus' ministry as a fulfillment of Old Testament prophecy and utilized Old Testament imagery to portray the coming crisis, he did not attach any significance to the Old Testament story itself. In contrast, Matthew portrays Jesus as the logical culmination of Israel's story. He structures it in that threefold way (Abraham, David, the exile), which interestingly ignores the exodus, like Chronicles. Matthew thus from the beginning makes a link with Israel's story and invites its readers to see themselves as living in light of a more substantial middle narrative than Mark's.

Luke's story extends the narrative further. First, it tells even more about the background to Jesus' birth, and does so in a way that implicitly links Jesus' story onto Chronicles-Ezra-Nehemiah. The community into which Jesus is born is the community that David, Ezra, and Nehemiah established. It's sometimes said that the Hebrew order of the Old Testament, closing with Chronicles, is a Jewish order, whereas the Greek order, ending with the Prophets and in particular with Malachi, is a Christian order. In origin it is quite likely that both are Jewish orders, and in content the Hebrew order leads just as suggestively into the New Testament as the Greek order does (furthermore, the last word in the Hebrew order, in the book of Malachi, is the word *herem*, annihilation, which is not too obvious a lead in to the gospel story). Luke incorporates a different account of Jesus' ancestry from Matthew's, and it is one that traces that ancestry back to Adam. Luke's account thus again recalls Chronicles. But Luke's much more striking extension of this middle narrative comes when Luke's Gospel leads into a second narrative, almost as long as the first, relating how the Jesus story spread through his home country and then around the Eastern Mediterranean to Rome. Once more Luke-Acts parallels Chronicles-Ezra-Nehemiah in the way it comes to a stop rather than to a conclusion. Readers know that more must have followed the last events that are related in Acts, but they do not discover the nature of the continuing story.

Again, there are other middle narratives that we could infer from the New Testament's non-narrative works.[4] But the issue I now wish to consider is the generating of a grand narrative from these middle narratives, a grand narrative that would be a key feature of a biblical theology. In calling them middle narratives I indicate that I am not giving up the idea of a grand narrative, though I have questions about the common form of the Christian grand narrative, which comprises creation, fall, redemption in Christ, and the second coming. I recognize that middle narratives are not so different from what Lyotard calls "little narratives" or "local narratives," which he regards as the nearest we can get to a "grand narrative."[5] Paul Ricoeur has likewise commented that "The birth of the concept of history as a collective singular, under which the collection of particular histories is placed, marks the bridging of the greatest gap imaginable between unitary history and the unlimited multiplicity of individual memories and the plurality of collective memories underscored by [Maurice] Halbwachs." The trouble is, Ricoeur comments, that human plurality "chips away from within the very concept of history as a col-

---

4. Cf. Miller, "Paul and Hebrews," 245–64.
5. See e.g., Lyotard, "Universal History," 314–23.

lective singular." Special histories resist globalization.[6] In examining the Jewish understanding of memory, Yosef Yerushalmi has noted that the Greeks did not see ultimate meaning in history as a whole.[7] Perhaps they were wise. One might see Ricoeur's observation as a comment on Qohelet's way of looking at things, in particular the lament that God has put "eternity" (*hāʿōlām*) in humanity's mind, yet has not enabled people to fathom it (Qoh 2:11). There is thus no total history in the Old Testament itself, even in Daniel, yet we have seen that there are some pretty grand narratives and that the adding of Daniel to Genesis-Kings and Chronicles-Ezra-Nehemiah within the Old Testament makes it not a huge leap to infer a grand narrative from the Old Testament. Likewise the narratives we might infer from John, Paul, and Revelation look pretty grand. In seeking to articulate a grand narrative on the basis of Scripture, then, we are undertaking a task of which the individual biblical writers did not dream, though no more so than in other aspects of biblical theology, and we are undertaking a task that is not alien to the scriptures as a whole.

Taken as a whole, the New Testament middle narratives embrace the Old Testament grand narrative and nuance it in light of Jesus. Or perhaps the point should be put the other way around: they set their own middle narratives in the context of the Old Testament grand narrative. They have nothing much to add to the Old Testament's account of the past up until the story of the last empire. What they do (in common with other Jewish understandings of the day) is extend and nuance the account of the empires in Daniel's visions by adding another empire that is a further embodiment of the beast. Their distinctive Christian angle is to present the story of Jesus as another intervention of the One on High who appears in Daniel 7. Like the visions in Daniel, these New Testament middle narratives describe this intervention as if it brings the ultimate end, but it does not do so. They are explicit about this point, in that they incorporate their own vision of events to follow Jesus' death and resurrection and the story that continues in Luke. They know that there will yet come the crisis that was historically constituted by the fall of Jerusalem, but that this crisis, too, will not be the end. The grand narrative they imply embraces creation, Abraham, Moses, Joshua, David; it embraces Assyria, Babylon, Medo-Persia, and Greece; it embraces Rome and Jesus' birth, ministry, death, and resurrection; it embraces the outpouring of

---

6. Ricoeur, *Memory, History, Forgetting*, 299, 301; see e.g., Halbwachs, *On Collective Memory*.

7. Yerushalmi, *Zakhor*, 7.

God's spirit, the proclamation of the gospel as far as Rome, the fall of Jerusalem, and the end still to come.

Considering this grand narrative when two thousand years have passed gives us a strangely new relationship with the middle narratives in both Old and New Testament. If we had been living in the year 50 or 60 AD, then like Mark we might have thought that not much significance attaches to the earlier middle narratives, but the passing of two thousand years gives them more significance. In the West, at least, the church lives in a context more like that which Chronicle-Ezra-Nehemiah addresses and describes than that of a Christian community in Mark's day. Our context is one in which God's promises have been partially fulfilled but in which nothing much seems now to be happening. We might even see ourselves as living in a situation like that of Judah in the exile. In some parts of the world and/or during some periods of history, the church finds itself living in a context more like the one addressed in Daniel's visions. One can see that the church in, say, Kenya in the 1950s might well find great encouragement in the middle narrative that pictures the rule of superpowers as not destined to go on forever. We would be unwise to live in light of one of those earlier middle narratives as if the events related in the later ones had not happened. Yet the church's greater danger is to live as if it makes no difference that we are living two thousand years after the events that look as if they were bringing the scriptural grand narrative to its climax. To put the point more sharply, Isaiah 52 declares that God's reign has arrived, but the world did not change as much as you might have expected. Jesus said that God's reign has arrived, but the world did not change as much as you might have expected.

In my thinking, biblical theology involves creating from the varied materials within scripture the big picture that might emerge from the whole, or using the building blocks constituted by this varied material to construct an edifice that makes good use of them all and doesn't involve either the importing of further materials from elsewhere or the casting aside of some of the materials in the conviction that they don't really belong in this building. But it also involves discerning which materials need highlighting in order to articulate the statement that needs making in the context in which the building is to be erected and to function.

Bibliography

Bultmann, Rudolf. "Prophecy and Fulfillment." In *Essays on Old Testament Interpretation*, edited by C. Westermann, 50–75. London: SCM, 1963.

Goldingay, John. *Do We Need the New Testament? Letting the Old Testament Speak for Itself*. Downers Grove, IL: InterVarsity, 2015.

Halbwachs, Maurice. *On Collective Memory*. Chicago: University of Chicago, 1992.

Lyotard, Jean-François. "Universal History and Cultural Differences." In *The Lyotard Reader*, edited by Andrew E. Benjamin, 314–23. Oxford: Blackwell, 1989.

Milgrom, Jacob. *Numbers*. Philadelphia: JPS, 1990.

Miller, James C. "Paul and Hebrews: A Comparison of Narrative Worlds." In *Hebrews: Contemporary Methods—New Insights*, edited by Gabriella Gelardini, 245–64. Leiden: Brill, 2005.

Rad, Gerhard von. *Gesammelte Studien zum Alten Testament*. Munich: Kaiser, 1973.

———. *Old Testament Theology*. Vol. 1. New York: Harper, 1962.

Ricoeur, Paul. *Memory, History, Forgetting*. Chicago: University of Chicago, 2004.

Yerushalmi, Yosef Hayim. *Zakhor: Jewish History and Jewish Memory*. Reprint. New York: Schocken, 1989.

The Book of Revelation and New Testament Theology

W. Gordon Campbell

INTRODUCTION

NEW TESTAMENT THEOLOGY REMAINS a "contested discipline,"[2] and the question of "how NT Theology is to be understood and done"[3] provokes a plethora of possible answers—a state of affairs admirably illustrated by *The Nature of New Testament Theology*, in honor of Robert Morgan, in 2006.[4] My approach here takes New Testament Theology to be an exercise in blending together polyphonically[5] the varied voices of the New Testament's distinct texts and corpora, all of which—I am assuming—deserve a hearing.[6] I will measure and assess the degree of audibility enjoyed by just one voice, Revelation,[7] and then suggest how it might be heard in the resulting unity-in-diversity.

---

1. The paper from which this contribution arose was first read at the Biblical Theology group of the *Society of Biblical Literature International Meeting* in St. Andrews, Scotland, in July 2013, then further refined for presentation at a joint meeting of the *Irish Biblical Association* and the *Queen's University Biblical Studies Postgraduate Seminar*, held in Belfast in November 2013.
2. To use Robert Morgan's words, "New Testament Theology," 138.
3. Hatina, *New Testament Theology*, 14.
4. Rowland and Tuckett, *Nature of New Testament Theology*, xi.
5. By "polyphony" I mean something closer to euphony than to cacophony.
6. In this instance I make no attempt to listen to voices from beyond the New Testament canon.
7. Theoretically, at least, it might seem self-evident today that Revelation *should* make its contribution alongside any and every New Testament document; this was

Whilst general scholarly interest in Revelation has increased in recent times, as a reflection of what Robert Morgan has called "the richness of this puzzling text,"[8] it remains rare enough for sustained attention to be paid to Revelation whenever constructive theologising is undertaken in relation to the whole New Testament corpus. It is my own conviction that Revelation has a unique and welcome contribution to make to the concert of New Testament Theology. My particular focus, here, will be on the cultic dimension of Revelation. In my estimation as a listener,[9] Revelation's voice owes its peculiar timbre and tone to this liturgical element: so crucial is its contribution to Revelation that, in and of itself, it amply justifies recourse to Revelation for the practice of New Testament Theology.

In part one I will take selective soundings concerning the role afforded Revelation in a recent introduction[10] and in two full-blown New Testament Theologies, regarded as representative;[11] I will reflect, as I go, on the quality of hearing being granted to Revelation and on the extent of receptiveness to the book's own dynamics being shown. In light of my findings I will then briefly revisit Richard Bauckham's suggestions about Revelation's relevance, made over twenty years ago.[12]

In part two, and arguing that Bauckham's challenge to scholarship and to the Church is still largely unmet today, I will offer my own proposal for giving Revelation a voice in the Church, the Academy, and the public square: Revelation's worship speech, I will claim, is a characteristic of the book's diction so fundamental and integral both to its shape and its purpose that it merits a hearing.

---

of course not always so. For a brief history of the development of New Testament Theology and of the contribution made by apocalypticism (and with it, *Revelation*), see Yarbro Collins, "Apocalypticism and NT Theology," 31–48.

8. Morgan, "New Testament Theology," 207.

9. In this piece I am more interested in how Revelation shapes readers than how readers shape Revelation; this is in pursuit of an attempt to gain a greater hearing for Revelation among NT theologians. Nevertheless, I readily acknowledge with Thomas Hatina that "a continuous dialogue between the subject and object" is desirable and unavoidable or, as he deftly puts it, that "texts and readers [are] in a dialectical dance," *New Testament Theology*, 208, 214.

10. Dunn, *New Testament Theology*, 2009.

11. Matera, *New Testament Theology*, 2007; and Vouga, *Une théologie du Nouveau Testament*, 2001.

12. In his well-known guide *The Theology of the Book of Revelation*, 1993.

PART ONE: REVELATION IN NEW TESTAMENT THEOLOGY

James Dunn

Dunn's declared aim is "to set out some of the key problems, the determining factors, and the main themes of a New Testament biblical theology."[13] To achieve this he develops a set of four themes which form an integrated whole;[14] since three of these involve Revelation it is appropriate for us to investigate how the book is featured in his integrative account.

The Theology of God

Two questions arise here: first, whether Jesus was worshiped as God, discussed in connection with angelic intermediaries in early Judaism; and second, the associated problem of possible confusion between angels and God in the literature, on which Rev 1:13-14 and 10:1 may shed some light.[15] Worship of the Lamb (in 5:13; 7:10), "*given to the Lamb unreservedly*,"[16] is of the sort also given to God, whose throne the Lamb shares, and is in contradistinction to angel-worship.[17] What worshiping Jesus as God might have meant for the first Christians generally, or how this dovetailed with their worship of the one God, is explained from "the absence of a sacrificial cult and sacrifice-offering priesthood within first-century Christianity."[18]

---

13. Dunn, *New Testament Theology*, 153. He describes his stated method as a conjunction of "*historical-critical description and theological reflection,*" 157, italics original.

14. Ibid., ix. These are: the Theology of God; the Theology of Salvation; the Church of God; and the Ethical Outworkings. Dunn offers justification for this core subject-matter on pages 38-39.

15. Ibid., 50-51.

16. Ibid., 65, italics original.

17. Ibid., 66.

18. Dunn suggests that "Jesus was revered more as the sacrificial victim who had made atonement for others, and not as the one to whom sacrifice should be made," (ibid.).

The Theology of Salvation

After brief treatment of the ark in the heavenly Temple (11:17), as part of a discussion of the continuity of covenant,[19] Dunn asks if the New Testament provides evidence for completion of the process of salvation: he answers "yes" but evidence is "*occasional*" and "*fragmentary*."[20] Revelation's contribution to this aspect of soteriology is fourfold: it addresses the process of salvation, through martyrs awaiting vindication; it features first resurrection; it offers powerful images of final judgment (19:20; 20:7–15); and it provides pictures of the creation restored.[21]

The Church of God

There is passing reference to Revelation, here, in relation to three motifs: the tribes of Israel; the language of election; and eschatological destruction of non-elect nations (19:17–21).[22]

The Ethical Outworkings

No reference is made here to Revelation.

Assessment

Given the limited scope of Dunn's project, there is only cursory treatment of Revelation overall. Yet it constitutes a promising start: Dunn touches on the very aspects of the book which, to my mind, especially characterize its own distinctive voice, namely, its Christology and its liturgical dimension; and what little Revelation does contribute to Dunn's synthesis is a faithful reflection of some of its key features.

---

19. Ibid., 84.
20. Ibid., 94, italics original.
21. Ibid., 94–95.
22. Ibid., 106. Somewhat surprisingly, in this connection, Dunn makes no mention whatever of the pilgrimage of the kings or nations into New Jerusalem.

BIBLICAL THEOLOGY | III. FUTURE

Frank Matera

Matera's method is to deal first with the diverse theologies of the New Testament books and then to endeavor, in his conclusion, to bring these together into unity: thus the chapter devoted to Revelation's distinctive voice[23] is distilled down to five paragraphs of his concluding proposal for the unique contribution which the book makes to "[t]he Diverse Unity of New Testament Theology."[24]

A THEOLOGY OF GOD'S FINAL VICTORY OVER EVIL

After sketching the shape of Revelation's narrative Matera draws out four aspects of its theology of victory: these relate in turn to God, Christ, God's people and to God's enemies and their defeat; a conclusion then follows.[25] Regarding God and his victory, Matera highlights the book's "summons to worship God"[26] and concludes that "[t]he book of Revelation expresses its understanding of God in terms of worship and praise[27] which, Matera acknowledges, elevate Christ to the status of God. Somewhat oddly, Matera does not carry this worship focus over into his consideration of Christ and his victory, where the emphasis falls instead on how that victory is portrayed as the need for local congregations (in Rev 1—3) to be victorious, through their suffering if necessary, and the final victory of God's eschatological people. Matera calls this victory "the victory of the Lamb,"[28] although how this is so is unclear to me, as is how the *already* and the *not yet* aspects of victory might affect "the eschatological people of God."[29]

A pessimistic claim follows: Revelation offers believers no "way to engage the world in a positive manner" or indeed any wherewithal to "develop a theology of positive engagement with the world."[30] This negative

23. See Matera, *New Testament Theology*, 400–422.

24. Ibid., 423–80, italics original.

25. Following an examination of the narrative (ibid., 402–12), around two pages are devoted to each of the four topics in question.

26. Ibid., 413.

27. "To worship God, he adds, is to affirm and participate in this victory" (ibid., 415).

28. Ibid., 419.

29. This exact phrase is used several times (ibid., 418–21).

30. Ibid., 422.

verdict appears to be the corollary of a failure to integrate theologically the churches' participation in worship of God and the Lamb, and their victory: to see created reality with God's eyes and from God's standpoint through the apocalyptic story, is for Matera to gain insight only into *future* outcomes; no new or positive perspective on the present emerges.

The Diverse Unity of New Testament Theology

Matera integrates the various New Testament writings into his account of the unity of New Testament Theology through five rubrics which he correlates with "an underlying narrative that guides the diverse writings of the New Testament . . . the implied master story to which these writings witness."[31] This overarching story is itself elaborated with one eye on recent proposals from five other scholars.[32]

Humanity in need of salvation.

Soteriology and anthropology combine, since "apart from the victory of the Lamb, humanity is under Satan's power."[33]

The bringer of salvation.

Concerning Revelation's Christology,[34] Matera sees the *traditional* (Jesus as Messiah, risen Lord or one like the Son of Man) combining with the *innovative* (the metaphor of the slaughtered Lamb and his faithful witness, for which he is vindicated by God; and his co-enthronement with God).[35]

---

31. Ibid., 427. Matera summarizes this story (427–28) in terms of a human predicament of alienation from God, to which God responds graciously and savingly.

32. The survey features F. Vouga (considered below), together with the contributions of Ferdinand Hahn, I. Howard Marshall, Peter Stuhlmacher, and Frank Thielman.

33. Ibid., 436.

34. Matera's previous work in this area may be found in his book *New Testament Christology*.

35. Matera, *New Testament Theology*, 447. Specifically, Jesus plays what Matera calls an "indispensable role in the salvation God offers to remedy the human predicament" (437).

The community of the sanctified.

Where soteriology and ecclesiology meet, Revelation addresses particular churches and their problems: Rev 2—3 shows how the Church must witness, resisting temptation and compromise, while the remainder of the book presents a victorious Church of Gentiles and Jews; these are Revelation's two distinctive contributions to the broader New Testament understanding of the Church.

The moral life of the sanctified.

For Matera, the various New Testament documents draw implications for ethical teaching from their particular understandings of soteriology. But since he has earlier taken Revelation to address the eschatological, rather than the present, dimension of the Christian life, all it can deliver here is the assurance that believers will one day "be victorious if they are faithful."[36]

The hope of the sanctified.

Matera therefore describes an exclusively *future* hope. Having previously argued that the distinctive perspective of Revelation on "God's final (or transcendent) victory in Christ,"[37] was of a victory *already* won by the slaughtered Lamb,[38] he now abandons this key point: even if "God has been and will be victorious,"[39] this apparently says nothing about how believers might live victoriously in the *present* or apply Christ's *past* victory now, or how in light of both they might anticipate its *future* consummation.

---

36. Ibid., 467.

37. Ibid., 468, 478.

38. Compare the following statements, at the beginning and end: "[Revelation's] purpose is not so much to predict the future as it is to remind listeners that God has already won the decisive victory over evil" (401); and "Christ's death upon the cross was God's decisive victory over Satan . . . [and a]lthough the decisive victory has already been won, its final consummation has not yet occurred" (ibid., 421–22). Christ's past victory is also evoked at various points in between.

39. Ibid., 406.

Assessment

Casting New Testament Theology as a set of five topical conversations does give a voice to all the texts, Revelation included; equally, however, it restricts to these five rubrics what any may contribute. I have indicated how, in his synthesis, Matera virtually discounts any practical relevance of Revelation for present Christian living; correspondingly, any distinctive message on worship found in Revelation also disappears. What remains is a rather truncated solo among a series of solos: Revelation's treatment of the five topics is not blended by Matera, whether symphonically or polyphonically, with the notes sounded out by other voices; there is no multi-voice concert, for unity drowns out diversity and renders inaudible Revelation's particular voice.

François Vouga

Vouga reserves only limited space for Revelation; yet its distinctive contribution to New Testament Theology is nevertheless recognized in several key ways.[40]

Revelation and liturgy

Vouga sees the liturgical component of Revelation as significant,[41] for it offers commentary on events within the visions, somewhat like a Greek chorus, and gives poetic expression to a fundamental christological conviction: the Lamb, in defeating the powers of evil through his death and resurrection, is lord over history; this fact grounds the life of believers in the world, energizing their witness in day-to-day living.[42] Vouga briefly examines six major liturgical moments in the book (4:1–11; 5:8–14; 7:9–16; 12:10–12; 15:1–4; 19:1–8) and identifies how they celebrate the activity of God, Christ, or Christ's followers.[43]

---

40. I readily acknowledge that Vouga's treatment considerably reflects my own intuitions.
41. Vouga, *Une théologie*, 77: "[t]he liturgy which the visions stage occupies a prominent place in the book's overall construction" (my translation).
42. Ibid.
43. Ibid., 78–81.

BIBLICAL THEOLOGY | III. FUTURE

Revelation and Hope

For Vouga, fidelity to the Christian hope in Revelation takes the form of outright critical opposition to imperial propaganda: the book's visions contest the political legitimacy of the Roman state's arrogant and absolutist claims, mediated by local elites in Roman Asia, and sound a wake-up call to a Church largely lulled by the reigning ideology.[44] The sovereignty of the Lamb rules out any compromise: "people either bear the name of the 'Father' or the name of the 'Monster' (Rev 13:16–18; 14:1–5)";[45] the christological conviction that Jesus is Lord entails active resistance to propaganda that portrays the lordship of Caesar.[46] Vouga locates the heart of this critique in Rev 12—13, a diptych which tells the same story twice: a mythical vision, seen from above (chapter 12), conveys the message that evil powers are already vanquished by the blood of the Lamb and by his followers' testimony (Rev 12:10–12); then a political analysis, conducted from below (chapter 13), exposes totalitarianism as a double monstrosity comprising the power of the state (the first beast) and its ideology and propaganda (the second beast).[47] In consequence, readers should listen up (13:9–10), exercise wisdom (13:18), and offer resistance.

Revelation and the Presence of the Risen One

Both Luke-Acts and Revelation, for Vouga, see a cosmic dimension to the presence of the Risen Christ.[48] In Revelation Christ who died and

---

44. For Vouga (192) Revelation sets about "demonizing the totalitarian State" (my translation). His is therefore a political reading of Revelation at this point, in line with an important recent interpretative consensus. In Revelation's sharp critique of the prevailing political order, over against the defense of that order's God-given legitimacy offered in Paul, Acts or 1 Pet, Vouga sees a contrast in focus, rather than a contradiction in principle.

45. Ibid., my translation; John, he says, is reacting to coercion from the imperial cult as practiced at Pergamum, boosted by imperial propaganda with an explicitly religious twist an promoted by local elites.

46. "[F]aced with [the Empire's] seductive manipulation of individual consciences, Christianity can only adopt a position of radical opposition and bear the irreducible testimony of a confessing Church" (ibid., 191; my translation).

47. "[T]he strength of totalitarianism derives from its combination of brutal use of force with ideological seduction via propaganda" (ibid., 196; my translation).

48. Where Revelation is concerned, "the presence of the Risen One as sovereign Lord and the consequences of this for the history of the inhabited earth provide both the subject and the viewpoint of the visions proffered by Revelation" (ibid., 268; my

has risen is: the one whom the book reveals (1:1), on whose authority it is sent forth (1:5); the danielic Son of Man figure in the inaugural vision, guarantor of John's prophetic ministry to the churches (2:1—3:22); the power behind history, figured as a rider (5:1–2; 19:11–16); and the co-regent with God over history and revealer of its meaning, as the slaughtered but victorious Lamb (5:6, 8, 12, 13; 6:1, 16; 7:9, 10, 14, 17; 12:11; 13:8, 11; 14:10; 15:3; 17:14; 19:7, 9; 21:9, 14, 22, 23, 27; 22:1, 3).[49]

Christ's shed blood as metonymy for witness faithfully given.

Somewhat against the consensus, Vouga does not see reference to the death of Jesus in Revelation as primarily soteriological: Christ's shed blood does not so much redeem; instead it is a metonymy, standing for witness faithfully given, as is confirmed in Christ's own case by the metaphor of the Son of Man's two-edged mouth-sword.[50]

The dialectic of God's presence in the world and the impact of active witness in history.

In Revelation 11 Vouga detects a kind of dialectic connecting the witness and the death of the Lamb or his followers, conveying John's sense both of how God is present in this world (11:1–2) and of the impact that active witness has upon history (11:3–14).

A double paradox: powerful testimony from weak persons and precarious-efficacious witness.

Vouga finds especially remarkable chapter 11's core contrast between the irresistible power of the witnesses' testimony (11:5–6) and the vulnerability of their person, once their task is fulfilled (11:7); yet their death becomes their vindication (11:11–12).[51] Since the witnesses' death

---

translation).

49. Ibid., 268-69. In summary, "[w]hat the seer sees is none other than contemporary reality as this appears when viewed from the standpoint of active witness to the confession that the Lamb is victorious" (my translation).

50. Says Vouga (269), "Jesus is not a witness through his death but by his word" (my translation).

51. It "seals their prophetic word, shows it to be true, and bestows on it its eternal character. It is their *passive testimony*" (ibid., 270; my translation, italics original).

causes both the city's collapse (11:13) and their enemies' terror (11:11b, 12b), implicitly their testimony must have been guaranteeing creation's stability hitherto. Vouga puts the two aspects together, crediting the seer with showing how God is present in the world and how witness acts powerfully, if paradoxically,[52] in history.

A triple figure: slain Lamb—Lamb's blood—Lamb's wedding.

The same paradox in turn conditions what Vouga calls the triple figure of the slain Lamb, the Lamb's blood and the Lamb whose wedding is to be celebrated: this configuration gives meaning to believers' active witness, providing a model for them to emulate. He makes four points.[53]

THE LAMB IS BOTH PERSONAL AND SYMBOLIC. Jesus crucified is combined with a seven-horned and seven-eyed personification of almightiness and of the activity of God and of his elect on earth.

THE LAMB CAN REVEAL WHAT HISTORY MEANS AND THE POWERS AT WORK WITHIN IT. By his faithful witness the Lamb is qualified to open the sealed scroll, revealing what history means and what powers are at work within it: the cultic language of his acclamation (5:9–10) celebrates the redemption achieved through his active and passive witness.

THE LAMB SYMBOLIZES BELIEVERS AS ACTIVE CONFESSING WITNESSES. The Lamb symbolizes the identity of believers as active confessing witnesses; their names are written in his book as his redeemed followers: they put their lives on the line as he did, defeating the dragon by their testimony.

THE STRUGGLE OF THE LAMB OR HIS OWN ANTICIPATES DELIVERANCE FOR ALL CREATION. The struggle of the Lamb and his own against the monster (chapter 17) is not about believers achieving victory, which is already won (chapter 7), but about the deliverance of all creation: this is symbolized

---

Similarly, Vouga detects *"revelation of the contrast between the precarious nature of the witnesses' personal destiny and the efficacy of their testimony"* (ibid.; my translation, italics original).

52. The paradox comprises "both *the dialectic of passive testimony and of active militancy (whose triumph it is)* and *the power lent to the prophetic word by the very weakness of those who bear it*" (ibid., 270; my translation, italics original).

53. Ibid., 270–71.

by the Lamb's wedding, anticipated in both the liturgy of Revelation 19 and the descent of his bride-city, New Jerusalem (in 21:1—22:5). For Vouga, a prior conviction underlies all this: the living Christ, the Risen One, holds the churches in his hand (1:16), knows them intimately (2:2, 9, 13, 19; 3:1, 8, 15) and calls them to respond.

The millennium as a new perspective on the period from Easter to Last Judgment.

Vouga's final brief consideration of Revelation[54] involves the millennium (20:1–6): like E. Cuvillier and others, he reads it as a new perspective on what was already recounted in 12:1—14:5, in the Lamb's defeat of the dragon: as complementary visions of the period separating Easter from the Last Judgment, chapter 20 pictures a time of the faithful witnesses' reign and judgment whereas 12:1—14:5 depicts the time of their testimony and militancy.[55] Witnessing and reigning are therefore one and the same, for testimony defeats the dragon: thus the thousand years are both a long period given over by God to the faithful witness of believers in history and a metaphor for the certainty that the triumphant Christ will have the last word.

Assessment

Although Vouga handles Revelation's particular contribution in a rather fragmentary way, he presents that which is most characteristic of the book with a remarkable degree of coherence. Heaven's liturgy or interpreting angels, as found in its visions or commentaries, do not bespeak some far-off future but describe how present reality is transformed for those who believe that God and the Lamb are reigning now. Vouga emphasizes how this perspective is played out primarily through believers' costly witness in a hostile environment, where they emulate their forerunner the Lamb, but he does acknowledge—tacitly, at least—how this perspective is predicated on the victory already won by Christ and how it receives its content and shape, for those same believers, in the very scenes of worship to which Vouga first directed his attention.

---

54. Ibid., 449. Apart from a one-page appendix where Vouga diagrams Revelation's structure.

55. Ibid., 399.

BIBLICAL THEOLOGY | III. FUTURE

Richard Bauckham

Bauckham's exploration of Revelation's theology remains the major recent contribution in English. Whilst he makes no claim to exhaustiveness, Bauckham's offers a stimulating concluding manifesto of ways in which Revelation might be relevant to contemporary readers, as so many "theological directions for contemporary reflection."[56] In the intervening years, it seems to me, scholarship has been slow to follow his lead.

CONTEMPORARY APPROPRIATION OF REVELATION

Here is my summary of Bauckham's eleven suggestions.[57] Revelation: uses powerful images to insist that truth is found only in God; counters absolutist human claims with its vision of a God who reigns over all; sees a future for the world, guaranteed by this God who reigns; corrects a defective understanding of this God; envisages a new creation co-extensive with original creation; enrolls the Church for extending God's reign throughout the world; *calls the Church to worship, thereby to find strength for active resistance; reminds the Church that authentic worship gives rise to her witness* (italics mine); purges and renews a Christian imagination, equipping it for resistance; promotes solidarity with this world's victims; and calls readers not to success but to faithfulness.

Christology does not come to the fore here—explicitly, at least—but, as my italics reveal, the topic of worship does emerge. In Revelation worship both conforms to Israel's hope, anticipating "the universal worship for which the whole creation is destined,"[58] and connects with life in the public sphere, first by inspiring believers to witness to justice and truth over against idolatry, and second by rendering feasible just such an outworking.[59]

---

56. Bauckham, *Book of Revelation*, 159.

57. Ibid., 159–64. My summary changes the order of the points somewhat; it is also unavoidably reductionist, reflecting somewhat perfunctorily Bauckham's invitation to further thought.

58. Ibid., 161.

59. It is worked out in that "the truth of God is known in genuine worship of God" (Ibid., 162); through this the Church's vision is also purified.

Worship of God and Jesus

Earlier in his study, Bauckham had given detailed consideration both to the worship of God[60] and the worship of Jesus.[61] Essentially, for Bauckham, acknowledgment of God as Creator leads to his worship, as in chapter 4 where the creatures and elders offer their unceasing adoration. The actions of Jesus, meanwhile, on God's behalf—as Saviour, Lord or Judge[62]—confer on him functional divinity, making him the object of explicit worship; yet, Bauckham argues, Revelation also recognizes Jesus' ontic divinity by designating God and Jesus alike as Alpha and Omega, depicting Jesus in chapters 4—5 as the one who "shares in the glory due to God."[63] In both cases, Bauckham finds worship in Revelation to be directed polemically at "the idolatrous worship of merely human power"[64] implicit in the prevailing political ideology.

Assessment

I find Bauckham's account significant in three respects: it highlights the importance of the worship of Jesus in Revelation; it shows how this intersects with the theme of witness; and crucially it integrates the book's worship material with its theology and Christology. Among my interlocutors here, Dunn (somewhat cursorily), and Vouga (in more depth and detail) do pay this some attention, but more needs to be said: by treating Revelation as a writing originally intended for use in the setting of the worship service—where, he thinks, it must have functioned essentially as reported prophecy[65]—Bauckham has provided scholarship with a significant hermeneutical key for which, surprisingly, it has found little use in more than two decades.[66]

---

60. Ibid., 32–51 (at various points).
61. Ibid., 58–63.
62. For Bauckham's main discussion of Revelation's Christology see ibid., 54–76.
63. Ibid., 60.
64. Ibid., 59; see also 37–39.
65. Ibid., 2–5.
66. Recent political readings, of course, have followed Bauckham (or Vouga) in considering Revelation's worship speech to be directed polemically at the prevailing political ideology. Personally, I find this frequently-made claim to be both unfalsifiable and based, in any case, on speculative referential exegesis which Revelation's genre renders inappropriate. As I have said elsewhere (*Reading Revelation*, 135), "Revelation's

BIBLICAL THEOLOGY | III. FUTURE

PART TWO: A PROPOSAL

Revelation's worship setting

Revelation 4 is the first panel of a diptych devoted to heavenly acclamation of God enthroned and of the Lamb, which Bauckham calls "a scene of worship into which the reader who shares John's faith in God is almost inevitably drawn."[67] Bauckham comes close, here, to asserting something which, for me, is a fundamental presupposition: "Revelation was originally intended for oral communication or performance by one or more liturgists in a worship setting."[68] From this assumption I wish to draw three implications, each of which will be briefly worked out below:

1. Scholarship should no longer discount the frequency or underestimate the phenomenon of liturgical language and worship activity in Revelation, but recognize instead how cultic events, whether occurring in heaven or earth, permeate the book throughout with words or actions of worship which impact or comment on all its narrated action.

2. This worship setting should therefore be factored into any consideration of how Revelation constructs its implied reader.

3. Once the act of reading is over, it becomes worthwhile for real readers to consider the pertinence for their own experience of the book's irreducibly liturgical dimension.

Revelation's pervasive worship

Elsewhere I have already sought to substantiate, in some depth, the prominence of materials in Revelation with a strong cultic colouring and to establish the integral manner in which they contribute to the book's

---

author . . . is content to denounce idolatry without actually describing it"; thus for Revelation "precise identification of this false worship and of those who practised it... is of only passing interest": see also my whole section "Legitimate adoration and bogus worship," together with 166–67, note 38. Just as prophetically–motivated denunciations of idolatry in the Old Testament typically go beyond the narrowly political to confront, in principle, all human violation of worship of the one true God, so also in my view does Revelation.

67. Bauckham, *Book of Revelation*, 32.

68. Campbell, *Reading Revelation*, 163 n.5 (see also 113). In this I am following David L. Barr, "Oral Enactment," 243–56.

complex narrative world throughout.[69] Like liturgical book-ends, Revelation's prologue (1:1-8) and epilogue (22:6-21) together mark the beginning and end of a sustained worship encounter which is both opened and closed by liturgical dialogue.

To establish whether this is so, one need only for present purposes read beyond the opening sequence and examine evidence from the septet of oracles to Churches or the diptych in Rev 4—5. Thus the Christ of the opening dialogue (1:4-8) and inaugural vision (beginning in 1:9), who first speaks in 1:10, is found to continue speaking uninterruptedly throughout 1:17—3:22, in a proclamation which repeatedly alludes to objects, furnishings, and activities associated with worship or false worship. When his speech concludes, with the last oracle (in 3:22), the seer ascends to heaven (4:1-2) and liturgical time on earth immediately merges with heaven's praise: readers now observe adoration around the heavenly throne, first of the Creator (4:8-11), then of the Lamb (5:9-14).

Only if the remainder of the book (in 6:1—22:5) were to *dispense* with this cultic framework could we avoid the conclusion that the whole of Revelation depicts, on one level, a worship event: in fact, as my own previous work amply demonstrates, worship scenarios continue decisively to punctuate the narrative action, expanding its liturgical or doxological component as it develops.

Revelation's Implied Worshiper

The first point impacts, in turn, the book's implied reader. Revelation's opening sequence addresses this reader inclusively through *we-us* language: from the start, the opening dialogue quite deliberately incorporates implied readers into a chorus of speakers, assimilating them to active participants in the goings-on of worship. Thus from the beginning of the book, Revelation constructs what I wish to call *cultically-implicated readers*, who enter implicitly into the praise of God and the Lamb: we could also speak of these implied readers as *implied worshipers*, whom Revelation construes to be welcome participants in the worshiping assembly from beginning to end. Indeed, I have shown elsewhere how this implied worshiper in Revelation may be both identified and characterized, "while also attempting to address real readers by imagining ways

---

69. Ibid., 112-69.

that they might enjoy the fruit of their discoveries once the act of reading is over."[70]

Revelation's Relevance

If we may speak of the implied reader constructed by Revelation more specifically as an implied worshiper, then a particular question arises for real readers: how may they make empirical use, in the world in front of the text, of whatever experience has accrued for them as implied worshipers? To this question, which brings us straight back to Bauckham's issue of contemporary relevance, I would like to propose twin real-world responses, each of which corresponds to a pole of Thomas Hatina's dialectic of "New Testament Theology inside and outside the faith community"[71] or, we might also say, within the Church and within the wider culture.

Real readers: a) worshipers.

First of all, let us suppose the empirical reader of Revelation to be a worshiper in the Christian tradition. Personally, I am such a reader. In that case Revelation's portrayal of worship of God and Jesus, in heaven or earth, may provoke reflection on personal experience of public or private worship, including (for example) the influence of Revelation through religious art or Church music: thus, speaking from within my own Presbyterian tradition, I can see how the dynamic narrative Christology of Revelation[72] has had only limited impact on individual and corporate piety and spirituality alike. Therein I perceive a challenge for confessional contexts like the local church: how may desirable theological clarity or weight be given to Revelation's uniquely dramatic, pictured–and–storied Christology, or, how might the way this is mediated, in the book, be exploited through a sustained doxological encounter? How may the worshiped Jesus of Revelation be made accessible, let alone amenable, to ordinary Christians, whose Christology might typically reflect elements drawn from (say) Romans or John's Gospel, but in which the Christ of

---

70. "Apocalypse johannique et adorateur implicite"; the quotation is from the appended English summary.

71. Hatina, *New Testament Theology*, 181.

72. For having pioneered understanding of the Christology of Revelation in a storied way, with the Lamb as the narrative's central character, credit must go to Boring, "Narrative Christology," 702–723.

Revelation might have little or no place, or be seen mainly through the pervasive hermeneutical lens of eschatological schemes?

As for New Testament Theology itself, it seems to me that wherever scholarship *has* investigated Revelation's depicted cultic activity, this has usually been as part of the historical enterprise involving reconstruction of the *context* of the worship once offered by early Christians in Roman Asia. Whilst this might work for terrestrially-focussed activity, in first-century Ephesus or Laodicea, it entirely misses the book's depicted celestial worship before the divine throne. Surely the time has come for scrutinising the *content* of Revelation's carefully composed and arranged liturgical materials in unbreakable relation to their *form* and *function*, in keeping with Revelation's narrative shape and in respect for its literary integrity. The generally fragmentary nature of cultic elements embedded in the New Testament increases the importance of Revelation's data relating to worship: general neglect of these materials in discussion of the topic of worship in the New Testament is somewhat puzzling, to say the least, and needs corrected.

Real readers: b) non-worshipers.

In the second place, let us imagine the empirical reader of Revelation to be a non-participant in Christian worship in the real world. In this case, what Dan Via calls "the interpreter's posture and pre-understanding"[73] may have made somewhat challenging, even uncongenial, the experience of engagement in an implied revelatory worship encounter with God and the Lamb through hearing or reading the Book of Revelation. Yet, wherever Revelation—or any difficult or controversial text—is still acknowledged to have "the capacity to put the reader in question,"[74] the real reader's perceived perplexity or discomfort arising from the act of reading may yet prove to be a stimulus to further dealings with the text.[75]

---

73. Via, *What Is New Testament Theology?*, 127.

74. Ibid., 113.

75. Some recent readings perceive Revelation's message to be problematic to the point of requiring serious reconfiguration, if not outright rejection. In her essay "Apocalyptic Horror", Tina Pippin has dubbed Revelation a horror fantasy filled with "intense violence" (79) and its God "a destroyer, the leader of the ultimate massacre" (92), whilst in *Death and Desire* Pippin finds the victimized prostitute woman–city to be incapable of translation or reinterpretation in ways that today's female readers might find acceptable. Such outright dismissal is a minority verdict, but it shows how for some real readers Revelation's troublesome violence may render the book

As far as the task of New Testament Theology for the public square is concerned, today's pluralist environment may therefore open up unexpected interaction with Revelation, amid multi-voice conversations about the public pertinence of the New Testament for today. To a culture dismissive of the institution but welcoming of the event, or to people impatient with promises of utopia and scenarios of doomsday alike, yet open to the relevance of transformative encounters in the present, might not the Book of Revelation have something appropriate to say? Just as Revelation has had a long and complex history of reception and effects in Church or Academy, so the ricochets of its impact on today's public square may yet produce present or future enthusiasts or detractors who defy easy characterization.

Bibliography

Barr, David L. "The Apocalypse of John as Oral Enactment." *Interpretation* 50 (1986) 243–56.

Bauckham, Richard. *The Theology of the Book of Revelation* [NTT]. Cambridge: Cambridge University Press, 1993.

Boring, M. Eugene. "Narrative Christology in the Apocalypse." *CBQ* 54 (1992) 702–23.

Campbell, W. Gordon. "Apocalypse johannique et adorateur implicite." *Revue Théologique de Louvain* (2016) forthcoming.

———. "Facing Fire and Fury. One Reading of Revelation's Violence." In *The Book of Revelation. Currents in British Research on the Apocalypse* [WUNT II], edited by Garrick V. Allen et al., 147–73. Tübingen, DE: Mohr Siebeck, 2015.

———. *Reading Revelation: A Thematic Approach*. Cambridge: James Clarke, 2012.

Dunn, James D. G. *New Testament Theology. An Introduction*. Nashville: Abingdon, 2009.

Hatina, Thomas R. *New Testament Theology and its Quest for Relevance*. London: T. & T. Clark, 2013.

Matera, Frank J. *New Testament Christology*. Louisville, KY: WJK, 1999.

———. *New Testament Theology. Exploring Diversity and Unity*. Louisville, KY: WJK, 2007.

Morgan, Robert. "New Testament Theology in the Twentieth Century." In *Biblical Theology. Introducing the Conversation*, edited by Leo G. Perdue et al., 137–208. Nashville, TN: Abingdon, 2009.

Pippin, Tina. *Apocalyptic Bodies: The Biblical End of the World in Text and Image*. New York: Routledge, 1999.

———. *Death and Desire: The Rhetoric of Gender in the Apocalypse of John*. Louisville, KY: WJK, 1992.

---

irredeemable: I engage with this and other readings of Revelation's violent imagery, employing my own strategy for interpreting it, in "Facing Fire and Fury," forthcoming.

Via, Dan O. *What Is New Testament Theology* [GBS/NT]. Minneapolis: Augsburg Fortress, 2002.
Vouga, François. *Une théologie du Nouveau Testament*. Geneva: Labor et Fides, 2001.
Yarbro Collins, Adela. "Apocalypticism and NT Theology." In *The Nature of New Testament Theology*, edited by Christopher Rowland and Christopher Tuckett, 31–48. Malden, MA: Blackwell, 2006.

www.ingramcontent.com/pod-product-compliance
Lightning Source LLC
Chambersburg PA
CBHW020407230426
43664CB00009B/1216